FOREIGN POLICIES OF MAJOR POWERS

PRAKASH CHANDER
PREM ARORA

COSMOS ™ BOOKHIVE
PUBLISHING REDEFINED

Printed in India by Repro India Limited

Published by **Cosmos Bookhive Private Limited**
V-6/7 (2nd Floor), DLF City Phase -III,
Gurgaon, Haryana-122002. INDIA
Phones: +91-124-4371455 , + 91 9811282855

Bulk Sales

Cosmos Bookhive offers excellent discounts on this book when ordered in quantity for bulk purchases or special sales. Cosmos Bookhive books may be purchased for educational, business, or sales promotional use. For general information on our other products and services or to obtain technical support, please contact: 124-4371455, +91-9811282855 or cosmosbookhive@gmail.com and you can also buy books from online bookstore at www.CosmosBookhive.com.

Preface

The latest edition of *Foreign Policies of Major Powers* is in the hands of our valued readers. We have tried to give all latest sets of information regarding the political game plans and structural intricacies of major powers in this volume. We have explained the concept of power in detail and tried to include the comments and views of all authors on this subject. These views are very vital from the examination view-point.

The Cold War has already begun. It may get converted into a new full-fledged war between Russia and the USA. As of now, covert operations are being done to avoid a direct conflict in East Ukraine. But if an overt war escalates between these superpowers, the entire world may suffer to the hilt. That is what European leaders do not want.

Even as the world struggles to come out of the pangs of recession, the war covert between Iran and Saudi Arabia has taken an ugly turn. The direct attack of Yemen by coalition led by Saudi Arabia has indicated that the Gulf region would remain the centre of this new war.

We have described all aspects of the foreign policies of all major powers in this volume. The entire text fully covers the topics related to examinations and interview schedules. Students are advised to read the book from the first page onwards to develop a full theoretical base. This very base would help them succeed in examinations.

The publisher, authors, DTP staff and support staff have left no stone unturned to make the presented volume a fine work of publishing. However, mistakes may have crept in due to human or machine errors. We request our valued readers to point the same. Thus, we would be able to incorporate them in the next edition of this volume. That would help readers get the latest and best knowledge on the subject.

Happy reading and best of luck in examinations!

Authors

Contents

Why Study Foreign Policies of Major Powers

CHAPTER 1

Introduction

The contemporary political scenario of the world is full of turmoil. The new era has not augured well for most nations, given that most of them are going through pangs of agony. That is because of recession, unemployment, internal strife, threat from the forces of terror and a stealthy yet certain transformation in their respective socio-cultural values. Political leaders of all countries are not able to stop the onslaught of terrorism and cultural transformation, these two being the key divisive forces in any country. You can take many examples of nations that have seen terror and internal strife due to a host of reasons. The examples are Australia (attack on a coffee shop in the busy district centre of Sydney and recovery of an IED from the Opera House nearby that coffee house in December 2014), India (attacks of 26/11 are still fresh in the minds of Indian peoples), Kenya (attack on a shopping mall in 2014) and Indonesia (149 Indonesian nationals missing in a plane crash, total toll was 162 in December 2014). Further, the ISIS is running around the length and breadth of Middle East and gunning down people and army personnel in Iraq and Syria at its own will. The residents of these two nations are facing the worst crisis of their lives. In Pakistan 132 children were butchered by the Tehriq-e-Taliban of Pakistan (TTP) on December 16, 2014.

On February 15, 2015, ISIS cadres kidnapped 21 Christians from Libya and butchered them. Thus, the entire world watched these events with awe and agony. The powers of the West and East must unite now to eliminate the threats of terror from all parts of the world. Terror does not prophesize any religion. The nations of this globe must unite now to create a new peaceful order that must last long enough. Let there be no war or conflict on the basis of religion, class, race, colour or economic status. This must be the priority of all nations, given that enough blood has been shed in the past 20,000 years by man on these very grounds.

All terrorist organizations must be taken into confidence and efforts must be made to restore peace in the conflict-ridden regions of the globe. If this is not does not happen immediately, the human race may head towards self-destruction in no time. Cruelty and cruel people must be done away with at the earliest possible time. We have many problems at the global level and if we continue to indulge in useless wars, we would not be able to focus on those problems.

How can major powers bring about this shift from war to peace? This is an interesting question. Firstly, they can set their own houses in order. Then, they can influence their respective regions and neighbouring countries. Trade is a good medium for creating harmonious relationships with neighbouring countries. Then, these countries can use UN organizations and various other forums to make this entire world a peaceful place to live in. If they themselves face financial or political crises every now and then, we cannot hope that they would play useful roles for installing peace in various parts of the world. Only a stable leader can bring peaceful and stable followers behind him. Further, financial stability is also a matter of serious concern for many major powers and even Russia, a super power. If a major power does not have money to sustain its masses, its arms and weapon systems are useless. This brings us to another conclusion. The military capability of any nation must also be equated with its efforts to make and install peace in various parts of the world. If a major power is capable in military terms, it must not threaten its neighbour and other nations of the globe. If it does, it is viewed with suspicion. Developing military prowess is good because we have to defend our nation at all times. However, the blunt misuse of power is not warranted in the changed world scenario where every enemy nation is also a distant or direct trading partner. Gunfire is no alternative of wheat. Bullets do not fill bellies but wheat certainly can. Nearly 90 percent of have-nots are watching the latest happenings with awe and fear. Nearly ten percent of the masses of this world own huge resources. The wars going on in different parts of the world speak volumes of this growing hiatus. This hiatus must be filled up. Major powers can play vital roles to fill up this hiatus. They must decide when to start this noble task. The sooner, the better!

Terror groups roam freely in Pakistan and Afghanistan and the world just watches! In the wake of these gory developments, the major powers of the globe ought to alter their foreign policies so that peace and order could be restored in the affected regions. In some cases, across-the table talk would suffice. In some others, the power of barrel must be displayed to keep wrong elements at bay. The human race is going through a bad politico-economic-cultural phase. Major powers can change the scene only if they adopt rational, pragmatic policies in the interests of the entire set of human classes and creeds. This is easier said than done, though. Let us take a deeper look at the situation.

In February 2015, the President of Egypt spoke up against the forces of terror. Mr. Abdel Fattah Al-Sisi stated that a UN resolution must be passed in which coalition should be ordered to be created to intervene in Libya and save peoples of that country. He stated that rivals had surrounded Tripoli and that weapons must be supplied to the government of Libya. Thus, the global situation is very precarious because of the spread of terrorism activities in Libya, Kenya, Nigeria, Yemen, Iraq, Egypt, Syria and West Africa. The nations of the West quite often face this heat because fighters and terror elements spill over into the nations of the West (when they get opportunities) and harass or kill people at will.

A Framework of Reference

The current framework of reference in the context of foreign policies of major policies is fraught with uncertainties. That is because the problem of global or transnational terrorism has affected all nations in more or less the same manner. An interesting trend has been observed by Arvind Kumar, the author of this text. Earlier, terror outfits used to operate in their own countries and perpetuate terror activities. Now-a-days, these outfits have set up their branches in various countries and are exporting terror indirectly from their secluded offices and bunkers located anywhere in the world. Thus, they have their deputies to do various jobs. As an example, we would like to quote the bomb blasts conducted in Bodh Gaya (India). The local office of the terror group performed the necessary operations at the behest of its foreign masters. This trend is growing by the day. Political leaders all over the world are worried about this evil export of terror.

Another interesting observation of Arvind Kumar is that nations are not fighting against terror by joining hands under the aegis of the UNO. Rather, they are using regional strategic groups or mutual agreements to fight against terror. This gives enough space to terror outfits because they take quick decisions whereas country heads take decisions through meetings and legal sanctions. Thus, terror groups move much more swiftly than any nation or group in all war theatres of the world.

General Benny Ganz, the chief of armed forces of Israel, retired in February 2015. The General has retired at a time when the situation in Ghaza strip is very volatile. Israel is constructing homes for civilians in Ghaza strip. Palestine claims that the area of Ghaza strip is under the illegal occupation of Israel. But the government of Israel is not listening to their demands. The long-standing problem ought to be sorted now. The Palestinians are also suffering and their war-ravaged homes have not seen peace for more than 60 years. Israel has emerged as a powerful ally of the USA, much to the dismay of the Arab world. Although Saudi Arabia supports American policies about free trade and liberalization of religious processes, it is up and against Israel on the issue of return of land to Palestinians. Arafat had given up the gun even during his lifetime and India was primarily responsible for this change in attitude of a majority of Palestinians. But now, Lebanon, Jordan and other fighter groups of the Arab world are attacking Israel every now and then. The USA has always used its clout in the UNO to save Israel from the wrath of the Arab world. We hope that the year 2015 would bring cheers among the families of Palestinian peoples. They must also learn to live along with their staunch opponents, the Israelis. We do not see any policy shift in Tel Aviv or the highest echelons of the Palestinian Authority. All we hope is that peace may prevail on the Palestine–Israel border at least for a couple of years. That is because the problems being faced by the masses of Libya, Iraq, Syria, Lebanon, Jordan and Yemen are too big to be handled by all major powers. Peace has been eluding these Arab nations. The families and fighters are facing hard times in the Gulf region. There are no solutions in sight for any one of the nations in conflict. The USA has assumed a passive role after the starting of the second term of Mr. Barrack Obama in office. Russia is busy handling Ukrainian government through a handful of rebels located in the eastern part of Ukraine. Thus, it is no longer keen to fight any war in the Gulf region. The super powers are out of this conflict zone. Since both of them are busy, rebels are killing hostages at their will in war zones of the Gulf. You would realize, after reading this chapter, that this is the outcome of covert conflict between Iran (a traditional Shia community) and Saudi Arabia (a traditional Sunni community).

Further, guerilla warfare is the key behind the success of every terror attack around the world. Ordinary masses are vulnerable to bomb blasts, kidnapping operations, day-light murders due to firing, secretively planted IEDs etc. Security forces are supposed to conduct full enquiry behind the incident and then they take necessary actions after the commandant orders them to do so. In the meanwhile, attackers quickly move to another target to complete the kill. The terror outfits and their cohorts are after the ordinary masses, not the security forces, paramilitary staff or armed cadres. They are after the ordinary masses which are soft targets by any norm. The irony is the foreign policy of any country does not have a single iota of deterrence against the ordinary common man who walks down the street and has vegetables which he must take home to cook dinner. This is not only scary by any global security standard, but also beyond the comprehension of political pundits of any country. There are no solutions in sight. We can quote examples of very recent times in this context. They are as follows:

1. London Tube Bombings
2. 26/11 attacks in Mumbai
3. Attack on the office of *Charlie Hebdo* magazine
4. Attack on an army school of Peshawar (Pakistan) in which 132 children were killed, the overall death toll being much higher
5. Attack on a café in Sydney
6. Death of the pilot of the Jordanian Air Force; he was burnt alive!
7. Kidnapping of girls by Boko Harem, a fundamentalist organization.

If you are a student of political science, you would probably not realize what is common in all these incidents. But if you are a student of strategy (a military term), you would immediately recognize that all victims in each and every case mentioned above were taken unaware by attackers. The element of surprise makes us believe that all major powers, even superpowers, have still not understood how terror factories operate around the world. We do not know how enemy operates and yet we have created blockades and security check systems for him all over the area under threat. Then, a few men come, fire at will, take hostages at will and kill people by firing indiscriminately. They are also killed but they do their duties well!

Thus, the problem before the major powers of the world is not a dwindling economy but terror threats and actual acts of terror that take heavy tolls of life and property. Before we grow, we must stop and look at what the terror factories have given to us all. They have given chaos, instability and above all agonies. This evil cycle must stop, for it is against the desires of Holy Jesus Christ, the penance of Holy Prophet Mohammed and the *modus operandi* of Lord Vishnu, who currently runs this universe. Ordinary people are getting killed and the same city or country is enjoying a party! How could these two poles exist together? We must resolve the problem of terrorism in all parts of the world. Nations must deliberate over the issue. Boundary disputes must be resolved. People must be allowed to practice their religions. Unemployed youths must be given jobs. Prophets must not be made subjects of caricatures. We must learn to tolerate the faults of others, lest we should suffer in the future, just like we are, today!

Major Powers: Basic Perspectives, Ambitions and Ideologies

The broad framework for study in this volume includes the basic strengths and weaknesses of each power, the problems being faced by each power and the economic problems each one of them is facing. We shall study, in detail, what ails global economy and what the reactions of major powers to the economic fluctuations are. Most events and offshoots thereof were due to extreme variations in oil prices in the period starting from 2010 to 2015. The year 2015 saw a steep fall in oil prices. The Saudi Arabian oil industry refuses to stop or cut down oil production due to political reasons. As a consequence of this move, the oil markets witnessed an oil glut in December 2014 to January 2015. This oil glut has led to a fall in the prices of oil crude to below 50 dollars per BBL. The political scene of the globe is being dominated by oil economy now-a-days. Russia is facing serious financial crisis due to its weak rouble. Its status as a super power may be questioned if it does not come out of the current quagmire of oil crisis.

Another issue that looms large over the political horizon of the globe is the covert war between Iran and Saudi Arabia. The supporters of these two countries are using other countries as their battlegrounds. Iran is also a target of the American forces in the sense that the US has threatened it time and again because of its ability to make nuclear weapons. Nuclear inspectors had examined Iranian sites but the IAEA did not find a single nuclear weapon. Thus, Iran is facing flak from the world because of its nuclear programme which has not shown up any nuclear weapon till date. Secondly, it is fighting against the Saudi-backed organizations because of the rift created by two sects.

China is also facing communal problems in its own territories. Nearly seven to ten percent of Chinese are Muslims and China cannot afford to ignore them. Many of them had migrated from central Asian countries to China. They are a power to reckon with even in a communist nation like China. Thus, China is also facing the threat of terror in its various forms. That is why it has joined hands with India and Russia and taken a vow to eliminate terror from its soil. On the contrary, China supports Pakistan, which is a terror factory and is home to the top terror organizations and terrorist of the world. China would have to come out of its dual foreign policy. On the one hand, it joins India and Russia and declares that terrorism is to be curbed at all costs. On the other hand, it shares very cozy relationships with Pakistan's fragile democracy which uses terrorism as its major foreign policy statement with weird elan.

Major Powers: Terror Trails

The other issue is terrorism. Attacks in India, France, Australia, Kenya and elsewhere have been discussed briefly. These incidents happened between 2011 and 2015. Major powers have to grapple with this serious issue by cutting across national or communal boundaries. That is because terror affects all of us. Thus, no humane and sane mind would support this evil Satan in any form whatsoever. We can observe that even highly equipped armed forces and police forces of major powers turn pygmies in the wake of a terror attack. France was taken to ransom in the second week of January 2015 by a handful of persons who had modern weapons. Australia had also faced a crisis like this one; we have mentioned the details in this very volume. Major powers must focus on the rising clout of terror groups among the masses at the grass root level. People link themselves up with these elements for the sake of money, political ideologies, religious fundamentalism or thrill. Major powers must transform their societies and teach their peoples to be liberal and fault tolerant. Currently, this is not happening. That is, people are getting training in arms operations in foreign lands, come back to their countries of work and executing deadly acts in those countries which had given them the permission to live and work. Most of these countries are located in the West. Despite the spread of modern education, many people are returning to Dark Age. This is a strange problem and every major power is trying to grapple with it in its own way. Religious fundamentalism is a major threat to the safety and dignity of any major power. Even countries like China and Russia, the big communist powers, have been facing the heat of religious fundamentalism due to their few sects which are highly polarized. Many of them are trying to become violent to the core.

Then, national orientations are also changing. Eastern Ukraine wants to get out of the control of the government of Ukraine. The eastern Ukrainian people want to join Russia. This national feeling is weird. If they had decided to remain part of Ukraine in 1989, why are they trying to change their camp now? Russian influence do not let the 20 CIS States grow independently. The Russian bear still rules over them. This is an example of broken national mandate. Communal reason may be behind the move of East Ukraine to secede from Ukraine. However, overt signs indicate that this bifurcation would be done purely on national grounds, not religious ones. Russia would gain from this separation.

Terror elements come from the mass-base level and are capable of shaking the biggest powers on the earth. The world has been facing terror attacks for quite some time now. In recent years, they have come fully trained and well armed. They executed plans with perfection. They killed people at will and they themselves died or got caught when they themselves decided. This is a weird strategy of terror groups. This can hurt the morale of security forces worldwide.

Major Powers: Three Categories

We shall also study the basic definitions of major power, super power and regional power in this text. It is hoped that our valued readers would be able to differentiate among these three concepts with finesse. The differentiation is vital from the view point of examination.

Major Powers: Affiliation with a Major Power is a Childish Idea

Affiliation with major powers is an issue that should be taken up with utter seriousness. If one gets close to Russia, one feels one is Russian and starts behaving like one. If one is close to America, one feels, as if American spirit has entered one's body. This world has business, terror, poverty alleviation and social transformation on its agenda. These petty issues (like alignment with one power or the other) should be done away with. We have to live peacefully with all peoples of this world. You cannot change your neighbours; all you can do is align some thoughts with your neighbours so that peaceful coexistence is feasible. This must be done in the interest of all the masses of this world. Religious differences must be given a back-seat in the interest of industrial growth worldwide. Major powers should influence business operations of their allies, not their strategic ambitions.

Economic growth of the masses is effected only if a major power adopts a country that is its ally and friend to the core. A coalition only for meeting strategic demands would not suffice. Rather, it would put that major power and its ally in bad perspective. Take the example of China and its strong ally, North Korea. The North Koreans have offended the USA time and again and even threatened to attack the White House. They have nuclear capabilities. How can North Korea even imagine of doing or stating all this? The reason is single and lethal—China is supporting North Korea and giving it strategic support of all genres. It is also training Pakistan to become a major terror state. Thus, Pakistan and North Korea are the two nations have been playing negative roles since the time they tied the knot with China. This is well known to the world that every act of subversion or terror against a person, firm or country ultimately ends up in devastation. The dominance of the West in the UNO and in North America irritates all traditional societies. But the West is also a growth engine of the world. Its negative points may not be imbibed but its positive points must be taken in for the sake of the growth of a country. No one stops you from praying in a temple, church, synagogue or mosque. The peoples of the West are free beyond compare, so let them live in their styles. However, we do not have any right to object to the living styles of peoples living in the West. At best, we may avoid copying those styles. We cannot pick guns and bombs to threaten any society on the plea that we are against their abilities, ideologies or *modus operandi*. Major powers can inform their allies about this cold fact. They cannot transform other societies. They can only protect their own interests as well as the interests of their allies in the most peaceful and rational ways. Tolerance is no longer the forte of the societies of the East. Otherwise, so much bloodshed would not have been witnessed since the start of the 1980s.

Major Powers: The Wannabes

Many other nations are aspiring to become major powers. They should try to improve the living standards of their masses. Economic prosperity and not military capability ought to be the most sought after goal of any nation that aspires to become a major power in the present era. More than one half of the peoples of this world are unable to make their two ends meet. Poverty has claimed millions of lives in Africa. Those, who have some resources, are also on the edge, literally! There is no scope of survival for them, leave alone growth. In such a scenario, major powers must consolidate their financial and industrial positions so that they could sustain the lives of their subjects. Then, they can look after the interest of the allies who they need and love. In the third phase, they all can join hands to make the UNO stronger and more powerful so that all masses of this world should be able to lead decent, agony-free lives. Today, even major powers are reeling under a host of problems, most of them arising from their own cultures, economies and social transformations. Let them put their houses in order first.

Major Powers: Must Unite against Communal Forces

Communal forces are raising their heads even in a communist nation like China. Elsewhere, religious sentiments flare up every now and then. The wars in Iraq and Syria are basically the clashes between Shiites and Sunnis, two major sects of Islam. Similarly, Pakistan has also witnessed many Shiite-Sunni riots in the past three decades, most of them bloody ones. This senseless violence must come to an end. Shiite and Sunnis are brothers from the same fold. There is no communal riot between any Shiite or Sunni community in India. Why is that so? The reason is that India is gradually shifting towards a culture of secular growth, despite media rhetoric and hate speeches of many religious leaders. Ours is a peaceful country which believes in peaceful coexistence of all sects and classes. Major powers must also address this issue and sort it out in the interest of our Muslim brothers and sisters.

Super Powers: Uncle Sam and Big Bear Still Dominate Major Powers

The USA and Russia dominate all powers because they are superpowers. If you closely observe, you would conclude that all major powers are under either of these two umbrellas. Overtly, they all support others in the UNO. But covertly, their policies are aligned towards one of the big bosses—Russia or America. As already stated, this system must be replaced by a rational system of ideologies and decision-making mechanisms. Why should Pakistan be called an ally of China? Why should India and China not settle their boundary issues in 2015 so that they could conduct more trade transactions with ease and élan in the time to come? Why are major powers trying to play games of hegemony, whereas they all know that wars would bring agonies for their respective peoples in the end? What happened to Germany, Italy and Japan at the end of the Second World War? We know that these three nations suffered the most.

Major Powers: Ecology and Environment are Key Issues

Environmental decay is the next major issue faced by major powers. They burn hydrocarbon fuels for the sake of their industrial growth. But these fuels generate toxic waste material. Thus, the soil, water and air of our planet have become polluted. Due to this, a host of diseases are taking birth and they are killing or hurting many lives. Ecological control and industrial efficiency must be on the agendas of Germany, India, Japan, China, the USA, Russia and other nations that are spending lots of fuels for the sake of industrial development. The Earth Summits do spring up plans and signature-worthy documents. But they do not stop major powers from polluting the environs of the mother earth. This is a serious issue because major powers and super powers are also the major polluters of the earth. They are squarely responsible for global warming, the extinction of 1000-plus plant and animal species and diseases like asthma, TB, lung cancer and others.

Major Powers: The Contemporary Scenario

Earlier, the role of a major power used to be only the protection of the interests of its peoples and those of its allies. Major powers like Russia and America used to follow this very policy. Then, times changed. The interests of other major powers started clashing with those of others. The human race suffered due to the extremely unipolar world during the Nineties and the first decade of the Twenty-first century. But then, the Russian Bear bounced back and started supplying oil and gas to Europe. That way, its financial prowess increased. It invested heavily on its defense arsenal and also on its allies. Hence, Putin found many avenues to challenge America. He kept Andrew Snowden, a whistle blower of the USA, at the Moscow International Airport for more than six months. Uncle Sam could not do anything to take Snowden out of the Russian Bear's hug. Thus, Putin showed his power.

This led to the initiation of a mini cold war between the two countries in question. If Russia does not supply oil to Europe, the latter would freeze forever in winters. That is why the EU could not tow American policies against Russia. Then, Russian forces or their allies promoted a rebellion within Ukraine. Thus, many Ukrainians voted in favour of secession from Ukraine and decided to join Russia without any fear or bias. Pro-Russian fighters also gunned down a plane of Malaysia in 2014 over the soil of Ukraine. The USA, just out of pangs of recession, did not try to venture out against Russia because it was trying to stabilize in economic terms. It was already fighting against the Taliban in FATA, Afghanistan and elsewhere. It did not want to open a direct front against the Russians who had many, many petro-dollars in their reserves and thus could prolong the new Cold War.

Believe it or not, there are only two super powers in the world. They are Uncle Sam and the Russian Bear. All others like China and India are still regional or major powers. Note that Major Powers include small players as well due to their technological advantages and close linkages with two superpowers. If this definition is given some leeway, we can conclude that Pakistan is also a major power. However, the defense establishment of Pakistan is very strong and its administrative set up has no control over either the army or the Taliban. That is why it was not included in the list of major powers. An unstable giant is likely to harm itself more than others. Pakistan is at its very best a regional power.

Stealthy to their cores, Chinese leaders are the thrust engines behind that country's economic and strategic growth graphs. China is not a democracy and shall never be one during the next 200 years. But how does that matter? China is a major power, moving ahead to become a super power, although the Bear and Uncle Sam do not admit this harsh fact. Thus, it is obviously a major power. The term super power is a bigger term and the term "major power" has different connotations, as we shall study in this book.

Recession had brought all countries on their knees. Now that the recession phase is slowly fading and as this world embraces the digital format of business slowly but surely, we have to understand concepts like "cyber warfare," "parallel diplomatic consultations," "satellite warfare," "religious affiliations in war" and "cultural resistance" to western cultural influences.

A Note on New Cold War

Since the US and Russia are members of the UNSC, leaders in the G-20 group and associates in many technological and scientific research activities, we cannot state that the New Cold war is really on. President Barrack Obama has not reacted strongly to the protection of Snowden, an enemy of the United States by all norms. This is his second terms as President and thus he would have to leave the stage in the next elections. Thus, he did not try to bother about the rising Russian influence over Europe and Asia. Thus, a mini cold war that is going on is likely to be resolved through diplomatic negotiations. The Russian rouble had plummeted in the wake of fall in the prices of crude oil in December 2014. A weak rouble forced the Russians to change their political stand. Thus, economy rules all countries in all parts of the world and major powers are not exception to this rule. A Cold War cannot be expected. Russia and the US are jointly working to eliminate terrorism. They have commercial interests which can be satisfied only of they work together at various global forums. Both nations are wise enough to understand that terror, not teasing, is the major issue faced by all five continents.

Thus, we need a decisive war against terror, not another Cold War. In any case, the previous cold war had ended as a damp squib. A new war between superpowers is only going to waste time and resources. Thus, it should not be initiated. If it has been, Putin and Obama can sort out their differences over a cup of tea.

Why Should We Study Foreign Policy of Major Powers

There are three aspects of this wide gamut of our deep-rooted study. We shall discuss them in detail in the text that follows:

(A) Religious Reasons:

Pakistan represents the active face of Jihad whereas Saudi Arabia represents the traditional Sunni face of Islam. The recent repercussions in all parts of the globe amply demonstrate this fact. The Islamic world has aligned with the West to get the vital information about the latter's strategies and plans. Although the Muslims and Christians are distant cousins, they are at daggers drawn with each other. This has been going on since the time of the sacrifice of grandson of the Prophet. All that we observe today is the revenge that is being taken by the forces of Islam against all those that are not Islamic and those whose posterity could be labeled as the one responsible for the martyrdom of Hussein, the (maternal) grandson of Holy Prophet. This is a new revelation because the Muslim world has become more volatile and hysteric after the death of Osama bin Laden and other religious leaders of his genre. In Pakistan, children were massacred as if they were army personnel (in December 2014). Religion is the opium of the masses. You cannot eliminate it from the mind of the masses. Hence, you cannot make this world grow to undefined heights till the time you are not able to eliminate the concept of religion from the minds of the masses.

(B) Political Reasons:

We must study the foreign policy of major powers because of political affiliations of various countries. Despite the critique heaped on the United Sates, it could not break its ties from Pakistan and Saudi Arabia. The major powers of the world are –the USA, Russia, Germany, China and Japan. Out of these, three powers have Christian majority and the other two have Buddhist minority. We cannot forget the ratio 3 to 2. The Christian race is ruling the roost, despite its reduced presence in India, Sri Lanka, Pakistan, Thailand, the Middle East and Africa. We cannot expect the entire world to come to the UN headquarters and take a unanimous decision simply because the future of a religion or race is at stake. Every religion must have its presence. We cannot stop any religious sect from spreading its wings in any part of the world; the only deterrent on its way could be the negative activities that it could plausibly execute to perpetuate its selfish interests. That step, if taken, leads to the destruction and massacre of innocent civilians, as we have witnessed in the past 100 years. Thus, political affiliations and motives must also be studied to get into the root of the problem.

(C) Economic Reasons:

Germany, despite its small size and GDP, wants to become a superpower. If it cannot become a superpower, it cannot enter major markets of the world. If it cannot become a superpower, it would like to become a major power at least. It is a technical super power, not a super power. German products are being sold in all parts of the world. Germany has collaborations with most nations of this globe. But you would hear about only the USA, China or Japan in technical trade agreements. Germany is a distant cousin in all these tech-games. Hence, if the USA can make Chevrolet, why cannot Germany make an Audi? That is the question of be or not to be! This is just an example. Talk of Japan. It has always been under the shadow of its own technology or the US. Japan was defeated by then United States in 1945 AD. Today, in 2015 AD, Japan is still a pygmy, a vestigial organ of Uncle Sam. Please note that Japan has armed forces only for namesake. The USA owns Japan!

(D) Socio-cultural Reasons:

Major powers, especially the USA and Russia, are trying to bring about cultural transformations in their own favour. They want to establish the markets of their products and services in the world due to their military or technological abilities. These markets must be established for achieving their commercial interests, for money the most important thing for a businessman. These countries are also business entities. Their billion-dollar budgets cannot be sustained until or unless they sell their products or services to those who need them.

(E) Academic Reasons:

The body of knowledge of any stream would grow only if it is studied with deep devotion. If we want to learn what the Chinese are trying to do in the future, we would be able to define our policies for the future. Then, our children would also be able to define or re-define their policies. Theory must be refined to give a new set of theory. New theories give rise to new sets of solutions. This had been done in the past as well; this shall be done in the future as well. Theory would be transformed into practice in international political circles. Time is the only deterrent. We must study foreign policy of major powers because we must know where this world is heading to. We want a peaceful planet and a human society which must learn to live, despite its diversities. Major powers would eventually decide what this human race would choose—life or death! The peoples of all countries look up to them and seek stability and prosperity for their families and countries. Thus, major powers, spread throughout the country, must have a common rationale to safeguard their interests. This can be done only if academicians study this process and reach correct conclusions.

(F) Regional Security Reasons:

The security of an entire country becomes a point of concern that takes part in anti-terror operations. Recently, the Australians were shocked when their own backyard, Sydney, was attacked by a few gunmen. Customers of the coffee shop were held as hostages for more than twelve hours. Note that Australia had sent its troops along with the US troops to Asia. The Australians got the reward of keeping their troops in a foreign country. India did not send its troops and even then, a shop in a busy street of Bengaluru was targeted by terror groups in 2014. We have become passive warriors and the results of this passive attitude are nasty by any norm. Just imagine—what would happen if we send our own troops to Afghanistan to fight against the Taliban? Regional security is also at stake because Pakistan is not willing to tame its army or terror groups. That is because the ongoing spate of operations in Pakistan is helping its politicians. They are having a ball even as children are dying. They would win—army or no army! They would quit if they are told to. Eventually, army rule would be imposed on Pakistan. It would continue for a few years. Then, the UN and a few members of the UNSC would prompt the Pakistani nation to restore democracy. Elections would be held. Another PM would arrive. Army would do its tasks. Terror groups would do their tasks. Everyone would be happy, except the common masses, elderly people and children of Pakistan, the latter being the latest targets of terror. This is a funny game that has been going on since the inception of Pakistan. There are no solutions for regional security. The only solution that could be implemented was the presence of foreign troops in Pakistan and Afghanistan. But the NATO ended its stay in Pakistan on December 30, 2014. Thus, the war theatre is open yet again for all terror elements operating in the FATA, North Waziristan, Peshawar and some parts of Afghanistan. Thus, the UN would have to devise a strategy under which a major power would always remain present in the terror-affected regions of Pakistan and Afghanistan. That is why we need to define clear, lucid foreign policies of all major policies.

(G) Futuristic Supply Reasons:

Any nation whose size is more than the size of Great Britain, already a major power, aspires to become a major power. Look at Nigeria, Kenya, Pakistan, Australia and South Africa. They all have ambitions to become major powers. They want to make their presence felt on the global political and strategic platforms. They ought to study how a nation can become a major power. That is why this study is essential. The emergence of a nation as a major power automatically opens up a host of possibilities for its citizens and allies. For example, Germany is a major power because of the technological progress it has made over the past 50 years. It can provide basic parts and equipment to superpowers that would be used in the most advanced war machinery. So, Germany would make either high-grade weapons or parts thereof. Behind the strategic and political supremacy of a country at the international stage, lies a very basic thought—commerce. Russia has been selling AK-47, AK56 and now, AK100 for more than 60 years. The USA has sold F-16 fighter aircraft to Pakistan and other allies. Currently, only the USA, China, Russia, Ukraine and a few other nations have become capable of supplying advanced weaponry to rebels, Jihadis, terror elements, smugglers, antisocial elements and a host of nations. This business is so vast and lucrative that our valued readers cannot fathom its exact depth. Countries want to become major powers because they would like to make weapons which would be easily usurped by many organizations across the globe. True! Some of them would not be countries but terror groups. But who cares about these aspects as long as cash counters are ticking!

(H) Personal Reasons:

When Colonel Muammar Qaddafi was alive, he had said that he would be the first one to buy a nuclear bomb, if it was made by a Muslim nation. Small countries become secure only if they acquire war machinery and lethal arsenal. Iran does not have a nuclear bomb but it certainly has nuclear capabilities; so does Pakistan. Personal vendetta is a crucial factor in this context. Had the Palestinians got a nuclear bomb, Israel would never have attacked them so ruthlessly in the past 60 years. They do not have it, so they are suffering. Israel has many of them, so it rules the roost in West Asia, Ghaza strip and elsewhere. We must study foreign policies of small nations like Palestine, Israel, Libya, Syria and Iraq so that we may learn what they would do if they acquire weapons of mass destruction. Their policies must have tinges of rationale, we pray!

CHAPTER 2 Concept and Bases of Power

Introduction

We human beings have layaways tried to acquire power. We love to be in the company of those who are in power. Countries form alliances with strong powers, called major powers. The world has become a highly volatile place due to the increasing number of acts of terror against the human kind. The security forces and armies of various nations are equally ruthless. One, who has some power, does not spare another who is not in power. The weak countries or groups organize and amass money, weapons and machines. Thus, they attack those who are in power. The reprisals of such attacks or wars take bloody hues. This vicious cycle has been going on since the end of the last century. Terror groups have become much stronger and full of resources after the breakdown of the Soviet empire. The US is also suffering due to terror elements spread across its length and breadth and also spread in other parts of the world.

Framework of Analysis

In the text that follows, we shall study power in detail. We have altered the text in the interest of our readers. We are studying power in the context of major powers of the globe. We have also included the text on personal power and country power to clarify both concepts. Country power makes a country a major power. An individual's power makes him a strong man among the masses; that is a totally different concept but quite basic to the tenet of country power, which is our focus in this volume. We shall discuss power, individual power, country power and the sub-classes of both these genres of power.

The following features of power are vital for defining a framework of analysis:

1. In this world, 10 percent people have control over 90 percent of resources. The World Economic Summit held in

Switzerland in January 2015 confirmed this fact. Poor nations were told to perform and deliver concrete economic results. They were accused of being inefficient. Thus, they are the haves and have enough power to decimate or overwhelm the rest 90 percent of the people of the world, the so-called have-nots.

2. If power is exercised, it gets reduced. However, reduced power can be enhanced only after making a lot of sacrifices. Recovery of power is not an easy task.
3. Powerful people attract the support of weak people. The same fact is true about organizations and countries.
4. Powerful people also attract the wrath of their enemies. If powerful people are rich enough, they become the targets of have-nots. Results could be bloody in many such cases.
5. Countries exercise power through forums. They cannot exercise power through bilateral relationships simply because the entire world is a place for free deliberations and friends and foes of each country play their respective roles for safe bailouts of their allies. For example, China and India fight against each other bitterly over the boundary dispute but they have not gone to war since 1962. The UNO and superpowers ensure that they keep their fists clenched. Hence, India a weak player out of the two players, acts slightly tactfully. China, on the other hand, cannot force India to decide the boundary issue in its own favour. Thus, the world watches carefully, even as China and India talk over various issues. They are friends as well foes. They are friends because Chinese investments in India are rising and the Tata group is setting up factories in China. They are foes because they seek territorial rights that the other party refuses to grant.
6. Country power can emanate from personal power. Mrs. Indira Gandhi, Winston Churchill, Harry Truman, George Washington, Garibaldi, Mussolini and many other able leaders of the old era are examples that can be quoted in this context.
7. Coercive power is the worst type of power. Expert power is the best type of power. In this context, examples can be cited of Germany (Germany, a technological giant of the

new era) and Adolf Hitler (a German, who decimated 60 million Jews but met his fate in 1945).

8. Individuals, groups, organizations, regional economic groups and nations can acquire power only if they either associate themselves with powerful entities or have enough resources and technologies to acquire supremacy in a field or two.

What Is Power?

We all are human beings. Still, we have some abilities that make us more capable of doing some things that others cannot do. Power is the ability to get something done from others without exerting any extra influence on others. This power can come to you due to your physical ability, authority (given by you in legal terms), your coercive prowess, your expertise (mental abilities), or political affiliations (due to your political party's powers or manipulations).

Power has many uses but it is mostly abused by those who have it. Take the examples of Idi Amin, Fidel Castro, Muammar Qaddafi, Indira Gandhi, Adolf Hitler and Joseph Stalin. All these leaders were famous for their arrogant, autocratic tactics even as they ruled their respective nations. However, Mahatma Gandhi, Martin Luther King, Vinoba Bhave, Dhiru Bhai Ambani, Bill Gates, Steve Jobs, Sunderlal Bahuguna, Medha Patkar and many more leaders of various fields did extremely well. They were not dictators. Remember the following typical features of power (and learn your lessons):

1. **Acquisition:** Power is not granted by any person or organization to you. Rather, you have to acquire it through your toil and guts. Expert power is the best power.
2. **Hues:** Power can be both negative and positive. Mostly, man longs for negative power. Coercive power is a negative power. It is better to become a university professor and teach management to students instead of running a mafia racket. Both of these posts carry power. The only thing is that power is its colour. You use blood of people to make it red and you yourself would get red. You use people to help people and you shall be showered Nobel

prizes, money and what not! Be on the positive side of the fence when you work to acquire power.

3. **Usage:** When power is exercised, it gets reduced. If you have power, your influence on the other person should be so much effective that he performs the tasks (which were to be done by him) on his own, without getting a single phone call from you. That is power. People laid down their lives for Gandhi, went to jail along with him and walked all paths to make him their own God. He had nothing in his hands. He did not have money, machine-guns, cars, bungalows, etc. he had only a vision—release India from the clutches of the British. His followers lived through that dream and eventually realized it too. Leaders do not use broom to clean up *ashrams* but Gandhi himself did it. He forced his wife to do so, for she was not ready to do the clean-up jobs. His humility was his greatest ability.
4. **Loss:** When one loses power, one feels as if the world has come to an end for him. That is not unusual. However, we repeat, expert power is best. It is also better than political power. Try to become an expert mechanic instead of PM of a nation; you would get more satisfaction that way. If a person or firm loses power, it can change its tactics to acquire it once again. But if a country loses power, it becomes very difficult for it to recover it. Pakistan lost the war of 1971 against India. General A.A.K. Niazi, who had surrendered to Indian troops in Bangladesh, lived for many years to live the painful moments of his surrender to General Jagjit Singh Arora at Dhaka in December 1971. The loss of 1971 was very telling for the general. That is why India has been facing terror attacks from Pakistan. We won at that time and we lose our men and equipment even today. A defeated neighbour is a hissing snake that can bite anytime. India also lost the 1962 war against China. But we decided not to extend the issue. India has not attacked any country for the past 10,000 years. Japan lost the Second World War. Its peoples still feel the agonies of Hiroshima and Nagasaki. These wounds cannot have any soothing balms; they are just there! Japan did rise from

the rubble of the War and became a technology major. But it is not a strategic power, a chief issue that we are discussing in this entire volume. When Germany lost the War, it was divided into two parts. Russia fiddled with East Germany like a toy for 50 years. The USA fiddled with West Germany like a cheesecake for 50 years. When the two Germany's united, they became one single entity once again. Today, Germany is a major power, a nation to be watched out for. Its size is small but its capabilities are amazing. Hail the Aryans!

5. **Friends:** When you join hand with people, you become more powerful. The strategic alliances of NATO, Warsaw Pact and KANU define and enhance the ambitions of their respective members. SAARC is not at a defence alliance. NATO is the most powerful strategic alliance, which was created to keep the EU nations under the American umbrella without keeping US troops in Europe. This was a wise and long-sighted maneuver of the USA and UK; it was decided long ago to keep American troops out of Europe because Europe is now a commercial and fashion hub of the world, not a war theatre. Two world wars were already fought for it and the human race could not afford a third one.
6. **Foes:** When one group becomes powerful, the members of that group also become powerful. The rival group feels the pressure and prepares, in turn, to strike with ever more strength. Thus, even if members are powerful within the group, they can be made timid by a rival group. Consider the alliance of NATO. No other group, except the Warsaw Pact nations had opposed it. But Russian Bear's grip over its members has weakened over time. Many nations of East Europe have also joined the NATO. Thus, Russia has only Ukraine, Moldavia, India, Cuba and some other nations by its side. India is not part of the Warsaw Pact Group. Thus, Russia's power has somewhat dwindled during the past thirty years or so. NATO is strong but Warsaw Pact Group is only for namesake. Yes! Russia itself is powerful enough to thwart any strategic challenge. It has love-and-hate relationship with Uncle Sam.

7. **Power Affiliation:** Everyone wants to get power. But this is not possible in every firm, group or country. Thus, every individual or firm of country tries to remain in the company of those who are in power. They think that they would acquire a part of the power possessed by them. In order to get closer to the echelons of power, an individual, group, firm or country has to make many a sacrifice.

Power in the Context of International Relations

Power in International Relations can be defined in different ways. Political scientists, historians and practitioners of international relations (diplomats) have used the following concepts of political power:

1. Power as a goal of States or leaders is the most important ambition of mankind. This very ambition forced man to wage battles and wars in the past and the future is also fraught with many bloody conflicts. Here, the term 'State' refers to a country or a nation ruled by a monarchy.
2. Power as a measure of influence or control over outcomes, events, actors and issues.
3. Power as reflecting victory in the time of conflict and the attainment of security.
4. Power as a control over resources and capabilities.
5. Power as a status, which some states or actors possess and others do not.

Today, experts speak in terms of State power, indicating both economic power and military power. Those States that have significant amounts of power within the international system are referred to as Middle Powers, Regional Powers, Great Powers, Super Powers, Hyper Powers or Hegemonic Powers, although there is no commonly accepted standard for defining a powerful State.

Entities other than States can also acquire and wield power in international circles. Such entities can include multilateral international organizations, Transnational Corporations (TNCs), military alliance organizations like the NATO, multinational corporations like Wal-Mart, Non-government Organizations, the Roman Catholic Church and militant groups.

Lethal Insinuations of Power in the Context of International Relations

There are five aspects of lethal insinuations of power in the international political arena. They are as follows:

1. Power Corrupts and Absolute Power Corrupts Absolutely

This is a centuries-old adage. Our valued readers must have read it in the books of management and political science. Recall the lives and times of Idi Amin (Uganda), Adolf Hitler (Germany), Mussolini (Italy), Joesph Stalin (Russia), Imelda Marcos (the Philippines), Zia-ul-Haque (Pakistan) and Julius Caesar (Rome). Recall the name of General Pinochet as well as all those dictators whose names may have faded into the oblivion. In an artificial democracy, an autocratic leader always uses the power of the gun to occupy the top spot. Then, he enjoys his spoils. Finally, he meets his gory end. His ouster is a matter of international observation and pondering over. In a real democracy, the person willing to acquire power uses democratic institutions to get to the highest echelons of power. Then, he starts enjoying his power. If he becomes corrupt or dictatorial or both, he is democratically removed. The masses suffer in both cases. The only plus point in a democracy is that the dictator or corrupt leader can be removed through democratic means. For example, General Pervez Musharraf was banned from fighting elections in Pakistan for his lifetime.

2. An Autocratic State Makes Humanity Suffer

The leaders of an autocratic nation make their peoples cry. The peoples of neighbouring countries also suffer due to the deeds of such leaders.

3. Power Breeds Terror

If a democratic setup is missing in a nation, its top leaders would use illicit means to collect revenues. They would also torture their own peoples or force other nations to follow their commands. These nations can be tiny in geographical and economic terms. They want to increase their clout in their regions. Even in a democratic setup, powerful people exploit those who are either out of power or are too weak to resist exploitation. In the global context, we can cite the name of Saddam Hussein (Iraq). Saddam mercilessly killed his opponents in 1966 and captured power in Baghdad. He used every resource at his command to maintain his supremacy.

4. Poor and Oppressed Groups Oppose Power through Gory Reprisals

These weak people then rise to the occasion and create anti-oppression outfits. Exploitation by the State has not become a major issue although reprisals to State exploitation are being witnessed in all parts of the world. For example, the Naxalite movement of Bihar, Andhra Pradesh and West Bengal had started from a village called Naxalbari (West Bengal). It was a reply to the exploitation of the innocent masses of those states by the corrupt system. The Maoists also came to the fore to express their demands in bloody ways. As a result of their gory reprisals, the eastern states of India are fearful and the masses extend all kinds of support to them. In the global context, Fidel Castro (Cuba) and Che Guewara (South America) opposed the oppression of the State.

5. Groups Use Global Support to Fight Battles and Wars

Many countries support outfits according to their commercial, political and geo-political ambitions. That is why many outfits are roaming around the globe and dictating their terms. The masses of any country are soft targets. These groups kidnap people, kill them, cut their limbs or keep them as captives as per their own wishes. That is why we must contend that the use of weapons must be restricted to only paramilitary forces, military and security organizations. But we can observe the dramatic, nee lethal proliferation of arms around the world. People fiddle with arms and learn how to use them. Unemployed youth are the best targets of nations that want to perpetrate terror in other countries. The 26/11 massacre of Mumbai was masterminded by Pakistani terror outfits in full collusion with the Pakistani army. The same terror leaders are roaming freely in that country. Note that perpetrating terror is a big business. The youth are sent to other countries to spread terror and kill innocent civilians. The common people do not have weapons. Thus, they succumb to coercive pressures in most cases. Two Japanese citizens were captured and beheaded by terrorists in February 2015. Japan could not pay the ransom to get them released. Every global terror group gets sufficient funds from one country or another. Otherwise, it cannot survive in the tough global conditions of today.

Dimensions of Power

Leopold von Ranke had tried to scientifically document great powers. For many, power capabilities were the sole criterion to categorize a nation into a proper set or subset of countries. In his essay, 'French Diplomacy in the Postwar Period,' the French historian Jean-Baptiste Duroselle spoke of the concept of multi-polarity. Thus, he wrote (we quote him): "A Great power is one which is capable of preserving its own independence against any other single power."

This was quite different from views given by earlier writers, notably from Leopold von Ranke. Thus, Ranke had a different idea of the world situation. In his essay 'The Great Powers,' written in 1833, Leopold von Ranke wrote: "If one could establish as a definition of a Great Power that it must be able to maintain itself against all others, even when they are united, then Frederick has raised Prussia to that position." These positions have always attracted critical remarks of scholars and political thinkers around the globe.

Spatial Dimension

Every State has a geographic scope of interests, actions or projected power. This is a crucial factor in distinguishing a great power from a regional power. According to definition, the scope of a regional power is restricted to its region. It has been suggested that a great power should be possessed of actual influence throughout the scope of the prevailing international system. Arnold J. Toynbee observes, "Great power may be defined as a political force exerting an effect co-extensive with the widest range of the society in which it operates. The Great Powers of 1914 were world powers because Western society had recently become worldwide."

Other suggestions have been made that a great power should have the capacity to engage in extra-regional affairs and that a great power ought to be possessed of extra-regional interests, two propositions which are often closely connected.

Status Dimension

Formal or informal acknowledgment of a nation's great power status has also been a criterion for being a great power. George Modelski avers, "The status of Great Power is sometimes confused with the condition of being powerful, The office, as it is known, did in fact evolve from the role played by the great military states in earlier periods. But the Great Power system institutionalizes the position of the powerful state in a web of rights and obligations."

This approach restricts analysis to the post-Congress of the Vienna epoch. In Vienna, great powers were first formally recognized. In the absence of such a formal act of recognition, it has been suggested that great power status can arise by implication, by judging the nature of a state's relations with other great powers.

A further option is to examine a State's willingness to act as a great power. As a nation will seldom declare that it is acting as such, this usually calls for the retrospective examination of that State's overt and covert behaviours around the globe. This is of much limited use in establishing the nature of contemporary powers, at least not without the exercise of subjective observation. No country would declare that it has nuclear weapons or is trying to acquire the same. However, every country would try to acquire them. In the heart of every nation's CEO, there is a desire to become a power. People support him or her in that thinking and finally, the country starts calling itself a power. The real strengths and weaknesses of the State are forgotten. How can a poor nation be a power? This is a big question. But still, India is called a regional power. China is called a regional or major power that would become a superpower later. China's poverty levels are not known to India, unlike those of India. Thus, many nations defy Abraham Henry Maslow's hierarchy of needs and try to leap to the topmost wrung of the power ladder, oblivious to the fact that many or most of their subjects do not have enough to eat on a daily basis. Developing countries can influence others but they cannot change the political and economic processes going around the world, just like Russia and the USA, who are capable of doing so.

True, if a nation has resources, it can act as a power. Saudi Arabia has oil. Hence, it can influence other Arab nations and can even alter their military and political policies. However, oil is but one part of the entire energy sector and it would not last forever. Hence, if you do not have a magic stick, you become powerless. So long as you wield it, you have power. Oil-rich nations have powers but these powers (born out of their respective resources) cannot be taken as firm bases to give these nations clear-cut designations on the chessboard of power and politics of the globe.

Other important criteria throughout history are that great powers should have enough influence to be included in discussions of political and diplomatic questions of the day, and have influence on the final outcome and resolution. When major political questions were addressed, several great powers used to meet to discuss the same. Before the era of the United Nations, participants of such meetings were not officially named. They used to be decided on the basis of their great power status. Conferences used to settle important questions based on major historical events. This might mean deciding the political resolution of various geographical and nationalist claims following a major conflict. But this concept is out of use now. Historical conferences and treaties display this very pattern such as the Congress of Vienna, the Congress of Berlin, the discussions of the Treaty of Versailles which redrew the map of Europe and finally, the Treaty of Westphalia.

Defining Four Types of Country Power

1. Superpowers:

In 1944, Fox defined superpower as great power plus great mobility of power. Thus, he identified three states, the British Empire, the Soviet Union and the United States of America. With the decline of the British Empire and the breakup of the Soviet Union, the United States is currently the only country considered a superpower, with Brazil, China, Russia, India and the European Union being potential superpowers. However, Russia has assumed the status of superpower yet again, given that it has the largest Red Army and the most sophisticated weapons and ammunitions, which are next only to those of the USA. China is a distant third but we cannot categorize it as a superpower. Thus, there are only two superpowers in the world. They are Russia and the United States of America.

2. Great Powers:

The term great power used to refer to any nation that had strong political, cultural and economic influence over nations around it and across the globe. Thus, China, France, Germany, Japan, Russia and the United Kingdom are often considered current great powers.

3. Regional Powers:

This concept used to describe a country that exercised influence and power within a region. Being a regional power is not mutually exclusive with any of the other categories of power. Many countries are often described as regional powers. They are Australia, Brazil, Canada, India, Italy, Mexico, South Korea and Spain.

4. Middle Powers:

They are second-tier influential States that are never described as great powers. They are Argentina, Pakistan, Netherlands, Indonesia, Israel, Poland and South Africa. They work to serve their regional interests but are never in limelight because of their internal strife or weak financial prowess. The Netherlands is a strong nation in this group. But it has not shown political ambitions as a power. That is why it does not have much say in most political forms. Israel is the right hand of the USA. Its identity has been defined and maintained by the Americans. On its own, Israel cannot fight against the Arabs. In the war of 1967, Arab states had lost to Israel because of the technology and military supremacy of the USA. Israel was still a state in formative years at that time. The Arabs were not able to penetrate Israeli territory simply because American intelligence agencies were very alert and powerful. They did not allow the Arab States to overpower Israel for a single moment.

Major Power: the Latest Concept

So, we should now come out of the jargon of description of powers. Instead of describing concepts and definitions, we should delineate the concept of major power in the interest of the human race. Thus, let us finally describe what a major power really is. Arvind Kumar gives the following definition:

"A major power is a democratically governed country that enjoys political, economic, cultural, social, nuclear and military superiority over other nations and wishes to (and acts to) ensure the benefit of all masses of the world on a consistent basis, without indulging in cheap or subversive degradation of any human's physical, social or higher-order needs."

Firstly, a major power is one that has a democratic system. Most major powers are democracies. Russia and China are not democracies but they have partially become democracies. Secondly, these nations must have some superiority over other nations. It is a fact and we admit that all major powers have some sort of edge over others. Thirdly, these nations must work hard for the benefit of all masses of the world. Well, these countries are taking care of or are trying to look after their own populations. Fourthly, these nations must respect the physical, social, and higher-order needs of man—physical needs are physiological, social needs demand relationships and higher-order needs demand the human being to become self-actualized. The concept of needs hierarchy was taken from the theory of A.H. Maslow.

The current major powers do not come up to the standards described in this definition, if we carefully scan their past records and current over or covert ambitions. However, Rome was not built in a day. There is always time for improvement. There is always scope for working in the right direction. This is an ideal definition, which has echoes of just one phrase.... "the entire mankind is just one single entity..."

Major Power: Names of Nations

We are not using the aforementioned definition to give examples of major powers because they have already been identified due to political, geographical, military or economic considerations. Thus, we have conducted a deep study in this context to arrive at the conclusion that the following nations are the powers of the world and have been categorized by various authors according to different definitions.

Major Powers of World	Major Five (Part of the UNSC)
1. The United States of America	1. The United States of America
2. Russia and CIS States	2. Russia
3. China	3. China
4. Germany	4. France
5. Japan	5. The United Kingdom
6. India	**Regional Powers**
7. Pakistan	1. Brazil
8. France	2. China
9. The European Union	3. India
10. The United Kingdom	4. South Africa
	5. Saudi Arabia
Superpowers	**EU's Big Three**
1. The United States of America	1. Germany
2. Russia and CIS States	2. The United Kingdom
	3. France
The Great Four	**Energy Superpowers**
1. Brazil	1. Saudi Arabia
2. Germany	2. Russia
3. India	3. Canada (likely to become)
4. Japan	4. Australia (likely to become)
Cultural or Entertainment Superpowers	
1. The UK	3. Japan
2. The USA	4. South Korea

Usage of Power

Power can be used in the following five ways:

1. Power as a Goal:

The primary usage of power as a goal in international relations belongs to political theorists, such as Niccolò Machiavelli and Hans Morgenthau. Classical Realist thinkers aver that power is an inherent goal of mankind and of States. Economic growth, military growth, cultural spread etc. can all be considered as working towards the ultimate goal of international power.

2. Power as Influence:

The NATO accounts for over 70 percent of global military expenditure. The USA is responsible for 43 percent of global military expenditure. Political scientists use power in terms of an actor's ability to exercise influence over other actors within the international political realm. This influence can be coercive, attractive, cooperative, or competitive. Many mechanisms of influence can be used. Examples are threat, political influence through a friendly nation, economic pressure, dinner diplomacy and cultural exchange.

3. Power as Security:

Power is also used when describing states or actors that have achieved military victories or security for their state in the international system. This general usage is most commonly found among the writings of historians or popular writers. For instance, a state that has achieved a string of combat victories in a military campaign against other states can be described as powerful. An actor that has succeeded in protecting its security, sovereignty, or strategic interests from repeated or significant challenge can also be described as powerful.

4. Power as Capability:

Charles W. Freeman, Jr. described power as the following: "Power is the capacity to direct the decisions and actions of others. Power derives from strength and will. Strength comes from the transformation of resources into capabilities." Note that will infuses objectives with a steely resolve. Strategy marshals capabilities and brings in a perfect alignment with precision. Statecraft seeks through strategy to magnify the mass, relevance, impact and irresistibility of power. It guides the ways the State deploys and applies its power abroad. These ways embrace the arts of war, espionage, and diplomacy. Power is also used to describe resources and capabilities of a State. This definition is quantitative and is most often used by geo-politicians and the military. Capabilities are thought of intangible terms—they are measurable, weighable and quantifiable assets.

Thomas Hobbes talks of power as a means of obtaining some future apparent good. Hard power can be treated as a potential and is not often enforced on the international arena. Chinese strategists have a concept of national power which can be measured quantitatively. They use an index known as Comprehensive National Power or CNP.

5. Power as Status:

Much effort in academic and popular writing is devoted to deciding which countries have the status of power and how this can be measured. If a country has power (as influence) in military, diplomatic, cultural and economic spheres, it can be called Power (as status). There are several categories of power. Thus, the inclusion of a State in one category or another is fraught with difficulties and confusion.

What is Sphere?

Under certain circumstances, States can organize a sphere of influence or a bloc within which they exercise predominant influence. Examples of spheres include the spheres of influence recognized under the Concert of Europe, or the recognition of spheres during the Cold War following the Yalta Conference. The Warsaw Pact, the Free World, and the Non-Aligned Movement were the blocs that arose out of the Cold War contest. Military alliances like NATO and the Warsaw Pact are another forum through which influence is exercised. However, the realist theory often attempts to stay away from the creation of powerful blocs/spheres that can create a hegemonic entity within the region. British foreign policy, for example, has always sided against the hegemonic forces on the European continent, i.e. Nazi Germany, Napoleonic France or Habsburg Austria.

What is Bloc?

A bloc is an entity that comprises many nations with close geographic boundaries or common interests. It may or may not be created for economic cooperation. The Shanghai Cooperation Organization (SCO), to quote an example, is a bloc that has been created by China to exert its influence over the members of this bloc.

Note that the SCO is a Eurasian political, economic and military organization. It was founded in 2001 in Shanghai by the leaders of China, Kazakhstan, Kyrgyzstan, Russia, Tajikistan and Uzbekistan. Four members of the Shanghai Five are part of the SCO. Note that Shanghai Five was created in 1996. The fifth member of the SCO is Uzbekistan which joined SCO in 2001. Thus, Shanghai Five became SCO and is a regional organization run mainly by the communist dictators of Beijing. This proves, and it would prove later too, that a visibly political or economic bloc of countries may not be serving the purpose for which it was created with a few overt official goals. Further, the ASEAN is a cooperation bloc that has economics and trade on its agenda, to quote an example. It does not have political ambitions in the ASEAN region. G-20 and G-8 are two blocs that have clear rules, goals and procedures. Their primary concern is economic development of the entire world.

What is Alliance?

Alliances are created for achieving military superiority or for proving to the world that the group or alliance members must not be harmed in any way. NATO and Warsaw Pact are two strategic alliances. In our view, all alliances have military connotations. If countries want to indulge in regional trade, they form economic zones like SAFTA, NAFTA or the EU. Then, they do not create alliances.

Bases of Power

In this context, we shall divide our study into two parts—Personal Power and Country Power. We are studying foreign policies of major powers. Hence, we must understand the concept of power and its bases from a country's viewpoint as well. In the text that follows, we shall discuss both types of power—**Personal Power** and **Country** Power.

Personal Power

There are nine bases of personal power. They have been divided into two genres—**Formal Power** and **Personal Power**. Let us study them in brief.

Formal Power

It is the power acquired by a person by virtue of his or her formal authority in a government office, private organization, NGO, the UNO or elsewhere. It is granted to him or her because of his or her academic background, experience, typical abilities to deliver concrete results and finally, his or her integrity of character during his years in service. People may have formal power but no one may obey them. The example of Indian bureaucratic departments can be quoted in this context. Formally appointed officers are handled in a formal way. If they cannot be handled that way, they are bribed to settle many issues. Formal power has four subcategories, as follows:

1. Formal Power (Reward)

This power enables the power owner to give reward to people for the pieces of work they do for him or her. Money and non-monetary incentives are part of every business organization. In the context of international relations, these rewards are very much fat and lucrative. Diplomats (Chinese ambassador in the USA), scholars (peace mongers, environmental activists (Sunderlal Bahuguna, Medha Patkar), bank CEOs (Raghuram Rajan), chiefs of UN organizations, negotiators of arms and equipment deals (Ottavio Quattrocci), health care workers and social activists (Mr. Kailash Satyarthi) get good rewards and honours for the services rendered by them. Example: Malala Yusufzai and Mr. Satyarthi shared the Nobel Peace Prize for 2013. The Nobel Committee considered them fit for this prize due to their expertise (peaceful solutions of problems); the Nobel Committee has formal power (reward).

2. Formal Power (Legitimate)

A judge can punish you by imposing a fine of Rs. 1,000 because you had crossed a red light. If you speak and protest, the fine is increased to say, Rs. 1,500. You cannot speak in front of a judge. This task is done by your counsel. A school headmaster, a college principal, a university's VC, a manager in a private firm, a commander in the army—all of them have formal powers. They cannot go beyond the power circles allocated to them. If they do, they are punished. A judge has legitimate power; it has been granted to him by his country's Constitution. He cannot give unduly long sentence terms to a convict.

3. Formal Power (Information)

Information is the latest power. If you have a set of information about a person, you can use or misuse it to manipulate him. If you know how he acts and behaves in public, you can manipulate him to your advantage. If you know his weaknesses, you can win him over in a jiffy. Such is the power of information. Ironically, we are going through an Information Boom in which most information on the internet is either wrong or not fully confirmed or validated. Thus, we have to use this power with extreme care, lest we should use wrong sets of information for wrong people (and end up in a mess).

4. Formal Power (Democratic)

This is the formal power granted to a person or group of persons through the right of adult franchise that is exercised by the masses of a nation. Arvind Kejriwal was elected as the CM of Delhi state. He worked for 49 days and had to quit because democracy had worked. Similarly, A.B. Vajpayee worked as PM for 13 days, 13 months and finally, for six years due to the power of democratic forces given to him; he was awarded the prestigious Bharat Ratna by the President of India in December 2014. If the masses are behind you, you can become God! But beware of your indulgences. The masses also know how to pull the carpet off your feet. The examples of Mrs. Indira Gandhi (loss in elections of 1977) and President Zia-ul-Haq (assassination on board a military plane) can be quoted in this context.

Personal Power

1. Personal Power (Expert):

This is the power acquired by a person due to his expertise in a particular field. You may be a good teacher, author, electrician, car mechanic, painter, army general, head constable and what not! You have a gift that you either had in you or had developed over time within you. Out of all the powers that we have described in this text, expert power is the best. We should try to acquire it, even though we may have to sacrifice something for getting the same. Examples of this genre include Mr. Raghuram Rajan (a professionally qualified banker and Governor of the RBI), Bill Gates (software icon), Om Puri (professional actor), Sachin Tendulkar (the Master Blaster), any expert doctor (say the one who is an FRCS) and so on. Expertise is acquired through education, practice and dedication. Even experts can fail at times.

2. Personal Power (Referent):

This is the power acquired by a person by virtue of his linkages with other people who are really powerful in legitimate or coercive terms. If your uncle is in the police, say it and feel. Everyone would start respecting you. If your father is a UN ambassador, you would have the best company of friends. You would also get good opportunities in life due to your father. If the person in power is a goon and you mention his name and link yourself with him, you would be able to get all your tasks done. But your image in the market would suffer. People pay *hafta* (weekly fee) to hooligans in Mumbai. Political parties also take money (*rangdari*) from shopkeepers during election days. Such goons and parties do not last long. The face of a black shadow remains black, whatsoever name may be given to it for the sake of convenience. So, use reference power only in a positive way and using those people who are positively placed in society. As an example, we quote the name of Raghu, played by Sanjay Dutt, in the movie *Vastav*. He rolled in millions and wore a thick gold chain. He killed many people but did not have the guts to kill himself. Finally, his mother had to relieve him from this agonizing jail, nee world (in the end of the movie).

3. Personal Power (Charismatic)

This power is acquired by only a few people. These people do not work for themselves but they are dedicated to the cause that touches the lives of masses. Mahatma Gandhi's example can be quoted in this context. He remained hungry and parched throughout his life to win freedom for the Indians. He advocated the Hindu-Muslim unity and got the bullet. He was either a maniac or a God. We know that he was not a maniac, for he had been educated in England. Hence, he must have been a God, we humbly opine. Lakhs of people were jailed, tortured and beaten to death simply because Bapu had told them to launch protests against the British. When he entered the court room, British judges used to get up and salute him. He had a wife, a stick, a goat and a spinning wheel. He got us freedom, not the bomb blasts in assemblies or Kakori carnage or executions of thousands of people. Indira Gandhi was also a charismatic leader; so is A.B. Vajpayee. In India, Vinoba Bhave (Bhudan Movement), V.B. Patel (unification of India), Khudiram Bose (freedom fighter who was hanged), Bhagat Singh (freedom fighter who was hanged), Yatin Nath Das (freedom fighter who succumbed to hunger) and finally, Madam Bhikaiji Cama (who organized and funded anti-British movements between 1900 and 1910) impressed the masses with their charisma. Further, at the international front, Abraham Lincoln (US), George Washington (US), Napoleon (France), Bismarck (Germany), Garibaldi (Italy), Che Guewara (South America) and many others ruled the hearts of masses due to their amazing charismatic personalities and deeds. For example, Pandit Madan Mohan Malviya was awarded the Bharat Ratna (2014) due to his charisma.

4. Personal Power (Coercive)

It is the threatening attitude or the use of stick on the part of an official. Terror groups have coercive power. We may opine that the USA has coercive power but they are in the wrong. The US President has to get the approval of the US Senate before striking any part of Afghanistan of Pakistan. The US is a democracy whose each step is watched by its masses. On the contrary, Pakistani army takes up military actions at its own will. The PM of Pakistan does not play much role on strategic fronts. Terror elements are so strong in Pakistan and Afghanistan that the government officials of these countries are not able to run their businesses, although they have been selected or elected through formal routes. Power flows from the barrel of a gun! How can one speak in front of a mortar or AK-100, the latest weapon in the hands of terror elements? Peace is a fine concept but no one is talking peace in any part of the world now-a-days.

5. Personal Power (Monetary)

Rich people can call the shots. Rich businessmen can change the lives of people they meet or deal with. Money is a big power in any part of the world. This world has 6.5 billion people. Out of these nearly 1.0 billion people are super rich. Nearly 1.0 billion people of the rest are just rich. The rest, i.e., 4.5 billion people, are either in middle income strata or are struggling to make their two ends meet. In India, only 20 percent people own nearly 80 percent of the assets of the country. Nearly 26.0 percent of India's population lives below the poverty line. The rich-poor divide is increasing. If this hiatus is not filled up, a national-level movement may ensue. Rich people are becoming richer. Poor people are illiterate as well as wild. Money solves most problems, except only a few. Thus, the rich-poor divide must be removed or at least, filled up to some extent in all societies of the globe.

What is Country's Ability?

The ability of a country is its capability of achieving some goals as a result of its geophysical, diplomatic, technological, human resource, economic or military strengths. The ability of a country can be passive. If a country does not use a resource available to it, then it is able but not using the resource in question. An able country can become a regional power, major power or even a superpower. But if it does not use the resource it has, it cannot become an entity at global political and strategic forums.

Country's Power

A country's power is its influence over its global partners, regions or organizations due to which it can get results in its favour. A country's power is created when it uses its abilities and develops in strategic, human resource, diplomatic, economic and technological terms. A country may be able but still, it may not become a power. In every country, six M's are to be considered to make it a major power. They are Man, Machine, Methods, Material, Money and Management. This is the traditional viewpoint of management thinkers, for it basically puts business and nonbusiness firms in full focus, not nations. Our discussion has been based on this very tenet but we are going further deeper, insofar as major powers are concerned. That is because we are considering countries, not companies, in this volume.

Bases of a Country's Power

There are ten bases of a country's power, as follows:

1. Geographical Base

The country can have vast geographical resources like huge land area, petroleum reserves, gas, timber, ores, gold, silver, diamonds, mountains, forest reserves, lakes and other kinds of resource that can help it earn valuable foreign exchange. This geographical resource would also help its peoples survive and grow in economic terms. For example, Russia is the largest producer of crude oil in the world. Saudi Arabia, Kuwait, Iraq, Iran, Russia, Venezuela, the USA and India are also oil producers. So, they have powers which can influence the nations of the world that are sans oil resources. The current global economy that we see today is oil economy. We have not been able to find alternatives to oil, so the OPEC and other oil-rich nations are ruling the roost at all global political forums. The variation in the rates of Brent Crude on a daily basis is an indication of the crude fact that poor nations would soon be deprived of oil-based resources. Only rich nations would be able to import oil, gas, LPG and CNG. Russia has the largest land area and is full of many rich natural resources. Since Russia remains under the snow cover for ten months of a year, these resources could not be identified and exploited even today. The US has also rich mineral and oil resources but they seem somewhat less than those of Saudi Arabia, Iraq, Iran, Russia and Venezuela. The US is dependent upon Saudi Arabia for oil. Oil politics had taken ugly turns in the past. India is producing 40 percent of its oil at home. The rest (60 percent) is being imported by it at rates dictated by the global crude oil market. We are spending a huge chunk of our foreign exchange earnings on oil import.

2. Economic Base

A country can be dollar rich in the sense that its capital account could show huge dollar reserves. In today's world, no country can afford to state that it is dollar rich. That is because import and export are done by all nations. So, money keeps on going into and out of a country. The overall effect of this global trade leads to the trade surplus of only a few nations. Most nations have huge trade deficits. Even many developed nations are facing this problem. Recession and inflation hurt all nations. That is why they are unable to meet the food and other needs of their masses. Such nations are not able to become regional powers, leave alone major powers. They do not have valuable foreign exchange to buy machinery, weapons, ships and technology from advanced nations. That is why they are not able to get their presence felt at various forums of the UNO. Economy and geography are connected with each other in many ways. If geographical resources are available, they can help a country become an economic power. This happens over time, not years. It has been observed that nations of the West have earned money by supplying technological equipment and processes (like milk plant, missile technology, tanks, fighter aircraft, AK-100, arms and ammunition etc.). The nations of the East have earned money by supplying their geographical resources or natural outputs (like timber, wheat, apples, oranges, rice, vegetables and meat) to the West. Here, Japan and Korea are exceptions, for they also have used technology to enhance their standards of living. Economic prowess is the much wanted thing in every society. Africa is a land full of amazing resources. It is home to diamonds, minerals and other natural endowments. But most of its nations are living below the poverty line. Resource management is poor in such nations. Take the examples of Ethiopia and Eritrea. They are the poorest nations of the world and are often captured by famine or severe drought. In our own backyard, Bangladesh is an LDC. Pakistani economy is also in shambles. The US has come out of recession. There is good news on India's economic front too. The EU is running its affairs because of the financial advantages of three nations—Britain, France and Germany. Other nations of the EU are dependent on these three countries which are very rich by any norm. These three nations have achieved supremacy by virtue of their technological advancements.

3. Political Base

You must have noted that a democratic country is respected at all global platforms. A democratically sound nation can become eligible for getting the status of a major power. Pakistan has democracy for namesake. China does not have democracy. Russia has also a domineering single-party rule, although democratic forces are sweeping across its length and breadth with an uneasy calm. We have started believing in Russian democracy to some extent because rebels in Ukraine want to join Russia. Had Russia been so must autocratic as it was during the rule of Brezhnev or Stalin, then the Ukrainians would not have voted in favour of their merger with Russia. Note that Ukraine would automatically merge with Russia one day or the other. The Russians do not have to force Ukraine to merge with it. It is a natural affiliation which would bring them together. Russia's downing of a Malaysian aircraft was condemned the world over in 2014. However, Russia turned a deaf ear to all such genres of condemnation. Thus, Russia and China are two exceptions in the club of major powers which are not democracies or are partially democratic. All other nations are complete democracies.

4. Human Resource Base

The human capital is studied under the new subject now-a-days. It is called **Strategic Human Resource Management** or SHRM. The human capital is the biggest capital a country can have to become a major power. The USA has the best human capital in the world. Brain drain is a big problem for developing nations like India. Professionals earn degrees in India and go abroad for better life. They work as doctors, engineers, architects, CAs, business promoters and what not! They get lucrative jobs in foreign countries and enhance the technological and economic abilities of those very nations. Thus, nations like India suffer due to brain drain.

5. Technology Base

Technology has become the life and soul of many nations. Japan, the USA, Britain, Italy, France, Germany South Korea and India are technologically advanced nations. They have gadgets and devices that can be used to win territories and create new countries. They can use new technologies to build modern weapon systems, space stations, rockets, train tracks, tanks, modern weapons and even space travel equipment. For example, India successfully sent its Mangal Yaan to Mars in 2014. It did so without suffering any loss during the course of this mission. Other nations like the USA failed a few times before landing their missions at Mars. But most developing countries have a long way to go on the technological path of the modern era. Technology would decide which country becomes a major power.

6. Nuclear Power Base

Again, we are separating the terms 'ability' and 'power.' A nation can make a nuclear bomb and has the technology to do this task. But if it does not have a nuclear weapon, it would not be able to ward off a nuclear attack by any other country. Contrary to the popular belief, nuclear bombs and weapons are not made overnight. Radioactive Plutonium or Uranium is required to make them. These elements are to be refined and processed in most modern factories. The US and Russia have nuclear weapons; so have China and Britain. Beside them, some other nations are trying to acquire nuclear weapons but it is not easy to get them. Pakistan has nuclear grade material or bombs or both. India has nuclear technology but no bombs. We have missiles that can carry nuclear weapons but have not made a single nuclear bomb till date. Our nuclear power plants would be shut down by the IAEA if we choose to make a nuclear bomb. We would not get any fissile material or technology from the Nuclear Suppliers Group (NDG) in which China is a major player. So, we have the technology, not weapons. The Indo-US nuclear deal was jeopardized precisely because of this reason. If we sign on the dotted line, we would not be able to conduct nuclear test of a particular grade or weight (of fissile material). In Pakistan, terror elements would not take many more years to acquire a nuclear weapon; and they would certainly use it against India at the first instance. They killed 132 innocent children in December 2014 (in a Peshawar school). How can they afford to spare India, their staunch enemy?

7. Strategic Base

The army, navy and air force of a country can certainly make it a major power, if not a super power. India has dedicated 13,00,000 armed force personnel. However, as the defence report of January 1, 2015 states, our armed forces lack high-grade weapons and carbines, ammunition, tanks, fighter aircraft and other resources that are needed by a modern collection of armed forces. We have to depend upon the West for getting weapons and material of fine grades. Thus, global political relations start playing evil games. The USA can give F-16 aircraft to Pakistan, not India. France has given Mirage aircraft to India, not to Pakistan. B-52 bombers are any fighter pilot's dream but the US does not even give their pictures to any country. The USA has fine-quality defence arsenal. Its nuclear abilities are well know. Russia has nuclear weapons, modern combat weapons, ammunition and nuclear submarines. India is way behind in the realms of technological modernization of its armed forces. This is our weak point. Shri Narendra Modi had captured the seat of power in New Delhi on the plea that "good days" would come. The armed forces are looking up to him now. He must start defence production and modernization programmes with immediate effect, given that circumstances are taking evil turns by the day in Afghanistan and Pakistan. Today, wars can be started only by five-odd infiltrators from across the border. The President of India does not have to declare a state of emergency. In any case, India has remained under emergency conditions since the inception of Pakistan. Not a single day passes when firing is not opened by Pakistani rangers on Indian troops or BSF personnel. India is taking these events in its stride. There would be no war between India and Pakistan; only nuisance would transpire. Russia is sharing its defence technology with China. So, we can no longer depend upon Russia as our one-to-one secret supplier. In any case, technologies are stolen and revealed easily for hefty prices. The method of making atom bomb is available on the Internet. Hence, the concept "Make in India" given by Shri Narendra Modi (given by him in 2014) should become a reality of the modern era. India must produce war weapons and ammunition for its armed forces of all three genres. We must develop our own fighter aircraft and naval war vessels. That is because our terrain air space and oceanic conditions are typical. The M1G aircraft of India crash almost every third month. They were built to take care of Russia's strategic needs. Moreover, the parts and components needed for their maintenance are to be imported from Russia. When India uses its home-made parts, these aircraft crash. Thus, we lose our precious air power. In order to address all these issues, we should develop our own military technologies. What's more, we must tell the private sector to invest and participate in the production of arms and ammunition.

8. Information Base

If you have some sets of information about a country or organization, you can use or even misuse it. Use this power with care. Just imagine—the USA has all vital information sets in the world because the Internet belongs to it. All servers of the Net are installed in the USA. That is why the USA is a superpower. It has the latest information about every country and business or non-business firm today. We should set up our Internet servers in India. We must guard our defence information and movements of armed forces personnel. Sadly, the media is very free. If there is a slight movement on the Indo-Pakistan border, TV journalists move to the spot in a short duration and start reporting about the incidents of firing and infiltration. The army does not work that way. The intelligence units of the armed forces and RAW are supposed to work in a stealthy manner. Strategic information is the key to success in modern battlefields which are, in fact, guerilla war theatres.

9. Management Base

Most successful nations of this world have literacy rates between 95 to 99 percent. If a country has to become a major power, it must educate its masses first. In India, the position on the academic front is very bad. People are not literate; and those who really are, take no time to leave the country. Politicians are not literate, so they cannot make concrete economic and strategic plans or execute them later. Literate people are not allowed to take up good posts in government departments because of reservations. The backward parts of our society are given privileges but they are not competent enough to decide what inputs our nation needs and how it would acquire those inputs. Our good managers are skillfully sidelined. Our bad managers, nee politicians, are elevated to the echelons of power. Thus, management of the entire country suffers. We are still dealing with poverty, to quote an example, even 60 years after August 15, 1947. When would we make our country hunger free and educated? When this happens, India would also become a major power. Today, even if we claim, India is not a major power. The citizens of a real power do not ride camels; they ride B-52 bombers! Management of resources is the real issue in India. Resources are there but they are usurped by bad managers of the country. Thus, the country suffers in economic, political and strategic terms.

10. Machinery and Gadget Base

Modern plants and factories must be erected in all parts of a country to make it a major power. We can start from those machines that process or make food. We can eventually produce modern satellites and space navigation systems that would take us to remote parts of our galaxy. We must make machines in India. Defence analysts aver that India must make its weapons and tanks at home. It can also make nuclear submarines and naval war ships. That is because it has a huge technical manpower and a gargantuan labour base. South India lacks vital machinery for growth. Growth has occurred over the last 60 years in North India, not in South India or East India. The peaceful natural environment and stable industrial climate of south Indian states are conducive to defence and industrial production. Hence, more factories should be set up in south India. Further, there is no industrial development in the North-east. The government must start factories of DRDO in that region. It must also invite private players in defence production programmes. This would lead to the generation of more and more employment opportunities. Finally, modern equipment and gadgets can also be imported to enhance the strategic status of a country. AWACS is a technology for fighter aircraft. We have purchased it from other countries to modernize our air force. Further, the use of satellites, electronic warfare and guerilla warfare (using advanced weaponry) also make a country more capable in strategic terms. Currently, the USA and Russia have these three capabilities. Their reconnaissance satellites, Electronic Warfare equipment, surveillance techniques and modern communication devices put them at the top of the list of global powers.

Regional Powers

These powers are dominant regional players in their respective regions. However, they cannot be termed major powers. Pakistan is a regional power, to quote an example. India is also a regional power. In Africa, South Africa and Nigeria are regional powers. In Europe, France is a regional power. In Asia, North Korea is a regional power.

Major Powers

The USA, Russia, Germany, China, South Korea and Japan have been termed as major powers because of their economic, technological, political and geophysical assets. Germany does not have a strong army. But it is part of the EU, so it enjoys considerable influence over other nations of Europe due to its typical position within Europe and the power of much ignored Deutsche mark. The German mark is a strong European currency. Technology and societal growth are the main USPs of the Germany nation. This nation wants to acquire bigger roles within the EU and if possible, within the gamut of the United Nations. Its size does not matter; its peoples certainly do.

Super Powers

The USA and Russia continue to be two super powers. China is a major power and is on the way to becoming a super power. It works in a stealthy manner. Its poverty levels do not show up. Its entire work force is employed in one profession of the other. It is a hardware king in world markets. India cannot become a major power unless it removes its poverty and becomes a predominantly industrialized nation. Currently, 60 percent of its peoples are engaged in agricultural or activities directly dependent upon agricultural. Barring a few technological achievements, our overall growth scene in technology fields is not worth talking about. Imported technologies do well in India. The cellular phone market is an example in this context. However, our own technologies, like any the helicopter developed by the HAL, do not perform well anywhere. We have IITs, engineering institutions par excellence and IIMs. But we could not build a fine fighter aircraft or combat chopper till date. So, we had to place an order for Augusta Westland choppers. The shady deals of that contract were unearthed and so we had to cancel that deal. Thus, the Indian Air Force suffers even today, for its does not have high-quality combat flying machines. Our army personnel do not have carbines, mortars, tanks, anti-aircraft guns, bullets, armoured vehicles like Humvee (of the USA), combat gear for soldiers and modern communication systems. How would we win the wars? The image of the boat that had set out from Tek Bandar (Karachi) on December 31, 2014 was given to our intelligence agencies by the USA. Had they not given us these vital inputs, we would have become the victims of 26/11 Part II. Technology would be the decisive force in the wars that are likely to ensue in the future. India is behind most developed nations and a few developing ones on the strategic front. A country, which does not have gadgets to win battles and wars, cannot afford to wear the badge of Major Power. Still, we have discussed India in this book because we feel that politicians, technologists and strategic planners of this country would wake up to the challenges of the new millennium. If they rise and come up to the mark, we expect India to become a major power by 2050 AD. Currently, going by any positive norm, India is a regional power.

Conclusion

Major Powers include super powers. Definitions vary from author to author. We have given the widest spectrum to our readers.

Foreign Policy and Its Determinants

CHAPTER 3

Introduction

Every country has to survive in this global environment so that its peoples may be able to lead decent and prosperous lives. The country has to survive first; growth comes later. The global environment comprises political, geographical, economic, technological, strategic, cultural and social environments. These environments shape the country in question through their microscopic and macroscopic organs. No nation can remain aloof from the effects of the global environment that works silently. Thus, the foreign policy of a nation is dictated by the global environment because this nation is an integral part of this very global environment. We shall also study the definition and concept of foreign policy in this chapter.

Framework of Reference

We shall study the determinants of foreign policies of major powers because of the following reasons:

(a) Vicarious Political Growth

We must know how these super powers or major powers acquired so much clout or base so that they could arrive at the spots they are in now. That way, we would be able to understand how our own country can learn vital lessons from their growth and elevation to a super status. Then, we can try to emulate or at least we can try to take some positive clues from their stories. This is called Vicarious Political Growth of the learning country. For example, we should learn how America became a super power. We must study its physical assets, peoples, policies, academic systems, war strategies, experiences in two World wars and its negotiations in the UNO. Then, we can take clues from the history of the USA and try to do those actions that suit us and were also executed by the

USA to become a superpower. When one learns from the experiences of others, one is called Vicarious, hence the term Vicarious Political Growth.

(b) Concerted Economic Growth

A major or super power also grows in economic terms, otherwise it cannot dictate its terms to the world. All major or super powers have economic resources at their command, whether or not they have been converted into hard currencies. We must study how these powers acquired essential financial clout or assets. We would also try to acquire the same clout and or resources to emulate these powers in the future. For example, the major thrust of China is on export of its goods. Chinese goods are not very superior to those made in the West. But they are cheap and sold worldwide. We must learn how we can reduce the cost of production achieve economies of scale so that we may be able to increase employment levels at home. That way, we would also increase productivity and foreign exchange reserves in our country. Hence, we must grow (in economic terms) along with major powers to become a major power.

(c) Preferential Human Growth

We must study major powers and their foreign policies to understand how they have incorporated the humane side of society in their policies. We must understand American liberalism, freedom of speech in Europe, freedom to do any task in India and the ability to tolerate the ideas and beliefs of others in any part of the world. Today, religion, communalism, caste and creed, colour of skin and many other issues dominate international scenarios and debates. The major powers have become mature enough to understand the human side of any issue. They would support only those societies that are rational, secular and growth oriented. They would thwart the attempts of all other societies that try to annihilate the human race on various pleas. So, they want preferential human growth, not just the growth of humans due to their multiplication. The major powers of the world want the world to have only those citizens who have enough tolerance and those who think for the protection of the human race.

(d) Selective Galactic Growth

Our eyes are on Mars, Jupiter and the solar systems beyond our own solar system. We want to dominate this part of the galaxy. A major power that would do this first would dominate later. For example, India, Russia, the USA and EU have successfully conducted missions to Mars. So, they all can stake their claims on Mars if it is developed as a new human colony in the future. Major powers and superpowers would have an edge over all other nations in the fields of industrial production, science and technology. Hence, we must study the success stories as well as fiascos of major powers even as they explore distant galactic systems and try to create human colonies there. If we become a major power at a later date, we would also like to own planets, land areas on mars or even stars. This seems a Utopian possibility today but we must not forget that space is the ultimate frontier for any super power or major power. We must expand our horizon and go beyond the moon! That is possible only if we study the foreign policies, economic initiatives and strategic moves of major and super powers.

Determinants of Foreign Policy: A Brief Overview

They are as follows (we have taken):

(A) Internal Factors

A1. Size of Country
A2. Geography
A3. Culture.
A4. History.
A5. Economic development.
A6. Technology.
A7. National Capacity.
A7. Social Structure.
A8. Public Mood.
A9. Political organization.
A10. Role of Press.
A11. Political accountability.
A12. Leadership.
A13. The willingness of the masses to change according to time.

(B) **External Factors**

B1. Power structure.
B2. International organization.
B3. Reactions of Other Countries.
B4. Alliances (economic and strategic).
B5. World Public Opinion

This is a suggestive list which has been prepared by Arvind Kumar after a lot of research. However, our valued readers can think beyond this general framework as well.

Difference between Bases and Determinants of Foreign Policy

Bases of power emanate from the country's geography, military prowess, manpower, technological advancement, nuclear abilities and the superiority of its personnel in various technical and strategic fields. On the contrary, the determinants of foreign policy of a country depend upon its relationships with the external world and also, upon how other players are placed on various economic, strategic and political fronts. The base of a nation can be good but its determinant may not be so strong. That is why a strong country may not be able to do well as a major power, even if it has enough resources at its command.

> *"Foreign policy is the key element in the process by which a state translates its broadly conceived goals and interests into concrete courses of action to attain these objectives and preserve interests."*
>
> —**Padelford and Lincoln**

In modern times no state can avoid involvement in the international sphere. This involvement must be systematic and based on some well-defined principles. The principles and the purpose of a state is reflected in its foreign policy. The importance of the foreign policy has been highlighted by scholars in various ways. According to one scholar, a state without a foreign policy is like a ship without a radar which drifts aimlessly without any direction by every storm and sweep of events. According to Prof. Taylor "Foreign Policy of a sort will go on so long as there are sovereign states."

Meaning of Foreign Policy

There is no unanimity amongst scholars regarding the meaning of foreign policy and various definitions have been offered. According to Padelford and Lincoln: "A state's foreign policy is the totality of its dealings with the external environment. Foreign policy is more than a collection of official documents, formal records of actions and public statements. A foreign policy statement can be simple and succinct ... or it may be complicated and imprecise ... Policy is the overall result of the process by which a state translates its broadly conceived goals and interests into specific courses of action in order to achieve its objective and preserve its interest."[1]

F.S. Northedge says that foreign policy implies "the use of political influence in order to induce other states to exercise their law making power in a manner desired by the state concerned: it is an interaction between forces originating outside the country's borders and those working within them."[2]

Joseph Frankel says that "foreign policy consists of decisions and actions which involve to some appreciable extent relations between one state and others."[3] Huge Gibson defines foreign policy as a well-rounded comprehensive plan on knowledge and experience for conducting the business of government with the rest of the world. It is aimed at promoting and protecting the interests of the nations. This calls for a clear understanding of what those interests are and how far we can hope to go with the means at our disposal. Anything less than this falls short of being a foreign policy."[4]

George Modelski says that foreign policy is "the system of activities evolved by communities for changing the behaviour of other states and for adjusting their own activities to the international environment."[5] According to Rodee," Foreign policy involves the formulation and implementation of a group of principles which shape the behaviour pattern of a state while negotiating with other states to protect or further its interests."

The Brookings Institution in its book *Major Problems of United States Foreign Policy 1952-53*, used the term foreign policy

1. Norman J. Padelford and George A. Lincoln, *The Dunamics of International Politics*. p. 195.
2. F.S. Northedge.
3. Joseph Frankel, *The Making of Foreign Policy*, p.l.
4. Huge Gibson, *The Road to Foreign Policy*, p.9.
5. George Modelstic, *The Theory of Foreign Policy*, p. 6

to refer to the complex and dynamic political course that a nation follows in relation to other states. According to it the foreign policy of a nation is more than the sum total of its foreign policy (thought out courses of action for achieving objectives), for also includes its commitment, the current forms of its *interests* and *objectives* and the principles of right conduct that it professes.

Crabb has offered a simple yet very effective definition of foreign policy. He says "Reduced to its most fundamental ingredients, foreign policy consists of two elements national objectives to be achieved, and means for achieving them."

Charles Burton Marshall defines foreign policy as the "course of action undertaken by authority of state and intended to affect situations beyond the span of its jurisdiction." This definition emphasises two points: first, foreign policy generates in action; secondly the things acted upon in foreign policy are beyond the jurisdiction of the state.

A perusal of the above definitions of foreign policy shows that scholars have laid emphasis either on the plan of action or policy as executed. However, they all agree that the foreign policy is concerned with the behaviour of a state towards other states.

Objectives of Foreign Policy

The main objectives which the foreign policy of a country seeks to achieve are as follows:

Firstly, it seeks to protect the territorial integrity of the country and protect the interests of its citizens, both within and outside the country. Generally, for this purpose the states prefer to follow policy of *status quo*. If a state pursues a policy which seeks to upset the *status quo* it is branded as revisionist and arouses the suspicion of other members of the international community. It has to protect the interests of its citizens both inside and outside the state, for the maintenance of its prestige.

Secondly, the objective of foreign policy is maintenance of links with other members of international community and adoption of policy of conflict or cooperation towards them with a view to promote its own interests. It is well known that India has deliberately avoided exchange of diplomatic relations with Israel so that its relations with the Arab countries do not get strained, primarily because of close trade relations with the Arab countries.

Thirdly, the foreign policy of a country seeks to promote and further the national interests of the country. The primary interest of each state is self-preservation, security and well being of its citizens. Often the interests of various states come in clash and the states have to protect their interests bearing in mind this factor.

Fourthly, the foreign policy aims at promotion of economic interests of the country. As the status of a state in international arena is largely determined by its economic status, the states try to pursue a foreign policy which can contribute to their economic prosperity and enable it in turn to play a more effective role in international politics. Most of the treaties and agreements concluded by the states with other members of international community are essentially designed to protect and promote the economic interests of these states. The importance of this factor is evident from the fact that India opted to keep out of two power blocs, which had come into existence when she gained independence, and adopted policy of non-alignment chiefly because she was keen to concentrate on her economic development. Further, she hoped to get every possible help and assistance from both the superpowers to accelerate the process of economic development. Similarly USA and China were obliged to patch up their differences, despite their ideological differences, due to economic considerations.

Fifthly, the foreign policy aims at enhancement of the influence of the state either by expanding its area of influence and reducing of other states to the position of dependency. The policy of United States and Soviet Union in the post-World War II period have been largely motivated by these considerations.

Determinants of Foreign Policy (Factors Influencing Foreign Policy)

The foreign policy of a country is influenced by so many factors that it is not possible to enumerate all of them here. Some of the important factors which influence the foreign policy of a country or constitute the inputs of the foreign policy are given hereunder. Broadly speaking these factors fall into two categories, viz., internal and external.

Internal Factors

1. Size.

In the first place the size of a states territory as well as its population greatly influences its foreign policy. Generally, the leaders and people of countries with small territory and population do not expect their country to carry great weight in international affairs. On the other hand, the leaders and people of large countries are ready to assume special responsibilities. However, sometimes even small states which have rich resources also leave a deep impact on world politics. For example Britain, a small country, played leading role in world politics in the nineteenth and early twentieth century. In our own times the oil-rich countries of the Middle East, though small in size are playing a significant role in international politics. Likewise Japan, another small sized state is playing a dominant role in international relations. On the other hand, large states like Canada and Australia have not been able to pursue effective foreign policy. Commonwealth of Independent States (CIS) which came into existence after the disintegration of the Soviet Union, though quite large in size, is not able to play an effective role in contemporary international relations.

2. Geography

The geography of a country, including its fertility, climate, location in relation to other land masses, and water-ways, etc. also influence the country's foreign policy. It is a major factor in determining self-sufficiency of a country. Generally landlocked countries, nations in the tropics and those bordering a superpower are less self-sufficient in comparison to the countries which have access to warm-water ports or are located in the temperate zones and far removed from superpowers. For example, in the nineteenth century USA adopted isolationist policy chiefly on account of its geographical location. Though the importance of geographic factors is acknowledged almost at all hands, its importance has considerably declined due to technological and scientific developments. For example, due to improvement in the means of transport and communication the world has greatly shrunk and the perception of large bodies of water as natural barriers to military attack has greatly diminished. But still geographical location of a country has a deep impact on the determination of its foreign policy. India adopted policy of non-alignment because of geographical location. The presence of two major powers on its borders (USSR and China) deterred it from joining power blocs.

3. *Culture and History*

The cultural and historical traditions of a country also deeply influence the foreign policy. Generally people possessing a unified common culture and historical experience can pursue an effective foreign policy because of the support of all sections of society who share the same values and memories. On the other hand, a country which is culturally and historically fragmented cannot pursue an equally effective foreign policy. According to Prof. Rosenau, "the influence of cultural factors is not limited to the impact of societal unity upon the formulation and implementation of foreign policy. Equally important are the processes through which the contents of shared norms and practices of society, as distinguished from the degree of unity that supports them, shape the plans that are made and the activities that are undertaken with respect to the external world."

4. *Economic Development.*

The stage of economic development which a country has attained also has its impact on its foreign policy. Generally the industrially advanced countries feel more deeply involved in relations with other countries because they have to import different kinds of raw materials and commodities from other countries. They are also on the look out for latest knowledge and technical know-how. Therefore they maintain intimate trade relations with their trading partners. All this leads to intimate links between the groups and people of one country with their counterparts in the other country. Again, an industrial country is expected to have a higher Gross National Product (GNP) and can devote greater funds for external purpose, viz., economic aid programme, military ventures and extensive diplomatic commitments. On the other hand, industrially backward countries are not able to actively involve themselves in external affairs. The lack of scientists, engineers and other specialists in the country prevents them from taking advantage of the technological break-through abroad. In recent years United States has been able to pursue more vigorous foreign policy and secure its national objectives, mainly on account of its high degree of economic development. It has made liberal use of foreign aid as an instrument for the promotion of its foreign policy goals. It is a matter of common knowledge that in our times the industrially developed countries (popularly known as G-7) are playing an effective role in international politics as compared to other developed or under-developed countries. This is but natural in view of the fact that economically developed countries possess greater military capability than the less developed countries, and can exert greater influence on international relations. In our own times the decline of Russia's economic power has considerably undermined her political role in the international arena.

5. *Technology*

Advancement in technology, which effects the military and economic capabilities of a state, also exercises profound influence on the foreign policy. However, this factor influences the foreign policy only in an indirect manner, viz., by influencing other sources of foreign policy. It has been observed that countries which possess advanced technology are able to provide technical know-how to less developed and developing nations and thus exert necessary influence on their foreign policies. Rosenau has rightly observed Technological changes can alter the military and economic capabilities of a society and thus its status and role in the international system. The dominant role which countries like France, China, Germany and Japan have been able to play in recent years is largely due to excellent technological developments in these countries.

6. *National Capacity*

The national capacity of a state also exercises profound influence on the foreign policy of a state. National capacity of a state depends on its military preparedness, its technological advancement and economic development. It is well known that United States which continued to pursue policy of isolation till the beginning of the present century got deeply involved in the international arena in the present century mainly due to tremendous increase in her national capacity due to rapid economic development. Similarly, the foreign policy of Britain underwent great transformation in the post-World War II period, mainly due to decline in her national capacity.

7. *Social Structure*

The social structure of a society also exercises profound influence on its foreign policy. A society which is sharply divided on the basis of wealth, religion, regional imbalances, etc., cannot pursue effective foreign policy on account of division and lack of co-operation among various groups. On the other hand, a homogeneous society possessing strong sense of national unity can pursue a more effective foreign policy. It is well known that Britain stood as one person under the leadership of Churchill during the Second World War and the people gladly suffered all kinds of hardships to preserve their unity because of social solidarity. No doubt, it is not easy to trace the impact of social structure on the foreign policy plans and behaviour because of the involved subtleties, but no student of foreign policy can afford to ignore the external consequences of the internal social structure and of the slow changes it may be undergoing.

8. *Public Mood*

Public mood is another important determinant of a country's foreign policy. Though it is generally held that the public mood usually follows rather than guides the foreign policy making process, it can exercise lot of influence on the determination of a foreign policy of basic realignment in the prevailing great power structure takes place and the state becomes more involved or more isolated from the world affairs. It may be noted that generally in an authoritarian system the public mood does not influence the foreign policy, but in a democratic system based on political accountability considerable weight has to be accorded to the changing public mood and sentiments.

9. *Political Organisation*

The political organisation found in a country also greatly influences the foreign policy. Generally under authoritarian systems quick foreign policy decisions are possible because the decision making power rests with an individual assisted by his clique. But as the leaders under this system are isolated from the operational environments and the subordinate policy makers provide the information which is perceived by the superiors, there is every possibility of a discrepancy between the psychological and operational aspects of the foreign policy. Further, under this system undesirable opposition can be suppressed through censorship and promulgation of regulations. On the other hand, in a country possessing a democratic structure the citizens can freely express their opinion on the domestic as well as foreign policy which naturally leaves its impact on the foreign policy of the country. Under democratic system there is very little discrepancy between what the officials want to believe about the state of world politics and the actual position because the subordinate policy makers make available critical and detached information.

Within the democratic system itself the difference in political structure has its impact on foreign policy. For example, under a parliamentary system of government based on co-operation between the Legislature and the Executive, the cordial relations between the two wings have an impact on countrys foreign policy. On the other hand, under presidential system based on the principle of separation of powers, the relation between the two wings are likely to be more strained which affect the ambiguity or continuity of foreign policy. Similarly, different foreign policy is likely to emerge under bi-party system and multi-party systems. Generally under bi-party system the government is likely to have a clear-cut majority and conduct itself in a more decisive manner regarding the conduct of foreign relations. In contrast of this, under multi-party system conflicting view points and interests may have to be reconciled. This may lead either to the avoidance or postponement of the decision.

10. Role of Press

The press also plays a vital role in the foreign policy formulation process. The press contributes to this process by supplying factual information on the basis of which the people take decision; by publishing specialised articles on current international developments which enable the people to understand the significance of developments in their country in relation to the past developments, and by analysing the policy of the government in regard to foreign affairs. The press also plays an important role in publicising the foreign policy of the country.

The role of the press, however, depends on the political system prevailing in the country, the rate of literacy as well as the attitude of government.

11. Political Accountability

The nature of political accountability prevailing in a system also greatly influences the foreign policy of the country. Generally in an open political system, the demands of citizen and groups get articulated and transmitted to foreign policy formulators. The framers of foreign policy cannot ignore these demands. In fact quite often the policy formulators anticipate these demands while formulating the foreign policy. On the other hand under a closed system the public reactions are neither available nor given much importance.

12. Leadership

The leadership also plays a vital role in the shaping of a country's foreign policy. According to Rosenau: "A leader's beliefs about the nature of international arena and the goals that ought to be pursued therein, his or her peculiar intellectual strengths and weakness for analysing information and making decisions, his or her past background and the extent of its relevance to the requirements of the role, his or her emotional needs and most of other personality traits these are but a *few* of the idiosyncratic factors that can influence the planning and execution of foreign policy." No doubt, the qualities of leadership have a deep impact on the country's foreign policy but their role is greatly constrained by the governmental and social structure. Further the role of leadership is not identical in all countries. In less developed countries their role is greater as compared to industrialised societies. In industrialised societies the individuals enjoy very limited discretion in high governmental and non-governmental positions.

External Factors

In addition to the internal factors which influence a country's foreign policy discussed above, a number of external factors also exercise considerable influence on the foreign policy of a country. In our times the world has become so interlinked that incidents in other countries have their immediate impact on other countries. Thus a *coup d'etat* in neighbouring country, or nationalisation of oil companies in Middle East or release of a proposed arms control agreements are events which influence the actions of leaders in other countries.

1. *Power-Structure*

The great power structure prevailing in the world politics also greatly influences the policy of a country. In this regard three possibilities can be envisaged. First, a number of powers may enjoy great power status and their relations may be based on balance of power system. Secondly, there may be only two powers which dominate the world scene and the other states are compelled to side with one or the other. Thirdly, more than two states attain great power status and the two powers at the poles are less able to command strict allegiance of those in the orbit (the system is known as loose-bipolar). The nature of power structure prevailing in the world has a substantial impact on the foreign policy of a country. Highlighting this point Prof. Rosenau says: "Wherever a nation is located in the prevailing hierarchy of world politics, rules governing the conduct of its foreign relations tend to be embedded in the arrangements whereby the great powers cope with then—conflicts or otherwise interact to frame and shape the major issue of an era. These rules may not be explicitly identified and their operation as inputs may take many forms, but their relevance to the deliberations of foreign policy officials is likely to be pervasive."

2. *International Organisation*

The contemporary international organisation also greatly influences the foreign policy of a country. While formulating its foreign policy the country has to take note of the international law, treaties and contracts. No country can ignore these factors without jeopardising its own interests. Apart from the structure at the global level, the structures at the regional and sub-regional levels also greatly influence the foreign policy of a country.

3. *Reaction of Other States*

While formulating its foreign policy a country has to take note of the reaction of other states to its various actions. No country can afford to pursue interests which are fundamentally against the interests of the other states because any policy based on narrow national interests is likely to evoke strong reaction from the concerned state and produce disastrous consequences. It is well known that in 1939 Hitler embarked upon invasion of Poland unmindful of the British reaction with disastrous consequences. Similarly Japan's attack on Pearl Harbour, unmindful of the strong American sentiments, produced disastrous effects for her.

4. Alliances

Alliances concluded by various states also greatly influence the foreign policy. The states parties to alliance have to respond to the requests and demands of their allies and refrain from formulating policies or taking actions which are offensive to them. It is true that generally the alliances give great amount of independence with regard to the plans and actions, yet they operate implicitly and explicitly as important elements in the process through which foreign policy is formulated and implemented.

5. World Public Opinion

The world public opinion also exercises profound influence on the foreign policy of a country. It is true that the world public opinion influences the foreign policy of a country only occasionally and is not a factor. Further, it is able to exercise influence on the foreign policy of a state only if it is supported by the domestic public opinion It is well known that U.S.Government was made to effect changes in its Vietnam policy largely due to hostile world opinion.

Thus it can be said that the foreign policy of a country is determined by the domestic factors as well as the international environments.

National Interests and Foreign Policy

Another issue which deserves consideration is how far the national interests influence the formulation of the foreign policy of a country. Though the states generally do not publically admit that their foreign policies are based on their self-interest, sometimes responsible people have admitted this fact. For example Hughes, American Secretary of State admitted in the 1920's that "Foreign policies are not abstractions but the results of practical concepts of national interest." Margenthau in his article "Another

Great Debate: The National Interest of United States" also asserts that the foreign policy "seeks the defence of the national interest by peaceful means" and to defend the national interest restrictively and rationally defined "against the national interests of other nations which may or may not be thus defined." Another scholar has observed : "national leaders as a rule never pursue national policies that are in the interest of any nation other than their own." Different national interests may overlap or be in harmony with one another but no president, prime minister or foreign secretary in full possession of his faculties—especially sense of his own political and personal survival would openly and knowingly initiate or implement policies that would favour another nation and damage his own. He further asserts "In planning, formulating, adopting and executing foreign policy, national leaders and their aides are confronted with a veritable spider's web of conflicting claims and values. Yet priorities, that is, the practical not ideal, contents of the national interest must finally be established in terms of preferred goals and in relation to the power of one's own nation and that of other nations. Both national goals and national means must simultaneously be related to dangers or opportunities on the international scene; not only other nation's power but also their intentions must be properly evaluated. In short, it has been asserted that the national interest is the predominant factor in the formulation of a country's foreign policy.

On the other hand Prof. Reynolds is of the view that it is not always possible to base the foreign policy of a state on its national interests alone. He argues that the foreign policy of a state can be based on national interest only if the interests of the various nations are homogeneous. On the other hand, it shall indeed, be a costly proposition to pursue a policy based on national interests, when the interests of the various nations are of a heterogeneous character. As each state shall try to resist the implementation of the alien values this is inevitably likely to lead to a war. As Reynolds puts it "Since self extending heterogeneous values of unlimited range must almost certainly lead to major armed conflict, national interests must require their limitations. National interests cannot, therefore always in all circumstances be identified with the values of the community; and when to this is added disagreement about the basic general purposes for which humans exist... the difficulty of giving any generally applicable empirical content to the notions of national interest becomes apparent."

Even if it is admitted that the national interest occupies a prominent position in the foreign policy of all countries, the leaders of the state do not necessarily always try to promote the national interest alone. Quite often they use foreign policy as a tool to strengthen their internal position. For example, Sukarno of Indonesia diverted the attention of the people from the acute economic and social problems by adopting the policy of confrontation towards Malaysia. Likewise, Pakistan has consistently raised the boggy of danger from India to divert the attention of people from the international problems.

Again, the vagueness of the concept of national interest makes the things quite difficult. Quite often the national interest comes to be equated with the maintenance of the existing political instiutions even at the cost of the interests of the general people. For example, the statesmen normally assume that the survival of the state, over which they preside, is the supreme national interest. Logically it may not always be so. For example, if attempts to preseve the state lead to the destruction of its people, then these attempts could not be in the national interest. It is an accepted fact that it is in the national interest of Britain that the standard of living of its people should rise even if it could be achieved by the complete merger of Britain into the EEC community and its ultimate disappearance. In other words the national interest of the people of Britain could be served by the demise of the state. But such an action is not likely to be approved by the political leaders, to whatever political party they may belong. This clearly shows that the decisions of the political leaders are not always taken in the larger national interest.

Prof. Reynolds asserts that "the concept of national interest is, therefore, an unfortunate and on the whole unhelpful one." It is normally attached to the notion of the state and so sacrifices stage goals. It directs attention to a particular advancement of which human ought to be organised—and the preservation and advancement of which accordingly ought to be the criteria for judgement of action. But if individuals are the proper referent, distinction needs to be drawn between strictly state goals and the goals that national interest prescribes. He further argues that in essence national interest "should relate to the real interests of the people, and this interest is not be seen as being necessarily contained within the state context. This notion of a 'real interest' is difficult to conceive... But even if it can be seen as a theoretical norm, it cannot in practice to be identified and will not serve as a means of judging particular decision or particular actions. State decision-makers who claim to be acting in the national interest misuse the notion, cannot have the perfect information necessary to validate their claims and so are pulling the wool over other people's eyes; and possibly over their own."

Constraints on National Interest

Any foreign policy which claims to operate in the national interest must have some reference to the physical, political and cultural entity called the nation. According to Morgenthau it must be determined in the light of possible usurpation by sub-national, other national and supranational interests, which are indeed serious constraints on the national interest. At the sub-national level we find group interest, represented particularly by ethnic and economic groups, which tend to identify themselves with the national interest and thus confuse the issue. Similarly, the other national interests can usurp the national interest of a state in two ways, *viz.*, through treason and criminology. For instance an individual may commit treason on behalf of a foreign government either out of conviction or out of monetary gains. Criminology may also prompt a person to promote the interests of a foreign government. In other words, there is every possibility of an ethnic minority of a country identifying itself with a foreign government and promote its interests under the guise of the national interests of its own country. Again the national interests of a country may be usurped by the supranational interests in two ways—through religious bodies and international organisations. Though religious bodies have ceased to be effective instruments of supra-national interests at present, the international organisations certainly operate against the national interests of the states by compelling them to pursue only such policies which do not operate against the interests of other member-states.

The international environments also exercise a profound influence on the decision-makers in the formulation of a country's foreign policy. As a unit of the international community the state is bound by certain regulations—-conventional, customary, ethical, legal or institutional and the framers of the foreign policy have to operate within these limitations. The framers of the policy have not only to keep the national interests in mind but also give due weightage to the interests of other states who are equally determined to fight for their national interests. They must keep a watchful eye on the policies and actions of other states and keep a track of various international developments. This naturally implies that a state which wants to play an active international role must take decisions keeping in mind the conditions prevailing around and should be willing to overhaul its foreign policy according to the exigencies of time. Failure to do so will only mean that the state is cut off from the main currents of the world affairs and its leadership is not far-sighted. In short, we can agree with the observation that "the major influence on foreign policy making thus derives from the fact that it is made with reference to other similarly acting bodies over which the policy-makers of the state in question have no authority or jurisdictian, and that the international arena within which policies are made is in high degree anarchical."

Prof. Morgenthau has also asserted the need of compromising the national interests with the interests of other nations. He says "the national interest of a nation which is conscious not only of its own interests, but also of that of other nations must be defined in terms compatible with the latter. In a multi-national world this is a requirement of political morality; in an age of total war it is also one of the conditions for survival."

Above all, in formulating the foreign policy the political leaders must not lose sight of the domestic factors like geography, natural resources, industrial capacity, demography, impacts of various groups and interests in the society, strategic position of the country etc. As the resources available for the pursuit of the national interest are necessarily limited in quantity and kind; and all the states cannot promote their objectives with equal vigour, it is of paramount importance that the states should allocate their scarce resources as rationally as possible.

CHAPTER 4 Foreign Policy Debacles and Challenges for the USA

Introduction

President Obama described US-India relationship as one of defining partnerships of 21st century. But Republican challenger, Mitt Romney, had said that Obama had failed to provide global leadership to the world. He promised to restore US foreign policy to its post-WW II role and exert itself as military and economic superpower. President Obama won because he had killed Osama. This machination worked. One big power overcame another. All is well that ends well! Obama basks in the glory created for him by the US marine Seals. He is in-charge of the economy but jobs are scarce. The economy has looked up in the middle of 2013. The economic and industrial woes would be overcome soon (three years, at the most). The incumbent administration would find it easy to focus on economic front. However, there are some issues that seem debacles in the US foreign policy. If they are not debacles by any norm, they ought to be treated as serious problems. Let us review them *in toto*.

A Framework of Analysis for the USA

The United States has come out of the dark phase of recession. The year 2015 seems to be a good start for American business people. The NATO has left Afghanistan. This was a major irritant for Islamic fundamentalists. However, the Americans are always at greatest risk due to their pro-democratic and anti-terror policies that they have been following. Today, US defence policy does not have Russia on its agenda. Its biggest agenda is terror. The Obama Administration was able to kill Osama bin Laden and in the future, it would also be able to weed out many more terror leaders from Asia. However, it had to pay dearly on 9/11. Its major allies, Australia and the UK, have also suffered many casualties, be there war or no war. America is a secular and rational face of democracy and there is no doubt about it. However, the biggest fiasco of its foreign policy is that despite the reprisals inflicted by NATO and other troops (which were masterminded or directed by Uncle Sam), the terror elements have come back again with more unity and strength than ever. Jihad is a word that rings bells in the ears of every terror group of Asia. The love and hate relationship with Pakistan continues. The US has stopped giving money to Pakistan on the pretext that it is no longer keen to wage bloody battles in North Waziristan, FATA, Peshawar, Afghanistan and other parts of Asia. The ISIS is going string in Syria and Iraq. The American military presence can only aggravate the situation there. India, as a passive ally in war against terror, is also a victim of this strategic alliance. There are sleeper cells of terror groups in every part of India. No railway station, aircraft, ship, train, bus or any other vehicle is safe in India. Terror networks are also spread in the US and the liberal and democratic Constitution of that country does not allow its courts to take serious actions against the masses at large.

Policy change would be clearly visible after Obama's exit. The party in power is not likely to come back to White House. Obama's term was peaceful. The next President may have to take harsh decisions. The ISIS would not spare any TV journalist, reporter, press person or any other person in Iraq and Syria. Most of them, who had gone there, were beheaded. Such is the hatred for the US in the minds of the Jihadis. This war of hatred has assumed gargantuan proportions. Ordinary peoples of Iraq and Syria are suffering. US help can only make their conditions worse. The biggest problem of the US foreign policy is that whosoever comes forward to support it in strategic, political or humane terms, suffers. Talks with terror elements do not yield fruits.

After coming out of the agonizing pangs of recession, the US ought to focus on industrial growth. But terror groups have gripped American policymakers. The major expenditure of the US exchequer is for anti-terror operations and for protecting the lives of its citizens in American embassies and consulates dotted across the globe. When the situation is so volatile and when a mortar or bullet can hit any American soldier, citizen or civilian aircraft from any direction, how can Uncle Sam think of growth in economic terms?

Traditional allies are with the US; there is no doubt about it. However, the conventional allies like Saudi Arabia, Kuwait, and

Egypt are not with it in this war against terror. They also have the same race as that of the Jihadis, so they would not harm them. Pakistan has a dual status. It is for and against terror. It has good Taliban as well as bad ones. Afghanistan cannot be termed as an ally of the USA. It is a land totally captured by the terror elements and democracy flourishes only under the shadows of guns there.

Some global think tanks suggest that America talk to terror elements and sort out things for an amicable settlement. However, we feel that this would be a futile effort. Both sides have lost enough. Therefore, neither would budge an inch from its place. London metro bombing, Australian café kidnapping, kidnapping of girls by Boko Haram in Nigeria, attack on a shopping mall in Nairobi—all these incidents are indications of the stiffened stance of ultra-religious terror organizations. The United Sates, a true democracy, cannot adequately deal with those who are truly bomb laden and can blow up themselves and people in their vicinity, irrespective of the consequences. Even the US military has the habit of talking across table before setting out for war. However, the terror elements it faces do not negotiate; they just shoot or explode! There is always space for democratic settlement, negotiation for mutual good and final curtain-raising for a peaceful show on the earth. But the situations in Iraq, Syria, Pakistan, Afghanistan, Libya, Kenya and Nigeria are the harbingers of the ever rising chaos whose perpetrators are very powerful. The situation is precarious for all other countries in general and for Uncle Sam in particular.

American citizens, not armed forces, are in danger of being attacked and that is what should be the top agenda item of foreign policy makers of Washington. A soldier is capable enough to save himself from the onslaught of a terror element, not an armless man or woman going down the street or buying cheese cake in a shopping mall. Thus, the strategy of the US must be re-defined in the interest of its people, plausibly the most vulnerable human beings in all parts of the earth.

Ideology Plays Role in Determining Foreign Policy

An international author has stated that ideology plays an important role in determining foreign policies. However, the received definition of ideology, which sees it as a set of beliefs or ideas about the world, makes for insuperable problems in mapping back and forth between ideology and the world. Instead, ideology can usefully be thought of as crystallized in policy instruments. It comprises organizationally structured activity sequences in which problems are linked to their concrete solutions in practical ways. Two examples of how policy instruments, as ideological, help throw light on great power interventions are as follows:

1. The eight-nation rescue mission in the Boxer Rebellion.
2. The US support for the Northern Alliance to overthrow the Taliban.

The USA at Camp David

The leaders of Britain, Canada, France, Germany, Italy, Japan and Russia joined Obama on May 18 and 19, 2012. They addressed major global economic, political and security challenges as well as energy, climate change, food security and nutrition, Afghanistan's economic transition and transitions taking place across Middle East and North Africa. The next day, US hosted the annual NATO Summit at Chicago. Leaders from 28 member countries of NATO took part. On May 21, 2012, International Security Assistance Force in Afghanistan met to discuss the transition of power in Afghanistan and set a goal for Afghan forces to take the lead for combat operations across the country in 2013. The US has left Iraq. It is present (in the form of NATO) in Afghanistan. The pullout year is near but US Administration can visualize time is tough. The Taliban has become stronger in Afghanistan and Pakistan. The inability of NATO to neutralize resistance of the Taliban and other ultra-fundamental forces has raised questions of mammoth size. Why is NATO working alone in the Af-Pak region, against the Taliban? Why doesn't the US talk to Taliban and sort out the matter in an amicable way? In fact, negotiations are going on but the Taliban commanders are not prepared to talk to US officials. They are also killing people in bomb blasts in Pakistan. All Afghan government offices are fortresses; only Allah knows when there would be a blast!

The policy of combat cannot work for US in Af-Pak because that region is living in the Medieval Age. The Taliban and Al-Qaeda cadres build upon the paradigm of religion-based supremacy.

The US cannot remove this paradigm. The policy should have been the following: make friends with Taliban and educate and transform them through education, industry, study abroad, interracial marriage and negotiations. There are nearly 18-20 tribes (*kabilahs*) in Af-Pak. They ought to be educated, trained for jobs and told vehemently that all other races and peoples also have a right to live. This strategy must transcend national boundaries. This can be a global human effort and the UN can take an initiative in this context. The tribes must be convinced that Malala Yusufzai has not done anything wrong by advocating the right to education of women.

War is not the right strategy for transforming the Af-Pak region. So, the present US policy towards this region would not suit any of the global or regional players. The policy was incorrect. That is why US and NATO have decided to withdraw troops in 2014 from Afghanistan, despite the fact that Karzai has no one to lean on in the absence of the exit of NATO forces.

War Theatres: US-dominated NATO in Afghanistan-Pakistan

On December 1, 2009, President put forth a new strategy for Afghanistan and Pakistan that is focused on disrupting, dismantling and defeating Al Qaeda and preventing its ability to threaten America and its allies. Obama said that for achieving that goal, the US would pursue three objectives, which are as follows:

1. Denying Al Qaeda a safe haven.
2. Reversing the Taliban's momentum.
3. Strengthening the capacity of Afghanistan's security forces and government so that they may take over for Afghan stability.

On June 22, 2013, President addressed American peoples about the way ahead in Afghanistan. President stated that US will begin the withdrawal of troops from a position of strength. He said that the forces had killed 20 of 30 top Al Qaeda commanders. US has broken the Taliban's momentum and trained 1,00,000 Afghan National Security Forces. It withdrew 10,000 U.S. troops from Afghanistan by the end of 2011 and the 33,000 surge troops he approved in December 2009 left Afghanistan by the end of summer 2012. Finally, the US troops withdrew completely from war zones of Afghanistan and Pakistan in 2014. By the end of 2014, all soldiers had pulled out of these two countries. Obama has followed the policy of minimal interference in his second term in office. That was primarily because he had directed NATO forces to search for and eliminate Osama bin laden. Now that Osama bin laden has been eliminated, he need not give fresh impetus to war against terror. The ISIS is going strong in the Gulf region. But Kurdish forces are getting support from the world so that they may fight against the ISIS. Similarly, Jordan has also started attacking ISIS targets in Iraq and Syria. The war has a communal tinge because it is basically a Shiite-Sunni clash. Obama does not want to interfere in this precarious situation. Peaceful solutions would be chalked out soon. The USA is exercising restrain for the good of its soldiers, who have been facing all kinds of danger in the war zones of Asia for many, many years in a row.

Hamid Karzai is considering a "zero option" and has stated that in 2014, there would be no American troops in Afghanistan. But before complete withdrawal is even official, opposition to it is high. House Armed Services Committee chairman Republican Buck McKeon—Republican lawmaker—got administration officials to assure him that they were not contemplating a zero option. The US wants its monitor-like presence in Asia. Afghanistan is the only option left for it. It wants to monitor Chinese troop movements from Afghanistan. It also wants to monitor the China-India conflict that may help it sell more weapons to India. Thus, its objective has two facets—strategic supremacy in India and commercial (weapon-based) deals with India. But it has central Asia in 2014. After its withdrawal, its interest in central Asia has reduced. After Obama, the US electorate is likely to elect a White President. The anti-incumbency wave may catapult the other party into power. America is currently improving its economy. It has given a backseat to geo-political confrontation. It is still not actively engaged in Pakistan, Afghanistan, Iraq, Syria and Nigeria. Its foreign policy has become defensive and it is not very keen to interfere in the affairs of chaotic States of the world. Obama's visit of 2014 to India is an indication that the US wants to be friendly with all now; it would prefer to be cozy with some others at a later stage.

Osama' Gory End

Obama got bin-Laden shot dead (May 2011) in Pakistan, under the nose of the Pak military, literally! He used drones in Afghanistan to kill the Taliban and Al-Qaeda cadres. He implemented a new strategy for Pakistan and Afghanistan that re-focuses US efforts on dismantling and crushing Al Qaeda.

Assistance to All, But Threat from Snowden

USA mobilized resources to help in relief efforts in Haiti, Japan, Pakistan and other parts of the globe. Despite the damage caused to American political façade from the Edward Snowden episode, the US continues to play vital military and diplomatic roles worldwide. Snowden is likely to reveal much more. He may be bumped off if he is not taken to US from the safe haven at the Moscow International Airport (in April and May 2013; he was still in Moscow on August 4, 2013, when this article was sent to press).

US Policy towards Nuclear Security and Disarmament

It announced a strategy to address international nuclear threat and convened a Nuclear Security Summit that took steps toward securing nuclear material worldwide. It built a broad coalition to pressurize Iran to abandon its nuclear program. Iran is not ready to give up its nuclear programme. Nuclear weapons were not found in Iran after inspection but the American intelligence sleuths claim it can make nuclear bombs. The North Korean defiance of the West has taken an ugly turn, this time in the shape of sky-pointing missiles. The North Korean dictator has installed missiles in all parts of the country and some of them are pointed towards the strategic targets of South Korea and some Western countries. It is prepared to wage a nuclear war. The US could not contain North Korean and Iranian nuclear programmes. This could be seen as its major foreign policy fiasco in recent times.

The joint Sino-Russian military exercises were plausibly a harbinger of the emerging Sino-Iranian-Russian nexus in which the indirect beneficiaries (India due to Russia and Pakistan due to China) might be forced to look away from the strategic alliances of the US and West (in the future). The nuclear capabilities of China and Russia are well known. As the key players of NSG, they may displace US from its top-notch post in NSG and start dictating their own terms.

Major Shift in US Foreign Policy

In a May 23, 2013 speech at the National Defense University, President Barrack Obama announced a shift in the national security strategy. After 9/11 attack on New York City and Washington, he averred, the United States "went to war." After 12 years, Al Qaida was decimated. Obama says that the American homeland is more secure. It ended or is ending large-scale military involvement in Iraq and Afghanistan. Terrorism still threatens but the nature of the threat has changed to an extent that US strategy should emphasize non-military tools rather than armed action.

Liz Cheney, a former Bush administration official and co-founder of "Keep America Safe," stated that President was retreating in the conflict with Al-Qaida. Peace is what we see now but Al-Qaida is known for giving surprises. Obama was censured for not being harsh to terror organizations in 2012 and 2013. He had taken a stand for withdrawal of troops in all conflict zones. This withdrawal policy may hurt American interests in the long run, claim many defence analysts and war connoisseurs.

US Policy towards Yemen

In February 2015, Huji Shia, an Islamic group attacked the capital of Yemen and captured it. It set up a council of 151 members to govern this war-ravaged nation. The new government was formed in November 2014. This government had the support of Saudi Arabia. The Huji Shiites have the support of Iran. Thus, we can observe that a proxy war is going on in various parts of the world and two masterminds—Saudi Arabia and Iran—are using armed people to impose their respective conditions on the Muslim communities of the globe. Iran is a Shiite-dominated nation. Iran also supports the organization called Muslim Brotherhood. Saudi Arabia promotes Sunni interests in most of cases, although the sacred mosques under the custodian of the royal Saudi family are meant for both these sects. Saudi Arabia promotes the interests of Sunni Muslims in Iraq and Syria. Yemen has great strategic and cultural importance for the Muslim world. It has a coastal area, which is vital for trade in the Gulf region. It has border with Saudi Arabia and the latter has enough clout in the Arab world and other political forums of the world. Yemen was the centre of activities of Al Qaeda till very recently. But there is a doubt whether this organization is actively working there or not. That is because the USA and UK have not been attacked one single time in 2014. The Al Qaeda cadres may be preparing for a big offensive against the USA in the near future. As on date, they are as silent as the lamb. That is what the reason behind worry probably is. Note that nearly 58 percent of the people of Yemen live below the poverty line. There are no healthcare, water, electricity, drainage and transport facilities for most of the populace of that country. Once upon a time, Osama bin Laden was active in that country. His footprints are still there, for the Yemen people and Saudi nationals may still be planning to strengthen the organization in a big way. Since the masses of Yemen are poor and lack basic amenities, they are easily tempted to join terror groups. That is what has been happening for the last 50-odd years there. Add to it, the Iranian connection of Huji Shia and you can expect a lethal concoction of mini wars, street battles and bomb explosions in Yemen and the entire neighbouring areas. The USA and UK ordered the closure of their embassies in Yemen on February 12, 2015. Yemen is the poorest among all nations of the Gulf region. Note that the Gulf nations earn their petro dollars because of the oil. But Yemen has lagged behind its sister nations in this field primarily due to internal strife and the impact of traditional Islamic groups on its peoples. Further, Saudi Arabia would never allow democracy to take deep roots in Yemen. It did not allow democracy to sit pretty in Egypt either. The management of a traditional society is easier for Saudi Arabia. It may be difficult for it to ignore the voices of people. Now, Saudi Arabia is a close associate of the United States and Britain. The cultures of Saudi Arabia and the US may be different but they are close strategic and economic partners. The USA wants Egypt to get peace and prosperity but Saudi Arabia denies this right to the Egyptians. You would read in this very volume that Egypt and Iran have good religious and cultural ties. Similarly, the USA wants the peoples of Yemen to get a democratically elected government. Saudi Arabia denies this right to the people of Yemen. King Abdullah had tried to pacify fundamentalist Muslims of Saudi Arabia. He had tried to pave the way for the modernization of the Islamic world. But he joined the great majority and his cousin has been given the charge of Saudi Arabia. We do not know how much liberal he would be able to become in the war-ridden Muslim regions of the world. But we are clear on the issue that traditional Islamic societies would not change so easily at the behest of a few leaders of Saudi Arabia. Thus, the proxy conflict of Iran and Saudi Arabia is talking its toll. People have died in Yemen, Afghanistan, Egypt, Pakistan, Syria and other parts of the world due to the sharp Shiite-Sunni divide. This is a painful situation for Muslim brothers and sisters of our world. The USA cannot afford to withdraw its support from the royal Saudi set-up because it needs oil. This oil can be supplied to it only by Saudi Arabia. If Saudi Arabia does not supply oil to the USA, the economy of the latter would go to doldrums in just six months! That is why developments in Yemen would be watched with keen interest by Obama. He cannot do much to change the precarious situation there.

The US Policy towards Cuba

Obama announced new policy steps towards Cuba. He focused on Asia-Pacific. He announced an international strategy for cyberspace issues. He reaffirmed support for military and their families.

End of War in Iraq

On February 27, 2009, Obama announced a plan to end the war in Iraq. On August 31, 2010, President announced the end of US combat mission in Iraq. Iraqi Security Forces assumed lead responsibility for their nation's security. On October 21, 2011, President announced that all US troops will move out of Iraq by the end of the year. Beyond 2011, decided to have a normal relationship with a sovereign Iraq. It was supposed to be a bilateral agreement in which both nations would work together as partners to promote common security and prosperity.

In December 2011, the last US troops left Iraq. When Obama took office, there were roughly 1,80,000 US troops serving in Iraq and Afghanistan. By the end of 2011, this number was cut to one half. Currently, there are no troops of NATO or US in Iraq and democracy is thriving there. The credit goes to the joint war machinery of Iraq and US as well as the peoples of Iraq. The bomb blasts of July 2013 amply proved the fear that fundamentalists would not let democracy have a simple ride. Oil wells of Kirkuk were attacked in July 2013 by terror elements. However, Iraqi administration managed the situation well.

The USA and Iran

During a trip to Iran, Hamas leader, Mr. Khaled Mashal, praised Iranian leaders for their support during the conflict in the Gaza Strip. This is a harbinger of the strengthening relationships between the Sunni Islamist group (defined by the USA as a terrorist organization) and the Shiite (also read as 'Shia' in this volume) regime in Tehran. The U.S. Treasury Department had given terror designations to Al-Qaeda leaders and operatives living in Iran. Latest examples of Sunni-Shiite cooperation raise new questions about whether Iran can improve its relationship with Egypt's Muslim Brotherhood.

Such a rapprochement is not unlikely. History suggests that it is far from impossible. Iran has maintained informal ties with the Muslim Brotherhood for many years and Shiite Islam probably has more appeal among Egyptian Sunnis than it does among the Sunnis of other Arab countries. Iran's sharp criticism of the former Egyptian President (Mr. Hosni Mubarak) is also likely to resonate with Egyptian radicals under the thumb of the regime in Cairo. If Iran were to develop close relations with Muslim Brotherhood, Iranian influence would grow considerably in the Arab world. That could Tehran a significant status among Arab radicals. That would certainly harm American interests in the region.

Egypt has long been suspicious of the connection between the Egyptian Muslim Brotherhood. Iran had strong ties with Hamas, an offshoot of Muslim Brotherhood. The conflict in Gaza is likely to arouse Cairo's suspicions. During the course of the Ghaza battle, Iran was highly vocal in their support of Hamas. Hamas leader, Mr. Khaled Mashal, had thanked Iran for its support of his organization Gaza. Thus, Iran openly supports the Palestinian cause and is against the settlement of Israelis in the controversial Ghaza strip.

Iran has also forged stronger working relations with other Sunni extremists. Saudi authorities allege that a leader of Al-Qaeda in the Persian Gulf, Abdullah al-Qaraqi, lives and moves freely in Iran. More than one hundred Saudis are working for him, they opine. The Treasury Department, in its recent enforcement action, announced that Saad bin Laden, son of Osama bin Laden, was arrested by Iranian authorities in early 2003 but he was no longer in Iranian custody. According to the Director of National Intelligence, Mr. Michael McConnell, Saad bin Laden is most likely in Pakistan at present.

While a breakthrough in relations between the Egyptian Muslim Brotherhood and Tehran remains unlikely, the consequences for the United States of such a union would be very damaging. Iran remains focused on expanding its influence in the Persian Gulf and beyond. Growing strategic and other ties between Iran and the Hamas and a look back at the relevant history make it clear that U.S. policymakers should monitor this trend very carefully. The USA could not find any nuclear weapons in Iran. But it knows something is wrong with the overt nuclear operations that were shown to IAEA operations. Muslim Brotherhood and Tehran may be hands in glove for making a nuclear bomb. On January 28, 2015 Muhammad Mahdi Akef, the current leader of the Muslim Brotherhood, said in an interview with a news agency, " Muslim Brotherhood supports the ideas and thoughts of the founder of Islamic Republic. Ayatollah Khomeini's idea, especially with regard to the Palestinian issue, is the continuation of the Muslim Brotherhood's attitude towards fighting occupation." These words must marked and remembered by American policy makers.

The Shia see the threat as not only military but stemming from the expanded influence over mainstream Sunni Islam of Wahhabism, the puritanical and intolerant version of Islam espoused by Saudi Arabia. The genre of Sunni Isalm being practiced in Saudi Arabia eschews Shia and other Islamic groups as non-Muslim apostates and polytheists. Iran is a Shia-dominated State. Saudi Arabia, on the contrary, is a traditional Sunni-ruled State. The conflict between these two States is assuming various Jihadi hues. However, the two sects must come to the negotiation table to chalk out a peace treaty soon. That is because both of them are from the same grand tree, the same lineage. Brothers must not kill brothers. Again, the USA has done its best to persuade both parties but to no avail.

The USA and Saudi Arabia

Saudi Arabia plays an important role in bringing it about by supporting the anti-Shia jihad in Iraq and Syria. Since the capture of Mosul (Iraq) by the Islamic State of Iraq and Syria (ISIS) on 10 June, 2014, Shia women and children were killed in villages south of Kirkuk and Shia air force cadets were machine-gunned and buried in mass graves near Tikrit. Note that the name of Syria in the terminology of ISIS is **Levant**. In Mosul, Shia shrines and mosques have been blown up and in the Shia Turkoman city of Tal Afar, 4,000 houses were taken over by ISIS fighters. The USA cannot help any one of the two major groups at war, for it is their personal issue.

The US Policy towards Egypt

The Egyptians are more receptive and positively disposed towards Shiism (the Shia ideology) than other Sunni Arabs. One reason is the Fatimid Dynasty that was established in Egypt during the Tenth century as an offshoot of the Shiite Ismaelite movement. This clan played an important role in the cross-fertilization between Iran and Egypt. Two centuries of the Fatimid rule in Egypt marks a high point in the history of Islamic civilization in terms of economic development and cultural prosperity. The art in Fatimid Egypt was also influenced by Iranian styles, aver historians.

The Fatimid period left a lasting impression on the Egyptians. Thus, vestiges of the country's long-ago Shiite rulers can be seen in Egyptian openness to Shiite traditions. This receptiveness is not found anywhere else in the Sunni world. The Egyptians still respect symbols, icons and sacred places of that period. The Egyptians believe that Hussein, the third Shiite Imam, and his family are buried in Cairo, not in Karbala, Iraq. For Sunni Egyptians, the tombs of Hussein, Sayyeda Zainab (his sister) and Assayeda Sakina (his daughter) are the most sacred places in the world, next only to the holy Mecca and Medina. Like their Shiite counterparts, the Sunnis (of Cairo) perform Ashura (the Shiite commemoration of the death of Hussein) every year. During the Nineteenth century, in Egypt, the Persian language was accepted as a language of literature and science. Thus, ties between Egypt and Iran have deep-rooted religious and cultural bedrocks.

Besides the influence of Egyptian political Islamists on Iranian clerics noted earlier, Iranian clerics in turn helped to shape Islamist revivalism in Egypt. One example I this context is the Nineteenth-century Islamist, Sayyed Jamal al-Din Asadabadi; he was also known as al-Afghani. When he arrived in Egypt from his native country, Iran, he claimed to be an Afghan so that he could be treated as a Sunni. His new ideology advocated the unity of Muslims and sought answers to the ills of various Muslim societies. As a result of this history, for many years, Shiism held some appeal in Egypt, despite the fact that the Egyptians, at the time of the Fatimids (and even today in 2015) are predominantly Sunnis.

The appeal of Shiism has been reduced in recent years as the Egyptian government has grown increasingly nervous about what it perceives as a rising Shiite tide in their country. In response, the Egyptian government and the State media began waging a campaign against Shiism and Shiite symbols. In November 2005, the then Egyptian President (Mr. Hosni Mubarak) stated, "Most Shiites are faithful to Iran, not to their own government." His comment provoked several Shiite demonstrations, including a grand march which was carried out by thousands of people in Najaf, a Shiite holy city in Iraq. Later, Mubarak explained that he meant that Shiites sympathized with Iran in terms of their religious, not political, viewpoints. Mubarak was murdered in broad daylight after a few years.

On several occasions, a prominent Egyptian cleric, Shaikh Yousef Qarzawi, a former member of Muslim Brotherhood, warned about the Shiite tide and the missionary activities of the Shiites and Iranian government, especially a few noticeable ones in Egypt. He had categorically that the increasing infiltration of Shiism in Egypt may lead to a civil war like the one in Iraq. The Egyptian government made efforts to mobilize powerful clerics and faculty associated with the Al-Azhar University against the Muslim Brotherhood to fight against the rising tide of Shiism.

There are no reliable statistics about the number of Shiites in Egypt. Since Shiites are under pressure from the Egyptian government, most of them avoid admitting their true faith. Some Western and Egyptian sources (like the Ibn Khaldun Research Center) indicate that the Shiites constitute less than one percent of the Egyptian population (approximately 6,57,000 persons). But Muhammad al-Darini, a prominent Sunni, who had converted into Shiism, puts the figure at 1.5 million persons. Al-Darini claims that Egyptian Shiites are Twelvers, which is the type of Shiism practised in Iran. But he denied any connection between the Shiite community and the Iranian government.

Shiism is not only and originally Iranian sect, but also an Arab one. The four traditional Sunni schools stem from Iran. The vital element of the attraction of Shiism in modern Egypt is political rather than doctrinal in nature. Some young Egyptians see conversion to Shiism as a way of protesting the regime, much as thousands of Iranian Shiite youths convert each year to various other faiths partially in reaction to the Shiite nature of their government.

The USA is at its wit's end even as it grapples with these new realities. It cannot send its troops to any part of the world, given that it has become notorious due to its past "interference moves" around the globe. So, its policy of "wait and watch" would help it protect its own forces from the blazing fires of battles in the Middle East. Political deliberations would continue with all nations in conflict, though.

Stopping Massacre and Supporting the Libyan Peoples

The US has supported pro-democracy fighters in Libya. After the death of Qaddafi, the situation in this African country is not much better. Stability would come only after the masses support democratically elected candidates. The USA is supporting democratic forces in Libya.

Keeping Nuclear Weapons Out of Hands of Terrorists

On April 5 2009 in Prague, Obama declared his vision for achieving the "peace and security of a world without nuclear weapons," laying out a plan for near term practical steps to move in that direction. He proposed measures to:

(a) reduce the number of nuclear weapons possessed by those States that already possess nuclear weapons (starting with Russia and US);

(b) prevent additional countries from acquiring nuclear weapons by strengthening the international non-proliferation regime and by holding accountable those nations that have violated their obligations (Iran and North Korea);

(c) prevent nuclear terrorism by securing vulnerable nuclear materials and strengthening international cooperation on nuclear security; and

(d) develop new mechanisms to support the growth of safe and secure nuclear power in ways that reduce the spread of dangerous technologies.

In April 2010, the President hosted the Nuclear Security Summit where leaders pledged specific steps to prevent nuclear terrorism and support the President's proposal to lock down all vulnerable nuclear materials in four years. The Administration oversaw the negotiation and ratification of the New START Treaty. Obama and Medvedev had signed it in April 2010 in Prague. Significantly reducing the levels of nuclear weapons installed by US and Russia, the Treaty represents a commitment by the world's two largest nuclear powers to the aim of disarmament. Hence, the two superpowers have complete understanding regarding the elimination of nuclear weapons, WMDs and missile systems.

The policies of US and Russia are determined to succeed on the nuclear disarmament front. The nuclear treaty could not be signed by US and India, though. Iran and North Korea are posing problems to world nuclear peace.

Promoting Peace and Security in Israel and the Middle East

The United States is committed to a comprehensive, just, and lasting peace in the Middle East, including two states for two peoples—Israel as a Jewish state and the homeland for the Jewish people and the State of Palestine as the homeland for the Palestinian people, each enjoying self-determination, mutual recognition and peace.

Obama's Views about Peace

President Obama believes that a key component of achieving peace is maintaining the unshakeable US commitment to Israel's security. He has also said that the core issues can only be negotiated in direct talks between the parties. That is why the President stated publicly principles on territory and security that can provide a foundation for an agreement to end the conflict and resolve all claims. Israel offered to release some prisoners of Palestine head of the crucial Arab-Israel talks in 2013. This step was welcomed by all parties. We hope US would be able to persuade Israel to make him give some concessions to Palestinians. Note that these talks are US-sponsored, so Washington would call the shots.

Further, Obama has also passed trite remarks about the communal situation of India. Note that after his visit to India on January 26, 2015, he has passed only one remark that could go against the warming up relationship between the USA and India. Otherwise, he has been appreciative of all efforts of Modi and his brigade.

Re-energizing America's Alliances

Since taking office, President Obama has strengthened America's old alliances, while building new partnerships to confront the challenges of the 21st century. On his first trip overseas, President visited Europe to begin this process, with the G-20 Summit, 60th Anniversary NATO Summit and US-EU Summit. During his May 2011 trip to Europe, President reaffirmed his commitment to the Transatlantic Partnership and its role in addressing global issues.

The President made clear in his speech to the Turkish Parliament and in Cairo that America's relationship with the Muslim world will be based on more than our shared opposition to terrorism. He stated in his policy that the US would seek broader engagement based on mutual interest and mutual respect. The US seeks to strengthen historic alliances in Asia while developing deeper bonds with all nations of the region so that US and other parties might work together to address the challenges of the Twenty-first century. He named challenges as follows: proliferation, climate change, pandemics and economic instability. Obama would be leaving the political stage of the world after the end of his second term at the White House. Obama has not changed relationships with most of America's allies. He came closer to India, albeit in a conscious way. He censured Russia due to its presence in Ukraine but did not supply advanced weapons to government of Ukraine due to the political pressures of Germany and France. Till the time the USA does not get a new President—he would be from a party different from that of Obama because we are tempted to extrapolate the general trends of the past—the US Administration would not indulge in serious global wars, battles, skirmishes against the terror elements and direct interventions. Political arm twisting would go on around the world, though.

The US and India

President Obama had visited India to attend the colourful Republic Day parade of January 26, 2015. Then, he left for Saudi Arabia the very next day to mourn the death of King Abdullah bin Saud in Saudi Arabia. Obama has made deep impact on the minds and psyche of the Indian Diaspora. He is the first ever President of the United States to have visited India and also attended the Republic Day Parade. This is not a very crucial win for Modi. But it is a big diplomatic win for Obama, contrary to the popular belief. Obama has balanced all forces that now operate at the international level. It has amended its walls with India and would like both nations to go ahead with the final draft of the nuclear deal. Many agreements were signed during the course of his visit. They included the areas of commerce, culture and technology. The nuclear deal with India is also in the backseat. He is not keen to address major issues since economic recovery is a major issue. The US has come out of the throes of recession. In July 2013, one single US dollar cost 60-plus Indian rupees. So, US economy is taking an upturn for the better. The US is focusing on trade deals as it is out of recession now (we are describing the scene of January 2015).

The USA and Jordan

Jordan is part of the US-led military coalition that had bombed ISIS targets in Syria. But a gory event took place in February 2015. A Jordanian fighter pilot was captured by ISIS cadres. His name was Lieutenant Muath al-Kasaebah. He was burnt alive by ISIS cadres and the video of this carnage was sent to Jordanian authorities. The entire country flew in to a rage. King Abdullah of Jordan took a vow that he would wage a harsh war against the ISIS. He also pledged his allegiance to the coalition led by the United States. The students of Jordan came into streets of various cities to protest the death of their hero pilot. Thus, Jordan and the USA have come much closer to each other after this heart-rendering incident. That way, a few pockets of the Arab world have taken a stand against terror elements. If this trend continues to develop and Arab leaders continue to give their military and economic support to the USA, the latter would certainly be able to establish peace in the Arab world. Currently, the entire Arab world is going through bloodbath and chaos. There are no solutions. The USA is also fighting for every inch of land in that region. Its policy of protecting its allies through thick and thin has been welcomed by its Arab allies and Pakistan. However, this policy may not have been viewed with pleasure in New Delhi, given that Pakistan is the major recipient of the economic-cum-military aid of the USA even today. Jordan has taken a tough stand against the militants and its peoples are hell-bent upon removing terror from the Arab soil. But Pakistan is the perpetrator as well as protector of terror. That is what its 66-year old history informs us. In Pakistan, there are good terror outfits (as per the government's versions) and there are bad ones. The government and courts give minor punishment to good terror outfits and releases them after keeping them in jail to please the global media. The staunch enemies of Pakistani army are the bad terror outfits who are really out of reach of any force of Pakistan. They had killed 132 children in an army school Peshawar. Pakistani armed forces could not do anything to protect innocent children and their teachers. Jordan, on the contrary, would come out in the open to wage a final battle. It would not play double games like Pakistan, experts opine. Thus, the USA would actually stand by Jordanian forces to establish peace in the entire Arab world.

US Is Getting Tired of Central Asia and Af-Pak Region

On June 26, 2013, Kyrgyz President Almazbek Atambayev formally signed a law annulling the country's agreement with US to host an air base in his country. The true significance of the law is hazy; it could be a bargaining measure to gain more favourable terms for a new agreement on the base which has been the most conspicuous presence of Uncle Sam in Central Asia since being established shortly after the 9/11 attacks. The passage of the law has highlighted how US interest in Central Asia is likely to reduce as the US leaves Afghanistan. In the short term, US interest in Central Asia will remain keen. As the Pentagon pulls out its forces and equipment from Afghanistan, it is setting up transit agreements with neighbouring States to allow material to be transported across their territories back home. The US already has such agreements for cargo going into Afghanistan—Northern Distribution Network (NDN)—there are issues with respect to cargo going out. The transport of cargo may call for new US diplomatic efforts in Central Asia.

The US Policy towards Japan

During the Cold War, the US-Japan alliance was variously described as the cornerstone and the linchpin of US Asia strategy but over the past decade, the role of this strategic alliance has come under scrutiny. Change in the Asia-Pacific region has forced a rethinking of American priorities in Asia. China's rise has called for a more complex assessment in both Tokyo and Washington of the circumstances under which the alliance might be tested. Japan's struggle with slow economic growth and poor political reforms has made strategic adjustment difficult. Similar concerns in the US over its own economic recovery and stalled politics in Washington during the Obama Administration's second term infuse the policy debate over the implementation of the rebalance to Asia.

For the past half century, Japan has played a supporting role in US regional strategy but while maintaining limited military forces and relying on the US to deter potential adversaries and helping in Japan's defence. America's extended deterrent was sufficient to keep Japan secure. The deployment of American forces in Japan provided a platform for US military presence in the Asia-Pacific. Much of the alliance-management agenda focused on Japan's provision of support for US operations elsewhere. Over the past decade, however, the regional strategic balance has shifted. Japan may become the target of attack. This doctrine is new and lethal for the Japanese. It has seeped into the minds of the security planning community in Tokyo.

Restoring American Leadership in Latin America

President Obama went to attend the Summit of the Americas in Trinidad and Tobago. He met all of leaders in the Western Hemisphere. The President also travelled to Brazil, Chile and El Salvador to strengthen partnerships in the Americas. The foreign policies towards these nations are friendly and commerce oriented.

Latest Determinants of Foreign Policy of the USA

They are as follows:

1. Regional Conflicts of Asia are No longer a Cause of concern: The USA would not like to send NATO forces or US marines to fight wars on behalf of its allies. Its economy has come out of the pangs of recession now. It would not like to impose fresh taxes on people to fight wars in foreign lands.
2. Proxy Clash with Russia May Be On Agenda: We sincerely feel that the USA may start supplying arms and ammunition to Kiev in a bid to exert its supremacy in global political affairs. Currently, Germany and France are dissuading it from doing so, for this is a harsh step by all norms. The security and economy of Europe would be affected if the USA supports Kiev to suppress the rebellion in eastern Ukraine.
3. A Strong Dollar: American economy is looking up. The standards of living of the American peoples have improved a lot over the past twenty-odd years. Hence, a rising dollar would be welcomed by the Americans. It might hurt American exports, though.
4. Policy towards Iran: Signing a nuclear deal with Iran is not easy game for any country. Yet, there is news that Iran

might get into a nuclear wedlock very soon. Israel has opposed the move. India is neutral to this concept. The USA assumes that through a nuclear deal it would be able to rein in Iran and its prestigious nuclear programme.

5. Policy towards India: President Obama had brought many good messages for India. Many contracts were signed and many more would be signed when the two nations interact with each other in the future. The USA has tried to move India away from the strong hug of the Russian bear. It has been successful in doing so, for the BJP-led government in New Delhi is in favour of the USA and its political ideologies. Due to this policy shift of New Delhi, Washington has also overly leaned towards New Delhi. China is also worried to learn that Indo-US honeymoon has begun. Pakistan is awestruck!
6. Oil Prices: Falling oil prices is happy news for America. Oil is a major headache for this country, for it is the largest consumer of energy resources in the world. Saudi oil supplies are meant to serve American interests only. If oil prices rise, Americans might stop buying it. Recession may ensue. Thus, oil prices must be made stable in the world so that the American economic system is able to grow at the rate of at least 0.6 to 1.0 percent per annum. Our economy is inextricably linked to American economy.

Foreign Economic Policy of America

Indian economy has grown 45-fold since 2000. In 2014, the real GDP of American economy grew at the rate of 2.4 percent. US economy is out of danger now. There is no recession in its markets. Its exports are increasing and it has a good balance of payment position. Thus, in 2015, the USA would grow by leaps and bounds. More jobs would be created for foreign nationals. Visa rules are liberal and workers are finding good work havens in that country. EU has not been able to give any reprieve to Greece where a new President has assumed power. The new President wants the debts of Greece totally or partially written off. The US is watching the scene with patience. Its EU connections through Britain may persuade it to be liberal with Greek economy. The

Chairperson of IMF has categorically stated in an interview on the CNN Television that most of economic pockets of this world are not performing. The USA was not part of that list, though. The chairperson was vocal about Greek recession and its failure to come out of the economic chaos. She had urged the weak economies to work harder and look for ways to come out of recession. A strong US economy would auger well for EU's economic health, which is anything but satisfactory as on date. We can keep France, Britain and Germany aside and we have a chaotic economic scene in entire Europe. India is also depending upon the USA for getting vital equipment, supplies and fuel for its nuclear plants. The deal has made headway but a lot more needs to be done. If US economy shines, India would get all benefits. The Americans are no longer to send troops in war zones of the world. They would like to sell weapons to rebels and governments around the world. This is a shift in the US foreign diplomacy. Now, they sell more weapons. They do not try to sell their concepts to the world to make it more democratic or humane. That is because they have seen their soldiers dying in the middle east, Afghanistan and Pakistan. Russia had also done well by exiting the war theatres of Asia. Now, the US has learnt its lessons. As a result, its economic revival has become a reality, much to the delight of all Americans. It would use its favourable balance of payment position to its advantage in the year 2015. It would not give much money to its allies because of its precarious foreign exchange position. When it is full out of the shadow of recession, which it certainly is as January 2015 data tells us, it would like to invest money in NATO, Pakistan, China and India. The FIIs of the US are currently choosy about investments. When they see that ample opportunities have come up in India and the EU, they would take the plunge and invest dollars in selected ventures. Currently, they are following the wait and watch policy. The situation in the middle-east is slightly precarious. The death of King Abdullah has created a vacuum in Saudi Arabia. The policies of the Late king may not be followed. Traditional societies like those of Saudi Arabia may be inclined to go back to the era of Medieval period. Most members of the 9/11 squad that hit America, were Saudis. King Abdualla was a picture of humility and progress. His demise may change Saudi policies towards America. That is why Obama had gone to Saudi Arabia after visiting India, given that Saudi Arabia is the major US ally that has always supported American policies.

Note that we have stated about the recovery of American economy and supported its growth. But if US comes out of the recession phase, it does not mean that world economy would get benefit from this recovery. The economies of Portugal, Ireland and Spain are facing recession. When these economies are suffering, American economy cannot remain aloof from their agonies. If America has to survive, it must export. But there are very few buyers in EU, Asia and Africa today. Thus, where are the markets for American products and services? The online shopping business is brisk now-a-days but it cannot sustain a big giant like American economy. Goods and services must be exported by American firms in 2015. Thus, experts have stated that the recent recovery of American economy should be watched with caution, not optimism.

Conclusion: Ensuring Energy Security and Opposing Climate Change

The US President has committed to put America on a path to a clean energy economy that improves its energy security, reduces the use of fossil fuels and drives a new era of American innovation. Obama recognized the need to break from old ways that were lethal for US economy and the blue-green planet. He committed to investing $150 billion in clean energy research and development over ten years. America, the biggest fuel guzzler and energy user of the world, will be a leader in addressing global climate change both by making contributions of its own and entreating other nations to do the same. Obama has demonstrated the American commitment to a low-carbon future, bilaterally and through the UN Framework Convention on Climate Change process by working with other major economies to reduce emissions and produce 'clean' energy. His positive approach to low-carbon emissions and inclination for the production of clean energy helped him win accolades around the globe. But let us see what happens in the year 2015.

CHAPTER 5 Few Friends in New Foreign Policy of Russia

Introduction

Russia is currently a sidelined nation because of the crisis in Ukraine. We shall discuss that crisis separately in this very chapter. A weak rouble has also taken its toll and Russian economy has been torn apart due to its consistent fall from October 2014 to February 2015. Russia is also worried about close relationships between India and the USA. China and Russia joined hands with India to fight a decisive war against terror. That is some solace for Russia. However, Putin is worried about its claim on the Ukrainian territory. The rebel cadres of Ukraine owe their allegiance to Russia and are being funded by Moscow. Russia is on cross-roads today. Its weak economy does not make it eligible to be called superpower. However, Russia would wake up to the challenges of economy and polity in the New Year 2015. We hope and pray it may do so on its own, just like it did in the past!

A Framework of Analysis for Russia

The Big Bear has come a long way since the eighties of the last century when we witnessed the break-up of the USSR and eventual polarization of Russia's allies in favour of the economic and strategic policies of the West. Russia supplies oil to Europe. Without oil, no economy can run. So, the jugular vein of EU is in the hands of Putin, literally the master of Russian destiny. China and Russia are coming close. The foreign policy of Russia has many pleasant bouquets for the Dragon and these seem brickbats for the Americans. Let us review the latest policy of Russia; we have added updates up to July 2013.

Putin's Changing Strategy

President Putin decisively turned the tendency towards a balanced foreign policy into one of the main pillars of his general strategy. For him, this task was no more difficult in his second term than during his first one. In 2000, he gained instant popularity that had remained the same through both his terms in office. His popularity rating has stayed well above 52 percent since then. Russians liked his tough approach toward Chechen terrorists, including those who emigrated, his attractive personal qualities (youth, seriousness, dedication and intelligence) and his determination to satisfy their wish for order, a strong nation (after the chaos of 1990s).

Voluntarily or due to coercion, the masses have given consent to Putin's new rules of the game and his supremacy in all realms of politics, including the foreign policy. During his first term in office, Putin carried out an upgrade of national security, military and foreign policy concepts to ensure nation's progress toward a multidirectional, balanced and pragmatic external superpower. During his second term in office, Putin continued to implement his new policy without facing serious resistance at home. Thus, he said (we quote): "It is important to make the foreign policy serve the comprehensive development and modernization of the country." We have learnt that Putin has dealt with rebels with an iron hand. Russia is not a true democracy. But Russia is a better option than USSR. The Russian foreign policy has shown signs of liberal consent and cooperation, both at home and outside it.

Russia and Chinese Immigrants

There was immigration of Chinese nationals into sparsely populated and backward regions of Eastern Russia that China claimed as her own in the past. The sheer diversity, both in character and geography, of security challenges led the Kremlin to develop a multidirectional, balanced strategy. Given Russia's geostrategic position and economic situation, the Kremlin could not afford to plunge into a new Cold War with the West, which Russia needs both as a valuable partner for the political and economic modernization of post-Soviet Russia as well as a balance to counter numerous security problems, which ranged from the real threat of terrorism to the potential challenge of the Chinese giant in the East. At the same time, Moscow realized that close cooperation with China would prevent US and NATO hegemony in world affairs and rebuff Islamic extremism in the south. The CIS zone also required a balanced policy in order to overcome conflicts and instability there.

Putin and Internal Reforms

At the beginning of his presidency, Putin recognized that internal reforms and modernization drive required the widest possible integration of Russia into the system of global economic interactions. Russia still needs the West as a valuable source of technology, capital and management know-how. However, Russia's leaders realized that in dealing with Western partners, Russia could not expect preferential treatment or concessions. Moscow faced competition and bargaining exercises on every economic issue. Putin also understood that the Russian Federation needed to increase economic cooperation in other directions. China and India looked attractive as markets for Russian weapons and other non-war products. India is the biggest buyer of Michael 1 Gushin (M1G) aircraft, to quote an example. Russia had to try to collect on debts owed by a score of Arab and African nations. CIS countries could develop into attractive economic partners of the Russian Federation. The changes in conditions of the energy markets due to the prolonged military campaigns in Afghanistan and Iraq have made the current oil price hike possible. Since 2004, Russia has been able to earn profit in its budget. In 2005, Russia created a reserve of gold and hard currency. We do not have the exact value of that fund since it would never be disclosed by the Russians.

Russia and the Paris Club

During Putin's second term, it became possible to repay ahead of schedule Russia's debt to the Paris Club. This served as the basis for changes in the tactics of Russian diplomacy in international relations. Putin continued his strategy to help Russia regain its superpower status. He did not do this by renewing the confrontation with the US. But the lowering of Russia's dependence on Western loans in 2005 and the breech by Western partners of their promise to renounce their discrimination against Russia in world trade (the preservation of the Jackson-Vanik amendment and America turning into the last obstacle to Russia's admission to the WTO) changed the situation. The changes in Russian foreign policy during the last year have also been related to the domestic situation. Putin's foreign fetched Russian popular support. But Putin's policy was rooted in the genuine needs of Russia and the prevailing mood of the society's elites. Nevertheless, liberals criticized Putin's excessive and unwarranted toughness towards the West.

Independent Foreign Policy

Vladimir Putin's desire to make Russia's foreign policy more independent corresponds to the moods of the conservative part of the Russian elite trying to relive the Soviet past. Kremlin continues to work for multi-polarity. It does not want to create enemies. It wants friends as business partners. Russia's population also needs computers, high-definition LED TVs, cars, disco culture, costly wine and all luxuries that were hitherto not available to it. Thus, Putin is going global. His foreign policies have shown a situation of win-win for all.

Like China, Russia is becoming one among few countries that will pursue an independent foreign policy course and play a significant role in a number of key regions—Europe, Northeast Asia Greater Middle East (areas with predominantly Muslim populations southward from Russia). The Russian leadership has declared that it in favour of a diversification of its customers and has begun using her energy resources to turn Russia into a great energy producer. It is very important for Moscow to restore Russia as a global center of power that needs the appropriate surrounding. Russia will not return to its imperial policy of the past. But it would continue to strengthen its influence by selling energy to the needy nations. Former Soviet republics have been losing their Russian preferences. The CIS has become internally unstable. Ukraine, Georgia, and Moldova have created the Union of Democratic Choice and orient themselves only to the US and the EU.

Russia and CIS States

Out of eleven CIS member countries, Russia has only five allies that are members of either one or both the Collective Security

Treaty Organization and the Eurasian Economic Community (EEC). They are Armenia, Belarus, Kazakhstan, Kyrgyzstan and Tajikistan. In November 2005, Russia concluded a treaty of alliance with Uzbekistan. These are practical alliances. The nature of a political regime in an allied state is of no relevance to the Russian leadership. During colour revolutions, troops at Russian bases did not interfere in the events going on in Georgia. Rather, Russia acted as an intermediary when political crises struck. Russia's political resources in the post-Soviet space are not depleted. It can compete with its main rivals in the struggle for influence—the US, EU and China. These resources are based on the economic and cultural attractiveness of Russia. It can live without exploiting its partners' resources. It can share with them its own resources and act as a leader of economic modernization and a guarantor of the security of the common space. Some of Russia's partners perceive the shift in world prices as a form of economic pressure. However, it is just the result of their refusal to have close allied relations with Russia that is providing the opportunity to dissociate themselves from the Russian hegemony and to act without the support they were fond of receiving. In future, they will have to look for new patrons in the West. The turn of Russia's interests toward Eurasia makes its policy in the Asia-Pacific region very crucial.

Russia and the Asia-Pacific Region

Developing good relations with the Asia Pacific Region (APR) is another goal of the Russian foreign policy. Moscow's priorities there are to protect its national safety, use the region's potential to develop Russian economy, consolidate multi-polarity in international relations and advance Russia as a respected pole of influence in the political international arena. The current situation in the APR seems conducive to Russian interests. There are no hostile blocs or states. Russia is not directly involved in local conflicts. Russian Federation is welcomed as a participant in the political and economic activities in APR.

Russia's foreign policy must respond to a host of problems in the region that have an impact on Russian interests. The most disparaging problem is the increasing gap in economic development between eastern Russia and its neighbouring Asian states. If the

Big bear fails to improve the economic situation in Siberia and its Far Eastern reaches, its neighbours will sense the weakness and begin to exert demographic and economic pressure. Russia cannot single-handedly overcome economic backwardness and must rely on assistance from its foreign partners.

Russia must also comprehend the problems that face its Asian neighbours. They are—reduced or nil natural resources, environmental degradation, overpopulation, terrorism, drug trafficking, unemployment and diseases. Finding solutions of these would call for international cooperation. Regional hot spots, principally the Korean and Taiwan issues and disputes over islands in the South China Sea, form the second group of problems. Moscow's approach to all these issues is straightforward. Russia encourages all relevant parties to search for a peaceful solution to conflict. The same position is taken towards the Russian-Japanese dispute over the South Kurile Islands.

The third set of problems is connected with the proliferation of nuclear weapons, particularly the nuclear programs of India and Pakistan. Russia also strongly opposes North Korea's missile and nuclear ambitions. It insists on a peaceful settlement in all these cases. Finally, the possibility of an arms race and increased tensions among leading Pacific powers (China, Japan, and US) raises a fourth set of problems. The Kremlin believes this rivalry can be toned down through improved multinational security and economic mechanisms. As for individual countries in the region, Russia's interests focus on China, Japan, and the two Korean states. Russian-Chinese relations have developed into a strategic partnership, and are characterized by both sides as "the best in their entire history." This development has been shaped by a combination of factors: the two sides have learned the bitter lessons of past confrontations; they have managed to solve some long-standing historical disputes over territory and concentration of troops on their common border; they have overcome political-ideological differences and feel an affinity as reforming societies in need of a peaceful, external environment; and they are economically interdependent. Common concerns in the international arena, including similar views on multi-polarity, hegemonism and the UN role, are also driving forces behind the Russian-Chinese partnership.

Difficulties do crop up in Russian-Chinese relations. One irritant is the growing number of Chinese immigrants moving into Russia's sparsely populated and economically backward Far East. Another potential problem may result from the changing balance of power between Russia and China. For the first time in modern history, China may become stronger than Russia. If this happens, China can overpower Russia even in strategic terms. Japan, unlike China, does not create this genre of tension in Russian society. Russians perceive Japan favourably and are impressed by the quality of Japanese goods and achievements in science and technology. Russia sees Japan's independent and strong status as a balance against the US and China. Japan and Russia are business partners as well.

Russia and Two Koreas

Regarding two Koreas, the Russian top brass has a lucid foreign policy. It maintains close and problem-free links with South Korea. As for North Korea, Moscow opposes military policies which could have negative consequences for APR and global security. Russia has somewhat improved relations with North Korea that were practically frozen after the collapse of the USSR. Kremlin insists that North Korea permanently renounce its nuclear ambitions in exchange for genuine security guarantees. Russia actively participates in the six-party talks on such problems. It supports dialogue between North Korea and South Korea. It supports the restoration of Trans-Korean Railroad. If it is linked to the Trans-Siberian Railroad, it would bring benefits to Russian economy as well.

The demand for energy and other resources and the economic growth of China, Japan, South Korea and India stimulate the development of Russian economy. Russia has to step up its activities in the eastern direction of its foreign policy. The growth of Asian economies and global power redistribution are increasing the chances for the creation of the real multi-polarity. Russia is also in favour of a multi-polar world. But it would like to retain its close allies as its Inner Circle members. India is one of them.

Asian Forums and Russia

APEC is a region Russia is focusing on. Its policies are friendly towards APEC. ASEAN Regional Forum (ARF) is another forum that offers unique opportunities. During the fag end of 2005, there was the first participation of the Russian president in ARF. It was followed by his visit to the APEC summit in Hanoi in November 2006. These developments show that Russia is increasingly active in building relations with all leading Asia-Pacific nations. It approach is global and its *modus operandi* supports its commercial mechanisms. The role of superpower, big boss or big bear has been relegated to a backseat, much to the changing of the traditional Russian thinkers who still advocate the emergence of Russia as a real second pole.

Impact of Iraq War on Russian Position

The crisis in Iraq has not changed Russia's foreign policy toward Asia, although it has paid more attention to "hot spots" in a bid to settle disputes peacefully on the basis of collective efforts of all parties. In 2002–2003, during the Afghan campaign, Russia gave coalition forces and US military secret data and maps of minefields. It extended diplomatic support and gave its resources to help deploy US military bases in Central Asia. Yet, the interaction encountered unwillingness to take into account Russia's interests. Hopes for an improvement in relations with the West proved useless. Another stage of NATO's eastward enlargement began in late 2002 which is a disputable theme for a Russian society that has not lost the momentum-generated vision of the Alliance as an enemy. In 2003, Russia sided with France and Germany when it opposed the US military intervention in Iraq without UN backing. In 2005, the members of the Shanghai Cooperation Organization (SCO) demanded that the US set deadlines for the withdrawal of US military forces from Central Asia. Uzbekistan's leader, frightened by the Western condemnation of his methods of suppression of riots in Andijan, managed to make the US troops leave his country. Andrew Kuchins called this a joint victory for Russia and China as the leading members of the SCO and the first weakening of US influence in the region where their geopolitical consolidation has been going on for two decades. Western political scientists often call the Shanghai Cooperation Organization an anti-NATO outfit. India, Pakistan, Iran and Mongolia were represented at the SCO summit on June 15, 2006 in Shanghai. Also, a contact group with Afghanistan was created. Putin said in an interview that since the creation of the SCO on June 15, 2001, it had rapidly gained weight and turned into an influential organization and an important element of stability in Eurasia. Even before the 9/11 attacks, the SCO leaders favoured the creation of a regional anti-terrorist structure. Russia and China see this region as a sphere of their interests. They long for regional stability.

The Iraq conflict put pro-Western opposition into motion. Moscow, Beijing and the central Asian countries are worried that the fire of the colour revolutions can bring about instability. Geopolitics is returning to Eurasia. Changes in the balance of power are accompanied by the return of the ideological component in China-Russia-America relations. The SCO leaders implement solutions to their concerns through firm resistance to the actions of the US and Europe for the promotion of democracy. Without opposing the idea of democratization, Russia offers its own version of sovereign democracy. It insists on the preservation of national traditions that do not coincide with American or West European traditions. It stands for a gradual development of democratic institutions Eurasia. The thrust of US and Europe in the promotion of democracy is dangerous, for it serves as a basis for new alliances in the countries that propose gradual steps. The Shanghai Cooperation Organization declares its goal to confront terrorism. The US and the US-initiated anti-terrorist coalition in Iraq do the same. It would seem that joint efforts may provide security for the whole Southern belt of Eurasia and Greater Middle East.

Russia's Policy towards Proliferation of Democracy

The desire of Russia's Western partners to speed up the "proliferation of democracy" and to support opposition in the post-Soviet states is causing fears that the war against terror might turn into a struggle for the West to gain new spheres of influence. Partly due to negative objective circumstances and partly through her own fault, Russia has lost her former allies. Now, she is mobilizing all available resources to preserve her partnership with the oil- and gas-rich Central Asian states. This region is turning into an area of great importance for Russia. On the other hand, the reaction of Moscow to the events in Iraq and Central Asia is transforming into an aspiration to increase her control over the internal politics there under the slogan of consolidation against outside forces. Some Western public opinion sees this as a threat to democracy and urges its leaders to put pressure on Moscow, thus increasing Russia's impression of outside threats. The circle becomes complete. Mutual distrust becomes stronger. But for Russia, it is very important that the war in Iraq caused discord in the camp of the Western allies and touched upon the fundamental issue of international relations. Sharp discussion on the question of forceful unilateral action without UN approval has cast doubts on the traditional principles of the world order. For Russia, these discords between her European partners and the US have had extremely negative consequences. Russia is the staunchest advocate of the UN. She stands for a careful attitude to its reform and for preservation of universally recognized traditions. The meeting at the summit in Shanghai between President Putin and the leader of Iran brought out different meanings of the term terrorism. Iran was labeled a Terrorist State by the former Vice President of America, Mr. Richard Cheney. Other nations, including Iran, do not think that Iran is a terror State. Pakistan also considers itself a great nation. This holier than thou attitude is sent to a trash can when the world media sadly covers the brutal killing of 132 school students in a school of Peshawar. Thus, global political thinkers give different views about terrorism and terror States. Even as they deliberate over this issue, thousands of people, children and women are killed or maimed by the bullets, bombs or ambushes of terror organizations. In our view, a person carrying an illegal arm and trying to offend, maim or annihilate a person, group, community or nation (of any age, caste, creed, culture or nationality) is a terrorist. Going by that norm, the people, who had killed many school students in American schools due to racial or economic inequalities, must also be branded terror elements. Thus, terror elements exist in all parts of the world. We must make global strategies to transform these people and accept their very reasonable demands, one of which could be a living full of plenty and dignity. If we fulfil some basic needs of these elements, most of them would join the mainstream of life very quickly. Currently, poverty, not religion, is the chief causative factor behind the unflinching wave of terror around the globe. True, religion does play its part. But no religion is as bad as one may deem it to be. Negotiations can be conducted across the table and concessions can be given on religious grounds.

Role of UN and Russia's Multi-polarity

The role of the UN in the definition of terrorism and in the legitimacy of any actions against terrorism has become greater. Organizations with the goal of fighting terrorism should unite different countries. Putin notes in his article published in China, India, Pakistan, and Iran that a spirit of Shanghai has taken shape and that the organization demonstrates an example of equal partnership of states with cultural differences and gathers the experience of interaction with new observer countries. Historically, Iran is similar to Iraq in terms of difficulty of dealing with. However, the efforts to engage Iran in discussion without the threat of military intervention are worth considering. Iraq crisis confirmed that the period of transition to a new world order is and this has led to permanent instability. There has hardly ever been another period with so many unresolved crises existing simultaneously. Russia is working to create such a world order in which every state will bear its share of responsibility for the future of mankind. The world communities will safeguard the lawful interests of each one of its members. The Russian principle of multi-polarity is prosperity and security through international interaction and the preservation of national identity. The majority of experts are sure it is possible to solve the problem of Iraq through joint efforts and to prevent US-Russian relations from deteriorating.

Critique of Multi-polarity Theory

Russia's multi-polarity theory is a bid to create many strategic poles and war theatres at one point of time. If there are many poles in the world, there would be more conflict. China wanted to become the third pole and is still working to become one. The rise of China could not be absorbed by the USA or Russia. India never became an ally of China. When multi-poles are formed, at least one of them would be anti-NATO. This cannot be tolerated by the West. The Third World War would come near if we have a multi-polar world in strategic terms. Secondly, Russia is advocating a multi-polar world concept which means it supports democratic forces. The Ground Zero situation in Russia clearly informs us that Russia is still not a democracy in the perfect sense of the word. China and Russia both are emerging autocracies which feign that they are democracies. They are not full-fledged democracies. Elections are held everywhere but we cannot take it for granted that democracy thrives in these two nations. Let Russia advocate democratic forces in her own land first. The concept of multi-polar world would come later.

Russia's Policy towards Iran

Russia and Iran plan to hold a combined naval exercise in the Caspian Sea. Russian Federation and Iran enjoy a good relationship regarding regional security issues. Iran has refused to intervene on behalf of the Muslim guerrillas fighting against Russia in Chechnya or elsewhere. Both nations helped opponents of Taliban in Afghanistan and opposed the expansion of Turkey's influence in their region. Russia considers Tehran as a partner to oppose the American influence in Eurasia.

Russia's Policy towards America

The stability in Afghanistan and eliminating Iran's nuclear threat are two key issues between the two superpowers. Besides, negotiations with the Taliban and the new government of Iranian President Hassan Rouhani also figure in the foreign policy agenda of Russia. If the reaction of U.S. pundits to the Obama administration's efforts to get Edward Snowden extradited are any indication, then the efforts needed to solve the Iran and Afghanistan crises are likely to be shelved. US cannot afford to let Snowden run as a berserk bull and disclose America's secrets. Political analysts perceive the President as weak. Countries are confident that they will pay no cost for defying Washington. Liberals are divided. For some in the Democratic foreign policy establishment, it is irritating that other countries do not realize the difference between unilateralist Republicans of the George W. Bush era and Democrats who they should now be more willing to accommodate. Others argue that Obama has been too willing to continue the policies of his predecessor and that only a clean dissociation from Republican programs would allow other countries to accept American requests. Note that many countries have refused to give asylum to Snowden. He was in Russia but left Moscow a few months ago.

Hillary Clinton effectively sounded the death-knell for the reset in US-Russia relations. Commenting on Russian proposals for creating a Eurasian Union comprising Russia and other former Soviet republics, Clinton bluntly described the plan as a move to re-Sovietize the region. She added that US was trying to figure out effective ways to slow down or prevent it. The proposal to develop the Eurasian Union was at the heart of the foreign policy platform that Russia had unveiled before his election. Hence, it is difficult to understand how Washington feels it can oppose the initiative and at the same time, retain cooperative relations with Moscow in other arenas.

Building on an existing customs union between Russia, Kazakhstan and Belarus, the new Eurasian Union (likely to be created by 2015) would be modeled on the EU. The ruling United Russia party has endorsed the project. Obama is fuming even as Putin is striving to form this union.

Russia and Europe

On July 12, 2004, Putin stressed at the ambassadors' meeting at the Foreign Ministry of Russia that Europe remains one of Russia's traditional priorities. Russia's relations with Europe have a much longer history than its contacts with America. These relations have been controversial and full of cooperation. But competition and hostility were also witnessed at times. Russian society was permanently split into Westernizers and Slavophiles. Westernizers pushed for the full integration of Russia with Europe, Slavophiles saw an alien and menacing civilization in Europe. They wanted to distance Russia from the West and orient the country toward the East.

Russia and the NATO

Another obstacle to improved Russian-European relations is posed by geopolitical differences. Russia is a Eurasian country in geographical terms. In cultural terms, it belongs to Europe. Russia has a long history as a great power and will not be satisfied with a minor, second-rate role on the European scene. NATO's expansion will not improve Russia's stature but at the same time, Russia cannot join NATO. China and India would oppose Russia's alliance with the Western military bloc. Iran and Arab countries would lose much of their confidence in Russia if it becomes a key player of NATO. Belgium, Canada, Denmark, France, Iceland, Italy, Luxembourg, the Netherlands, Norway, Portugal, UK and the US are the founding members of the NATO. The other members are Greece, Turkey, Germany, Spain, Czech Republic, Hungary, Poland, Bulgaria, Estonia, Latvia, Lithuania, Romania, Slovakia, Slovenia, Albania and Croatia. We can see that many nations of the Eastern Bloc are members of the NATO now. This alliance is a sore in the eyes of Russia. But it has to counter the NATO threat through careful cooperation and formation of powerful small alliances in all parts of the world. The policy of Putin is: cooperation with all but strengthen your position in all corners of the world (keeping Europe as most vital platform from a strategic angle).

NATO members do not welcome Russia as one of their own. Russian membership would be opposite to American interests because America does not want any competitors to its primary role in NATO. Germany, France and Britain also have issues about Russia's presence within NATO. East European members think that Russian membership in NATO would negate the purpose of their own partnership in the alliance. NATO is wary of China factor: should problems develop on the Russian-Chinese border, the NATO would have to side with Russia if it were a NATO member. This concern also applies to Russia's conflicts with separatists and extremists in the South. Such a prospect would not appeal to NATO members. The NATO's enlargement through the incorporation of CIS countries spells nothing good for Russia. The intense mutual distrust and suspicion accumulated during the 40 years of war makes Russia cautious. If Ukraine and Georgia join the NATO, it would mean a growing dependence of

Russia's former allies on NATO. Russia has already made its intentions clear about the eastern part of Ukraine. The NATO has not been able to put up resistance to anti-Ukraine fighter rebels through any covert or over tactic. Obama has been told to wait and watch the next move of the Russians.

Russia strives for the creation of Greater Europe united on the basis of common values and the capability to defend them jointly and to resolve regional conflicts (including the frozen conflicts in the Balkans, Cyprus or post-Soviet space). It is important to take into account the concerns of all parties. Imposition of variants of fast settlement and forceful pressure is counter-productive as it creates new grounds of security risk. Political-ideological problems also impede closer relations between Russia and Europe. Russia is in the initial stages of building a democratic society. Communists and nationalists who preach undemocratic and anti-Western ideas are prominent in public discussion. Russian officials pursue policies that add to Europe's anxieties. Authorities believe that their attempts to safeguard the Russian Federation and to prevent the collapse of the country are purposely opposed by unfriendly forces in the West.

Globalization and the Russian Dilemma

China, India and Southeast Asia are becoming increasingly interdependent. If Russia does not cooperate with this process of globalization, it may collapse. As Russia's economic and political values align increasingly with the realities of the globalizing world, Russia and Europe will share more security priorities. Russia will get a more definite role in the world. After this, Russia's uneasiness over NATO's possible new steps toward expansion will reduce while European countries will no longer depend on NATO as a shield against Russia. Military deterrence and the balance of power calculations will fade away from the agenda of Russian-European relations. Russia and Europe face the same threats. They will have to create a comprehensive security system for the entire Eurasian continent that would comprise Europe, Russia, China, Japan and unified Korea. Russia will become an indispensable partner in this procedure. Economic interdependence will also grow. With the Middle East unstable, Russia will most certainly reinforce its position as a principal supplier of oil and gas to the West. The West and Russia will forge cooperative efforts in the extraction, delivery, refining and distribution of energy supplies in Siberia, Caspian Sea and Russian Far East. Considering Russia's rich deposits of many other raw materials, Russian-European economic cooperation has endless vistas. As market reforms progress, Russia will eventually be a lucrative target for investments in other areas. Russia needs European cooperation, and this has already begun to develop in Afghanistan and Central Asia, where Russian-European cooperation is already under way to suppress the drug trade and illegal immigration.

As the social situation and standards improve, barriers to travel and to the movement of labor and students will begin to fall. The Schengen visa will expand to include Russia. More Russian students will study in Europe. This partnership will not result in Russia's full incorporation into the Western community. Because of its history, size, power, development, geography, security and economic requirements, Russia will remain a separate entity, a bridge between the West and East. Russia sees itself as the mentor of Europe and master of Eurasia but would never speak up about it, unlike the USA whose leaders declare their policies through media hype. Russia and China are silent global players and expect America to remain a vocal global player.

Sino-Russian Honeymoon

In addition to their growing energy and renewed arms trade, another sign of the strengthening Russia-China relationship was their recently concluded bilateral naval exercise. The drills were larger and more sophisticated than those held last year. But they are still far from establishing a Russia-China capacity for joint maritime combat operations, which does not appear a goal of either government in any case.

The active phase of the maneuvers took place on July 8-10 in the waters off of Vladivostok. Twelve Russian vessels from the Pacific Fleet participated in this year's drill, compared to seven warships and support craft in 2012. China sent fewer ships than last year, a total of seven vessels from its North Sea and South Sea fleets. But they included some of the People's Liberation Army Navy's most advanced warships, including a guided-missile destroyer with an Aegis-type radar system. The drills involved

4,000 military personnel, including Special Forces units from both countries.

Foreign Policy of Russia towards the Middle East

Due to the Middle East's vast human and natural resources as well as its geography, the region is tactically important to world peace and the world economy. For this reason alone, it is attracting Russia's attention. The nearness of the Middle East to Russia is further focusing Russia's attention on protecting four broad areas of interest.

Firstly, the security of Russia depends on the security of the Middle East. Any disturbance to the peace and stability of the region may undermine Russia's security, draw her into destructive conflicts, or damage her economic interests. Moscow must also assure that the states, movements, and citizens of the Middle East maintain a positive attitude towards the Russian Federation and not threaten Russia's territorial integrity, sovereignty, or internal peace.

Secondly, Russia has political goals in the Middle East. She wants to work closely with all states in the region to pursue peace and cooperation, solve global problems and create a stable, multipolar global system.

Thirdly, Russian government intends to actively participate in extracting Caspian oil and exporting it to world markets. Russia also needs access to the energy resources of the Persian Gulf and other parts of the Middle East. Russia wants to export technology and goods to the Middle East to import their products and attract Middle Eastern investors to the Russian economy. Moscow would also like to recover huge debts from Iraq, Syria, and Libya.

Fourthly, Russia's interest in the Middle East is cultural. Russia's Muslim population numbers over twenty million. Moscow must find a path that is conducive to religious, spiritual and ethnic contact between the peoples of Russia and Middle East but must steer away from any negative political consequences.

For promoting Russian interests in Middle East, Putin must give attention to resolving outstanding security threats. Islamic extremism and international terrorism are big problems. The cadres of extremist groups penetrate the areas of the Russian

Federation, fight in Chechnya, smuggle in weapons and money, recruit local youth and preach the separation of Muslim areas from Russia. Russia has joined with the US, international organizations and other governments in the region to remove terrorism. The Israeli-Arab conflict must also be resolved if we are to achieve lasting peace and stability in the Middle East. In Russia's view, a fair solution to the conflict must include a return of occupied lands to Arab nations, creation of a Palestinian state and security guarantees for every participant of the conflict. WMDs and missile capabilities threatens peace and stability of Middle East and Russia. Russia would certainly be vulnerable to attack if Middle Eastern states acquire either WMDs or medium- or long-range missiles. Russia wants total elimination and prohibition of WMD and lowest missile capabilities in Middle East.

Russian Policy towards Israel

Russia believes that Israeli efforts to acquire WMD and missile capabilities must not be condoned. Israel's neighbours would feel compelled to seek similar capabilities in self-defense. Further, the increase in exports of conventional weapons to this region must be halted. The influx of weapons is fueling an arms race spiraling ever further toward more sophisticated and destructive systems. Another particularly sore subject in the region is the preferential treatment accorded to various Middle Eastern nations on arms collection. The practice of generously providing some states with weapons while denying arms to others ignites distrust and fear.

Russia and Ukraine: New War Complications

On February 17 and 18, rebels and Ukraine confirmed that 139 ceasefire violations had already been committed on the first day of declaration and effectiveness of a ceasefire agreement. The rebels captured the eastern town of Debaltseve. They fought street-to-street against the Ukrainian soldiers and did not give up till they succeeded in capturing the town. They were able to capture nearly 80 percent of the town. This speaks volumes of their war-worthiness and also, of the strong support Kremlin has been giving to them for the past one-odd year. The EU-brokered peace deal has not brought relief to the people of Ukraine because rebels backed by Moscow keep firing at will. Kiev has stated in vehement terms that Russia is supplying tanks, artillery and soldiers to rebels. Kremlin denies such allegations. On the contrary, Putin claims that a new nation, called New Russia, would be formed soon. The observers of the OSCE group were barred from entering the town of Debaltseve by rebel fighters. Thus, the Russian resolve seems steely, insofar as the annexation of eastern part of Ukraine is concerned. The name of the Russian rebel commander is Eduard Basurin. He is guiding rebel forces at the behest of President Vladimir Putin. If Russia is able to capture east Ukraine after fierce battles, which are the order of the day in eastern part of Ukraine now, Basurin may be made the CEO of the liberated eastern Ukrainian territory soon.

Russia seeks to dissolve a large part of the territory of Ukraine within a period of five or six years from now. It is not afraid of bloodshed. It shot a Malaysian plane that flew over its territory. It had accused that the passenger plane was on a spy mission. Or, it could have followed Putin's aircraft and Ukrainian army, or air force cadres of Ukraine could have been present in it to kill Putin in the air. It gave unconditional support, money and weapons to Ukrainian rebels. It 'arranged' elections in Ukraine, albeit in a covert manner. Russia's increased military prowess is a cause for concern for NATO commanders. Kremlin has welcomed a constructive dialogue with European. The leaders of France and Germany headed to Kiev and Moscow to end the fighting in East Ukraine on February 5, 2015.

The eastern part of Ukraine is trying to join Russia. The rebels of the eastern part of this country are being funded by Russia. America wants to give lethal weapons to the armed forces of Ukraine. But this would amount to facing Russia, eye for an eye. If this happens, the Cold War may escalate to new heights. France and Germany want to prevent this clash from transpiring. That is why leaders of both these nations have been trying to convince Kremlin and Kiev to find a peaceful solution to the problem.

Russia is sitting pretty. It knows that the eastern part of Ukraine, if not all, would come to it sooner or later. The peoples of the eastern part of Ukraine have already voted in favour of Russia in their last mandate at the ballot box. Thus, NATO and the USA may not be able to stop this secession of Eastern Ukraine.

Ukraine is sending eight million American dollars per day to fight against the rebels of eastern Ukraine. Its economy is in doldrums. Its currency, the hryvnia, slid 46 percent against the US dollar on February 5, 2015. Ukraine must end this crisis soon, lest its masses should face chronic hunger and abject poverty within a few months.

Obama was also in a dilemma recently. He faced the question—whether to send aid or sophisticated arms to Ukraine? Good sense prevailed and he ordered John Kerry to send 16.4 million dollars as aid to this nation which has already been battered to the core by war and economic shortages. Clearly, the USA does not want to irritate Russia. Obama is an outgoing President. The other party would certainly come to power once he goes after completing eight years of his term in Washington. That is why Obama did not take a harsh decision against Russia. This has boosted the morale of the fighters (rebel cadres working at the behest of the Russians) operating in eastern Ukraine. The NATO is not likely to intervene in this game because it feels Russia is likely to take its part of the cake in Ukraine. The EU has also taken the diplomatic path to resolve the issue. All others organizations, the UN included, are watching the games of death and destruction being played in Ukraine. Rebels and army cadres of Ukraine fought gory battles in the past eight-odd months. No party is ready to budge an inch from its place. Those, who are suffering, are innocent masses of Ukraine.

Some New Aspects of Russian Foreign Policy

In European organizations, Russia stands in support of inter-civilization concord. The fact that a fifth of Russia's population is Muslim helps it establish constructive dialogue with Muslim communities in Europe. Russia wants to proliferate in Europe the initiative of "Alliance of Civilizations." It was propounded by the UN Secretary General, Turkey and Spain. Ukraine is resisting Russian dominance. But rebels of the eastern part of Ukraine state that they are willingly pro-Russia and that they have no coercive influences over them due to Kremlin. Russia does not want to escalate tension in Europe because of economic reasons.

Russia Is Capable But Not Growing

Politically self-willed Russia is not growing in economic terms. In May 2014 Putin completed the second year of his third presidential mandate. In 2015, barring the issue of falling oil prices, Russia has been doing well at all diplomatic fronts. The USA, dogged by wars in Asia and the middle-east, could not attend to its traditional rival with care. Putin was also silent at most G-8 and G-20 summits. Putin knows that oil export is an ace up Russia's sleeve. Hence, he would like the oil prices to shoot up. Saudi Arabia, Russia, the USA and Kuwait have not reduced their oil outputs. That is why the prices of crude oil in global markets have plummeted to below 47 dollars per BBL. Today, Russia is not growing. However, it would wake up to the challenges of the new era.

Its arms exports are stable. It is making AK 100 assault rifles, Sukhoi aircraft and modern tanks now. Its weapons are sold throughout the world. India and China are two major buyers of Russian defence equipment. Russia is also selling the same technology to China that it had sold to India. Thus, this free market world does not have friends or foes. Rather, they have only financial allies, the clients who ought to be satisfied at all costs.

Russia and the US

Vladimir Putin had given shelter to Andrew Snowden, the whistleblower, who had disclosed the topmost secrets of the Americans to the world. Now, the world is condemning Russia, including the US, for giving him shelter. The US-Russia relationship is strained, as for now. The exit of Obama after his second term in office may bring some respite for Putin. They met at G-20 and G-8 summits but did not make much headway, insofar as mutual relationships were concerned. However, Russia has more or less defied the arm-twisting tactics of Uncle Sam during the course of leadership of Putin. The oil politics of Europe has made Putin stronger. The present oil crisis may have made Russia weak in rouble terms. However, this country has enough resources and so it wields power over entire Europe. Eastern Europe is still under the covert control of the Russians. True, there is no eastern bloc left *per se* to comment on. Russia itself is a big bloc. The US understands its covert presence in all parts of Europe and in the UNO.

The US was engaged in war theatres of Pakistan and Afghanistan. Now, that it has come out of these war zones, it would focus on the shaky relationships it currently has with Russia. Obama would not tease Russia in any way. Only his successor can take a decision in this context. Changing political and military choices force both these nations to dig into new markets and find new clients for their equipment. Both are part of UN general Assembly, the Nuclear Suppliers Group, UNSC, G-8, G-20 and other major political blocs of the world. There is no direct confrontation. But the episode of granting asylum to Snowden did irritate the Americans. They may be on the lookout for a whistleblower from Russia. Better still, they might be looking for cracks (read 'traitors') in the armed cadres of east Ukrainian rebels. However, Russia's grip is so strong over rebels that it seems impossible that it would lose this war game. If that happens (and east Ukraine officially joins Russia as its newest state). Russia would be way ahead of the Americans in the realm of strategic warfare.

Russia and African Nations

Russia has observed with keen interest the terror attacks on cities of Nigeria and Kenya. Shopping malls and stores were attacked in these two countries during the period November 2014 to January 2015. Several people were killed. Russia is also facing threats for terror groups who operate from its soil. Thus, Russia has aligned its policy against terror with those of African nations.

Russia and China

Russo-Chinese relations are another essential vector which may determine Russia's global stance and ability to deal with rising powers in the times to arrive. The Balkans are emerging as a region of competing economic and energy interests between Moscow and Brussels. Russia must exploit the current Euro-crisis so that it may not lose its influence over that strategic area. In January 2015, America and India came closer. This would force the unique alliance of Russia and China in the future, given that India has made deep relationships with the USA in the past eight-odd months. They may like to raise objections on the civil nuclear deal that is being discussed in India and America. Both of them are part of NSG. The nuclear deal between India and the USA may not be viewed by them with pleasant remarks. China may also hinder the process of supply of vital equipment and fuel to India at a later date. Russia may not do this but China certainly can, at the behest of Pakistan. China and Pakistan would not like our nuclear plants to function. In that case, our traditional friend, Russia, may have to persuade the Chinese to give a concrete shape to the Indian nuclear power edifice.

Latest Determinants of Foreign Policy of Russia

They are as follows:

1. Relationships with Ukraine: Currently, these relationships are strained. If Ukraine does not part with its eastern part easily, Russia may attack Ukraine with its full force. But the Russians think that eastern Ukraine would join them sooner or later and that there would be no need to shed blood or tears.
2. Cold War with the USA: it is true that a kind of mini Cold war has started between these two super powers, after the granting of asylum to Andrew Snowden by Putin a few years ago. The USA has taken this issue with utter seriousness. Russia has been acting like a big brother during the past three years. Putin has acted arrogantly at most global platforms. The USA has taken a cold or sheepish stand in international relations.
3. Relationships with China: China is a commercial ally of Russia. After India, it is the biggest buyer of arms, equipment and technology from Russia. If India and the USA come closer to each other, Russia and China may also start some deep strategic partnerships to woo India to their camp. The American policy towards India may change after the exit of Obama from the White House. Russia and China are also worried about the entry of India to the NSG. In fact, it is not an entry but only a permission to get nuclear fuel and technology form the members of the NSG. Russia may be positive about this but China would certainly toe Pakistani stands on this issue.

4. Russia and the Middle East: It seems that Russia is not keen to interfere in the affairs of Gulf nations. It has not given any statement against the ISIS, Al Qaeda and terror outfits operating in Pakistan and Afghanistan. That is because a big chunk of its population is Muslim. It is also learning to accommodate new sects.
5. Poor Economic State: The Russian rouble is very weak. Thus, Russia may have make compromises at global strategic and political forums to keep its currency stable. A bankrupt nation cannot be called super power. Due to its weak economy, Russia has not been able to support the rebels operating in eastern Ukraine; nor it has been able to attack Ukraine to snatch the latter's eastern provinces.

Russia's Foreign Economic Policy

In the year 2014, the real GDP growth rate of Russia was 0.6 percent. In the end of 2014, the price of one barrel of crude oil fell below 70 dollars. In January 2015, the price of one barrel fell below 50 dollars, much to the dismay of Russians. Thus, a weak rouble has caused panic in Russian markets. Russia is a primary producer and exporter of oil to Europe. A weak rouble would not be able to fetch it enough money to sustain its economy. That is why Putin has resorted to strict austerity measures in the first quarter of 2015. Russian economy is in doldrums because its linkage with global oil supplies affects it squarely and even dangerously. The only solution is that Russia should reduce its oil production. If production is less, prices would go up. However, other oil producers are not keen to cut down production and Russia has to align its oil policy with other oil-producing nations in any case. This is a precarious situation for all oil majors. They would not be able to tide over this problem for at least six more months. Russian economy is facing a very serious crisis now. Its position as superpower would be hurt in a serious way if it does not earn valuable foreign exchange. The US is sitting with its hands on its cheeks; it is glad to observe that Russians are in trouble. American economy is out of the recession phase whereas Russian economy is plummeting to an abyss. Thus, in the UNO, Russia may not be able to dictate its terms on many issues. The foremost of them would be the voluntary exit of Greece from the EU. Reeling under the recession phase, Russia would not be able to affect EU policies in the ties to come. America would be able to rule the roost in the UN and EU for the next few years.

For Russia, the year 2014 was the "Year of Economic Doldrums." Its rouble had lost ground in all parts of the world. Oil had hit a new low at 47 dollars per BBL of crude in January 2015. Russia's exports suffered a lot. They were still suffering in January 2015 when this text was being written. A weak Russian economy may trigger a chain reaction in Europe and Asia. Many countries depend upon Russia because it imports goods and services from them. If the Russian rouble becomes unduly weak, Russia cannot import even basic necessities meant for its masses. Thus, a Greece-like situation may develop in Russia if oil prices do not rise. The fall of oil prices would lead the entire world to the state of deflation; that is what the specialists at BBC aver. Deflation means things would become very cheap. Earlier, goods were costly, so people would not buy them. If deflation arrives, goods would be so cheap that suppliers of these goods do not earn healthy margins in sales. Thus, deflation is equally harmful. In order for the Russian economy to grow, it must fetch better oil prices. Currently, this is not happening. Russia may face the wrath of deflation but it is facing inflationary pressures now-a-days. The only good news for it is the rising influx of tourists from abroad. Since the rouble is weak, it is easy for foreign tourists to see Russia and have a taste of its inclement weather.

Conclusion: Big Bear Will Bounce Back

The Bear has suffered in economic terms but around the globe Russian arms and defence equipment are sold like hot cakes. The Russian establishment has a small part that is totally pro-capitalistic and is always away from the public view. It may be protected by the communists, experts aver. Since corrupt practices were unearthed in China in recent years, we cannot rule out the fact that the capitalistic lobby of Russia may also be earning through wrong means, probably in collusion with senior government officials. We do not know what happens in Kremlin. But Kremlin has become a wee bit weak due to weak rouble. When currencies crumble, ordinary people find it hard to eke out a living. That is what is happening in modern-day Russia. However, its political and economic visions are intact, given that Putin has proved a strong leader of this nation, nee superpower. Russia would continue to dominate eastern Europe, the Balkan states of Europe and a part of south-eastern nations. It may not have enough political control over Africa, India (which has chosen to align with Obama under the leadership of Modi) and south America. India is in the US net now, at least for the time being. The US-Indian honeymoon has just begun and the Russians have painfully realized how their most trusted ally has become a cozy partner in trade and polity with the other nation, nee superpower, situated across the Atlantic ocean. The events of 2015 and 2016 must be watched with keen interest. Terror control is on the agenda of Russia but it has also decided, like the US, not to interfere too much in the present war zones of the globe. Global recession and a fallen rouble are the chief two reasons behind this policy shift.

CHAPTER 6 Foreign Policy of Germany

Introduction

Angela Merkel is the representative of a growth oriented German State. Under her leadership, Germany has grown by leaps and bounds. This article is devoted to German supremacy. It is a country to watch out for. It is an industrial giant. Its people are handsome, robust, witty and willing to do anything for their country. The foreign policy of this country is quite lucid—"Work hard with your partners and create a new economic order to bring prosperity to the masses worldwide." It has contributed to the EU Fund so that poor countries of Europe could get bailout and dole packages. This speaks volumes of the German psyche which is positive and human to the core. In this chapter, we shall study the history of foreign policy of Germany, its indulgences in the past and its future vision.

A Framework of Analysis for Germany

Following the Nazi rise to power, Adolf Hitler's government conducted a foreign policy aimed at the incorporation of ethnic Germans (Volksdeutsche) living outside German borders into the Reich; German domination of western Europe; and the acquisition of a vast new empire of living space (Lebensraum) in eastern Europe. The realization of German hegemony in Europe, Hitler calculated, would require war, especially in eastern Europe. Racially inferior Slavs would either be driven towards the east of the Urals, enslaved, or exterminated. Besides acquiring Lebensraum, Hitler anticipated that the drive to the East would destroy Bolshevism. He was a staunch opponent of Stalin and Bolsheviks. Sadly, he did not know how harsh Russian winter could be.

From 1933–1938, Konstantin von Neurath, a conservative career diplomat, served as German foreign minister. During his tenure, Germany followed a revisionist policy aimed at overcoming the restrictions imposed on Germany by the Treaty of Versailles and seizing the diplomatic initiative from Britain and France. Germany withdrew from the League of Nations; began rapid rearmament; signed a non-aggression pact with Poland; reacquired the Saar territory through a plebiscite; militarily assisted the supporters of Francisco Franco in the Spanish Civil War; and remilitarized the Rhineland.

From 1938–1945, Joachim von Ribbentrop, a Nazi party member and former ambassador to Great Britain, served as the foreign minister. During these years, Germany strengthened its ties to Fascist Italy and to Japan by signing the Anti-Comintern Pact, which aimed to combat international communism, the Pact of Steel (with Italy), and the wartime Three-Power Agreement (with Italy and Japan).

In 1938, Germany acquired new territories using the threat of war. In February, Hitler pressured Austrian chancellor Kurt Schuschnigg into signing the German-Austrian agreement (Berchtesgaden Diktat), which brought Nazis into the Austrian cabinet. The next month, Germany carried out the Anschluss, the annexation of Austria. Hitler then began demanding a solution to the Sudeten crisis, a conflict over the Sudetenland (a region of Czechoslovakia settled largely by ethnic Germans). On September 30, 1938, British prime minister Neville Chamberlain (an advocate of appeasement), French premier Edouard Daladier, Italian prime minister Benito Mussolini, and Hitler signed the Munich agreement, which ceded the Sudetenland to Germany. In March 1939, Germany occupied and dismembered the rump Czechoslovak state.

In August 1939, Ribbentrop signed the German-Soviet Nonaggression Pact. A temporary deviation from Germany's normally anti-Communist foreign policy, this agreement allowed Hitler the freedom to attack Poland on September 1, 1939, without fear of Soviet intervention. Britain and France, Poland's allies, declared war on Germany on September 3, 1939. Hitler's aggressive foreign policy resulted in the outbreak of World War II. What made this paradigm change in intra-European relations possible was that America after 1945 decided to stay in Europe, instead of withdrawing as it had done after World War I.

Unification of East Germany and West Germany

With more than 80 million peoples, Germany is the most populous EU country. German reunification created a colossus in the continent in the late eighties of the century gone by. A united Germany is capable of doing more than a major power can plausibly do. It has technology, educated manpower, machines, automated plants and above all, money! Only its size is small. The Aryan Master race rules the roost in Deutchland. Hitler was born in Austria but was proudly called Fuehrer in Germany. Volks Wagon, L&T, Audi, BMW and Pfizer are its most popular brand names.

Germany and American Influences over Europe

America turned into an "empire by invitation" (Geir Lundestad), and relations among Western European states became to a certain extent depoliticized. Washington took over control of Western European geopolitics, to the relief of most Europeans, who were exhausted by war and conflict. Under the U.S. umbrella, and pushed by the U.S., former enemies became deeply engaged with each other. Instead of being obsessed again with borders and national grandeur, Western Europeans became part of the consumer society, focusing on economic well-being and fair redistribution. European states started to integrate economically and politically. Old-style power politics and the harder elements of power were removed from intra-European relations. It was this geopolitical environment, shaped by the U.S. and increasingly also by autonomous European integration, which permitted Germany to recover from its wounds, to become successful as a nation again, to finally unite again and overcome the darkness spread by the Holocaust (in Auchwitz concentration camp of Austria during the 1941-45 period). Nearly 60 million Jews were killed by the Nazis during that era. Then, the War ensued and Italy, Germany and Japan (the Axis Powers) lost the game to Allied Powers. Germany was divided into two parts-Eastern Germany and Western Germany. The two nations united in the last decade of the past century after the end of the Soviet era. The effluent West Germans now met their brothers and sisters who had been reduced to big zeroes after the War. But Germany worked hard during the past 30-odd years to come up to the mark. Today, in 2015 AD, it is a technology leader and producer of high-technology equipment, cars, automobile parts, electrical products and precision devices. Its achievements have made the world sit up and look at them, literally! The Germans are hardworking, honest to the core, have firm belief in their nation and can bring about deep-rooted technological changes around the globe.

These achievements allow Germany today to take a leadership role in the European Union. Germany is the strongest nation in entire Europe. It calls the shot in all EU meetings. Greece, Italy and Spain have fallen economies. But German technology sings in all parts of the world. A nation, which is so technically sound and resource rich, should be elevated to a better designation than major power, avers Arvind Kumar, the author of this text.

In an environment that is largely defined by economic interaction—the European Union—German economic strength easily translates into power. The current weakness of Germany's traditional partner in Europe, France, makes Germany look even stronger. And the division of the euro zone into creditors and debtors as well strengthens Berlin's hand in intra-European affairs. Having been a frontier state during the Cold War, in the last twenty-five years Germany has become the economic and infrastructural center of Europe.

Relationships with Regional and Major Powers

Twenty-four years after reunification, Germany has become Europe's indispensable power. Berlin has quietly moved into a leadership position in the EU, as became most obvious during the euro crisis.

The Ukraine crisis clarified that German leadership is not limited to internal EU affairs, where Germany has always been a powerful player. Berlin also speaks and acts increasingly on behalf of the EU in foreign affairs, at least when it comes to relations with the EU's Eastern neighbours.

Global powers such as the United States and China acknowledge these developments by viewing Germany as their most important European interlocutor.

How Germany Became a Fuehrer in Europe?

Germany's position between Western Europe and Eastern Europe, between Scandinavia and the Mediterranean, makes the country the natural point of intersection of all kinds of streams: people, goods, information, ideas and mentalities. Germany's handicap—its geopolitical position—has turned into an advantage. From German unification in 1871 until World War II, fear of encirclement by a hostile alliance was a main driver for German foreign policy, with the well-known fatal consequences. But as European states have moved, in the second half of the twentieth century, from a system of competition to one of cooperation and coordination, Germany now can benefit from its geographical location, as it connects and reflects the continent's diversity.

Germany Benefited from US Presence in Europe

America turned into an "empire by invitation" (Geir Lundestad), and relations among Western European states became to a certain extent depoliticized. Washington took over control of Western European geopolitics, to the relief of most Europeans, who were exhausted by war and conflict. Under the U.S. umbrella, and pushed by the U.S., former enemies became deeply engaged with each other. Instead of being obsessed again with borders and national grandeur, Western Europeans became part of the consumer society, focusing on economic well-being and fair redistribution. European states started to integrate economically and politically. Old-style power politics and the harder elements of power were removed from intra-European relations. Relieved of competition in terms of power and feeling relatively safe in the U.S.-led system of collective security, Germans and their European partners were able to develop a system probably unique in history.

While retaining large parts of their sovereignty, they started to meddle in their neighbours' internal affairs, going far beyond traditionally international cooperation. Incrementally, Europeans were replacing deep-seated fear of each other with equally deep-seated trust. The EU's Eastern enlargement is another factor that has contributed to German power. New Europe now looks to Germany as its regional leader. Thus, Germany has been adequately termed as a major power in most syllabi of political studies.

Poland, the Czech Republic, and others have entered into the value chain of German business, and increasingly, they also expect leadership from Berlin. In November 2011, Poland's Foreign Minister Radek Sikorski said that he fears "German power less than German inactivity."

Warsaw has worked hard to become a core partner for Germany, a goal it has achieved to a large extent: in the coalition agreement of the current coalition, Poland has been acknowledged as Germany's second most important partner, after France. Poland is an eastern European player, so it would not be able to give full support to Germany. Holland and Denmark can help Germany, though.

Angela Merkel is respected in Europe, the United States, Russia, China and elsewhere. In office since 2005, she is generally seen as Europe's most powerful and most successful leader today. Germany's moment at the top may not last, though. The country doesn't invest enough in education and infrastructure, and its demography is highly problematic. France and Britain may reassert themselves on the European scene.

A successor to Angela Merkel in 2017 may turn out to be less skilled than she is at handling power. Whether German leadership lasts or not, what Berlin should do with the power it enjoys is to invest in the stability of the system which is a precondition for its national success.

Three major systems are vital for German freedom, security, and prosperity, systems into which German statehood is embedded. They are as follows:

1. The existence of a rules-based global order.
2. The transatlantic partnership.
3. The European Union.

All these three aforementioned systems were originally set up largely by the USA. They have been supported by Washington for decades. But all three systems have come under increasing stress in recent years. The EU could not become a free entity even after the declaration of its common currency. The nations of EU are also divided over immigration policies. Germany can lead the EU from front. But it may not be liked as a leader in the front. Rather, the USA would like to appoint the UK as the new leader of a changed European Union.

Preserving EU is Vital to Germany

The euro crisis has unveiled deep cracks in the common European house: an institutional mess, a lack of vision, growing fragmentation, and a dangerous centrifugal dynamic.

European nation-states are unwilling to make a great leap toward a more federalist design. And a possible British exit from the EU might shake the foundations of the system and would certainly diminish the EU's international position. What the EU lacks most is a re-definition of its role, a vision: should it still be guided by a federalist dream, should it be scaled down to a joint market, or should it become something new and different, a sui generis entity?

For decades, different views have co-existed. But with the euro crisis and Britain's potential exit, those ideas are coming into open conflict; narratives have started to clash. Germany, as the EU's current strongest player, should take the initiative and should, with like-minded European partners, work out new concepts for a future EU. Germany has a vital interest in keeping the EU strong and capable. A decline of the EU would not only put German prosperity at risk. It would also reopen the "German Question"—a dangerous insecurity about Germany's place in Europe—with the risk of a return of competition and confrontation between European states.

From a German perspective, the EU is a major dream. It provides the country with a ring of friends. It allows Berlin to multiply its own international presence. But Germany cannot displease the US and UK, given that they have always ruled the roost in Europe since the end of WW II. America has supremacy over Europe though its most trusted ally in Europe, which is Britain. Germany can be a dark horse in Europe, not a pawn for checkmating Britain in the game of European chess. German business firms can win the world, not Europe. Their presence is respected due to their quality. But Germany's strategic ambitions cannot be given a go-ahead by the UK or its elder brother across the Atlantic.

Transatlantic Security and German Concerns

The transatlantic security system is under stress as well. America is much less of a European power than it was during the Cold

War. Whether the United States is on the verge of a broader retreat from Europe, or even from world affairs in general, is difficult to say. Certainly, U.S. citizens have become much less willing to take responsibility for an extensive definition of American interests, and the role of global policeman certainly looks unattractive for most Americans today. Despite the appearance of a momentary U.S. comeback in Europe in the Ukraine crisis, Europeans must be prepared for the likelihood that Americans are going to be less and less willing to underwrite European security. For years Europeans have been discussing the need to fill the gap resulting from U.S. disengagement by doing more to keep their neighbourhood stable. But this talk has only partly been followed up by action; in the Balkans, the EU indeed became a key player. But in Europe's Southern neighbourhood (including the Middle East), the EU today is largely absent. In the Ukraine crisis, Germany has taken the lead, but only after years of neglect of the Eastern neighbourhood in favor of relations with Russia.

In the Ukrainian crisis, Uncle Sam has remained an important player, especially on the side of hard power, by taking measures to reassure NATO members in Europe.

Germany Can Change Course of EU History

That points to an important handicap on Germany's ability to play a larger foreign policy role, in particular when it comes to managing crises: the unwillingness to consider military means as a tool of foreign policy.

If the use of force is always a priori excluded, if measures such as military reassurance and deterrence and the build-up of military capabilities in other countries aren't part of the toolbox, foreign policy is very much constrained in its capability and efficiency. And the side that is ready to use force has a significant advantage. A deep aversion to the use of military power has characterized Germany since the end of the Second World War. Germans rearmed in the 1950s only under huge US pressure. During the 1990s, after German reunification, there was a lot of talk about normalization or Germany becoming more like Britain and France. The use of military force was accepted as a tool for turning tables on the enemy at the last moment. Under the red-green coalition of Gerhard Schröder and Joschka Fischer, Germany participated in two wars, one in Kosovo and the other one in Afghanistan.

Germany and US-NATO

In recent years, Germans have moved back into their comfort zone. The Iraq War and the conflict with TTA in Afghanistan are widely seen as a confirmation of the view that war can never be an instrument of foreign policy. Germany's decision in 2011 not to support its allies in a military intervention in Libya was not an accident; rather, it was an expression of a broad consensus in Germany. The Germans are peace-loving. They are sandwiched between many countries and have a small coast line to guard. They do not want to indulge in useless conflicts going on in the name of religion, for they do not culminate into good results. At the same time, they know that they are vulnerable and that their country relies on the United States as their ultimate security guarantor.

Even for German Foreign Minister Frank-Walter Steinmeier of the Social Democrats a party that is usually more critical of military power than Merkel's Christian Democrats are the transatlantic alliance remains the backbone of German security. But that foundation of German security cannot be taken for granted. The NATO will only remain relevant if major members invest in the alliance. Germany should be much more aware of that risk and become the driver of a new commitment to NATO; it should work on building a much stronger European core inside the alliance.

If the NATO is Germany's ultimate life insurance, Berlin must invest in it. Within the alliance, Germany should partner with Eastern neighbours who are committed to keeping the alliance strong, as a credible deterrence against Russian aggression. Making Central and Eastern Europe safe is in Berlin's interest, as it also makes Germany safe. But there is much more to the transatlantic alliance than a security guarantee for Europe. The United States, Canada, and the EU remain the core of the liberal West, together with like-minded partners in Asia and elsewhere.

These liberal democracies share a double interest: first, to remain safe, prosperous, and free at home, and second, to build a global order that is complementary—to make the world safe for liberal democracy and market economy. Securing and enlarging the sphere of liberal order, defending it against attacks by autocratic regimes and by forces of disorder are a major challenge for liberal democracies. Russia's attack on Ukraine is one of the test cases for the EU's preparedness to stand up for that order, the civil war in Syria another.

Germany and China

China presents a further major challenge, as it is slowly but surely changing the *status quo* in the seas to its south and east, thereby destabilizing a region on which European prosperity increasingly relies.

Germany as a Stabilizing Power

Germany, as a deeply globalized country, has huge stakes in this order. Germany's economic success relies on the ability to send goods, people, and information safely around the globe.

That requires the existence of a physical global infrastructure, but also a normative web of rules, institutions, and like-minded partners. Liberal democracies are the natural partners in that enterprise.

In a Hobbesian world, by contrast, Germany would have bad cards. Its power is not based on autonomy or autarky but on deep interconnectedness with neighbours and partners.

If the currency of global competition were military strength, Germany would either have to change its identity fundamentally or be fully at the mercy of other, much more ruthless players.

This country plays in the league of the top five most influential states. The biggest handicap on a more active foreign policy is domestic. The Germans are averse to their country's global role. They feel very comfortable staying on the sidelines. Germany's foreign policy culture remains weak, despite the country's growing international role at technological and economic platforms. In the past decades, Germany has become free, safe and rich. America is partly retiring from its role a mentor of Europe in toto. Germany has the resources to stabilize EU.

Policy against Religion

Pegida, Germany's new anti-Islamic movement, suddenly became a thing to be talked about in Germany in particular and in Europe in general. This new movement has risen to stardom. Pegida is dominating media headlines and television shows. Angela Merkel is using every moment to condemn it. Germany has ultra-Rightist Christian majority. The Germans are viewing currently going on massacres in Afghanistan and Pakistan with contempt, hence the trend of creating such organizations in Germany.

Germany and Greece Crisis

In 2015, Angel Merkel gave a nod to the exit of Greece from the EU. She has no objection if Greece leave the EU block. She even stated that the fallout would be managed well. On January 25, 2015, Greek voters would vote for or against anti-austerity Syriza. If Greece leaves the Euro fold, this currency would not be affected at all. That was because Greece was a minor player in EU economy. If Greece leaves the Euro Zone, it would have to enforce devaluation. This would lead to capital account control. Banks of Greece would be given fresh targets. Greece cannot pull its economy without the Euro, market experts aver. They state that if Greece leaves the Euro Zone, it would be akin to "Venezuela without oil." The exit of Greece from Euro Zone has been termed 'Grexit' by international financial experts. Germany is watching these happenings with keen interest. If Greece leaves the Euro Zone, Germany would become much more influential. Angela Merkel fully supports the Euro concept in Europe. Germany considers Euro Zone as a tool for uniting Europe. Experts also state that the likelihood of Greece leaving the Euro Zone is less than 25 percent. Nevertheless, Greece would continue to get aid from the EU. Portugal, Spain, Cyprus and Ireland also got bailouts due to the rising influence of Germany in the EU. Carsten Brzeski, the chief economist of ING-DiBa, stated in Frankfurt that it would be a nasty precedent if Greece leaves Euro Zone. That is because, he added, other nations of Europe would also do the same. This could lead to fragmentation of the Euro. That is what Merkel would despise from the core of her heart, other experts say. A fragmented mandate of Euro would lead to unstable economic scene in entire Europe. Germany would be able to overcome this crisis through its financial prowess, international observers aver with élan. Thus, Germany's foreign economic policy would be pro-Euro and neutral towards any nation like Greece that wants to leave the fold of the Euro Zone. That is because Germany is committed to the Euro and sees it as a tool for uniting Europe's small nations.

Latest Determinants of Foreign Policy of Germany

They are as follows:

1. **Ill Effects of Russia-Ukraine War:** The Germans feel that this war is being fought in their backyard, literally! Thus, Angela Merkel and Francois Holland had rushed to meet Putin in Kremlin to sort out the issue of eastern Ukraine. Germany does not want to irritate the USA by fully aligning its policy over Ukraine with that of Russia. However, Ukraine is also an important part of Europe. Thus, Germany would have to play a positive role to sort out the problem of rebellion in Ukraine. Currently, its role is positive but not very effective.
2. **Strong Economy Invites Applications for More Dole:** If German economy is very good, the poor nations call it even more good! Thus, they ask for more dole from the Germans. Greece has elected a new government. This new government refuses to accept the policy of reforms dictated by the EU. In the EU, Germany dictates most terms, along with Britain and France. Thus, poor nations of Europe are a big worry for Germany. In the EU, Germany may have to take bold steps to stop the flow of dole to countries like Greece, Ireland, Italy and Portugal.
3. **War in the Middle East:** Currently, Germany is not sending its troops to any one of the burning zones of the Middle East. Its stance is neutral. However, the events of the future may force it to change its passive policy towards the Middle East.
4. **NATO Influences:** German is very much under the control of NATO forces. It cannot come out of this cleavage in any way. If EU is supposed to become a single entity, the NATO would be its most prominent strategic face. The leadership of Germany can think about technological and political development. War strategies of the EU are likely to be designed, honed and altered by the NATO only.

5. **Relationships with Asia:** They are good and would not affect its marathon march towards technological perfection. India and Germany are big trade partners.
6. **Relationships with Africa:** Germany has good trade and political relations with all African nations.
7. **Racial Bias:** The Germans have thrown out many Asians out of their country in the recent past. Racialism is a big issue in Germany now-a-days. They do not want to let the Indians or Asians come to their country and settle there permanently. Thus, Germany will try to influence the immigration policy of the EU in the times to come.

Foreign Economic Policy of Germany

The real GDP growth rate of Germany was 1.5 percent in 2014. This West European nation is tiny but its technology has catapulted it to the economic stage of the globe. Germany is dollar rich as well as euro rich. Its GDP growth rate is nearly 10 percent per annum. The economic recession of the globe did not affect it in an adverse manner because its technology and machinery have always been hot items for exports. Thus, it can overcome recession cycles with ease and finesse. It is a contributor to the EU monetary fund that gives dole to poor nations of Europe. Naturally, Angela Merkel calls the shots during all such meetings as decide the future of Portugal, Ireland, Spain and Greece. France, Germany and Britain are driving the growth engine of Europe at present. Recently, the World economic Forum had conducted a meeting in Switzerland. German leaders expressed their will to help the poor have-nots during the course of that meeting.

Conclusion

Germany has emerged as a major European player in industrial and economic terms. Its rising political influence is also a harbinger of its supremacy in Europe. Britain and France are its leading competitors in Europe. However, they all are also friends because of their industrial growth rates and huge fund bases. Germany can be visualized as an economic cum political leader of Europe in the decade starting from 2015. This rise to power could irritate China and the USA. Trade policies of EU would be influenced, if not altered, by Germany in 2015. This country has the potential of leading the entire Europe. Its rising clout could make America and China sit up and look at it in utter disbelief. Germany has given dole to sick countries of Europe with a big heart. No other country has been able to help its sick EU partners with such a kind of liberalism. German philanthropy is an irritant for many a country of the globe. But its rise to power in Europe is inevitable. A new Europe is emerging under the combined leadership of Germany, France and Britain, Germany being the top in this trio. The attacks on French cities by terror elements have made France ever more vulnerable to threats of anti-social clans. In that case, German war machinery would come to the rescue of France and other countries that are facing or likely to face the threats of terror organizations. Thus, Germany would also lead Europe in strategic terms in the year 2015. The Germans made minimum mistakes in the last World Cup Soccer. That speaks volumes of its efficiency. It would repeat the same feat in strategic, industrial and economic fields in the times to come. It is a nation to watch in the EU. It is the future of Europe!

CHAPTER 7 Chinese Dragon Is Raising Its Ugly Head for Worse

Introduction

Mo Yan, the first non-imprisoned, non-émigré Chinese to win a Nobel Prize, straddles the line between critical and Communist Party success. Liu Xiaobo, the 2010 Nobel Peace Prize Laureate, is imprisoned in China. How could these two authors win the Nobel? China has produced guns and N-bombs in the past, not fine literary content! The peoples of China cry freedom but the Communist Party has chained them so heavily that freedom and democracy seem two Utopian words for the Chinese masses. This feature of Chinese nation reflects lucidly in its foreign policy too. The recent border disputes with many a nation prove that the dragon is flexing its muscles, including nuclear ones. Let us discuss China's foreign policy.

A Framework of Analysis for China

China has been fighting, overtly or covertly, against India, Vietnam, Japan and Russia due to its boundary disputes with these nations. In fact, it has boundary disputes with all those countries with which it shares international borders. The rise of China as a major power was basically a need of its masters to become strong enough so that the country could annex land areas from its neighbours. When our former defence minister (of the former UPA government) went to China in 2014, he was snubbed and even threatened due to the boundary disputes. Japan is also suffering due to its territory dispute with China. Thus, China's foreign policy has boundary disputes at its heart and soul; and the Chinese dragon would leave no stone unturned to annex land from its neighbours. Note that except Russia, no neighbour of China can withstand its merciless onslaught. Further, China has also emerged as a major supplier of consumer goods and electronics items to the entire world during the last 15 years. Its export markets are growing. It has well developed shipping and rail transport systems which have been dutifully linked with those of Korea, the USA, EU and India. Global trade has become a strong feature for this communist country. Nearly 15 percent of the Chinese people are enjoying all luxuries and comforts like the people of the West because they all are in the good books of the Communist Party. These 15 percent elite people are high-profile businessmen, politicians, industrialists and thinkers who support the Chinese ideology. All facilities of the Chinese nation are for them. The rest of the country is full of workers. China does not reveal its secrets. But it is a major industrial nation, a keen explorer of the space, a nuclear power, a part of the NSG and above all, the owner of the largest army of the world. It may be noted that The Great Red Army of Russia may be less in terms of number than the Chinese army. The numbers of either of these major armies have not been revealed by ether country. We feel that China may have an edge over Russia in terms of the number of active defence personnel. At all global platforms, China has been supporting Pakistan, North Korea and Vietnam. Its relationships with Pakistan are known to all. Its rise to power started when it became a member of the UNSC 50 years ago. At that time, it had a weak economy. Now, situation has changed for better. Its dollar power cannot be ignored. It has also mended walls with Arab world. You would be surprised to note that there are no communal riots in China. There are no terror attacks in Chinese cities. It is just possible that China may be supplying arms and ammunition to terror groups through its intermediaries in the global arms markets. India and China are two major customers of Russian arms and ammunition. China's Guangdong missile range is capable of carrying nuclear bombs. Hence, it is a befitting answer to Brahmos, the missile system jointly developed by Russia and India. China may also be supplying weapons and technology to Maoists in India. Its presence in Pakistan's Gwadar Port is a cause of concern for India. In fact, China has established complete or partial bases on the entire rim starting from Karachi up to Myanmar. This rim encircles Indian peninsula partially and covers Pakistan's most military establishments (on the side of Arabian sea). In a way, India has been surrounded by Chinese forces or their pawns in the Arabian Sea and Indian Ocean. Its intentions are clear—dilute Indian influence through strategic muscle show and then, get land territory from India. It has taken 5180 square kilometers of the Kashmiri territory from Pakistan. This disputed area is a bone of contention between two nations. China infiltrates into Indian territory in Kashmir and Ladkah. Then, it gets a snub from the global community. Thus, it withdraws its troops after a few days. This has been going on for two and a half years. It claims that Arunachal Pradesh is its territory. It has acquired Tibetan Autonomous region from India. It has given up its claim in Sikkim, which is now an integral part of India. However, many serious issues remain to be resolved. At the global front, it is a direct competitor of the US and Russia insofar as the race to become a super power is concerned. It is a major power but not a super power. It is quite comfortable with the Russian bear. Due to its friendship with Russia, it did not attack India after 1962. Its global trade is increasing. New Zealand, the USA, Britain, EU, India, Africa and Australia are flooded with Chinese goods every year. Due to low production cost per unit, China gets an edge over America, Australia, India and other nations of the world. It is a hardware king. Its technological prowess is growing by leaps and bounds. It may become a super power by 2060, avid strategic thinkers aver with elan.

History of Attacks on Neighbours

China's peaceful yet lethal rise is guaranteed in an environment full of domestic stability and international respect. China has started wars (on limited scales) with its neighbours. The new Chinese PM did not take more than 10 days to start small-scale conflict with at least five neighbours. India witnessed three intrusions in 2013, the last one in Ladakh in July. This and the scandal rocking its upper leadership are potential signs of real political instability. The Bo Xilai affair has tarnished the image of a united CCP. Bo was expelled from the party to face criminal charges.

Four Major Aspects of Foreign Policy

Four facets of foreign policy focus in China are being discussed here. They are as follows:

Firstly, China is trying to integrate economically with every country in the world. The current slowdown in its rate of economic growth is directly related to China's extensive integration with the world market. As Europe and the US face prolonged economic malaise, China's exporters have suffered. The poor-quality Chinese goods were censured around the globe. China may attempt to continue rapid economic growth by boosting the purchasing power of its hundreds of millions of rural and urban masses. The potential market for modern amenities such as washing machines, electric scooters and computers could be worth many trillions of dollars of economic growth in that country. The potential political and economic uncertainty in China will have drastic effects on its economically centered foreign policy. It is highly unlikely that China will retreat from the global markets. However, a more populist trend in the leadership, or the possible establishment of true democratic reforms, could see vast changes in the way the government uses the tremendous assets earned through international trade.

Secondly, China makes efforts to expand classic power projection capabilities. However, classic power projection will also feel the consequences of its political and economic uncertainties. The leadership has expended considerable resources in enhancing China's long-range military capabilities. The deployment of the PLA Navy along the Somali coast in counter-piracy operations, China's increased military support to United Nations peacekeeping missions, and the recent launch of the country's first aircraft carrier are good examples of this trend.

Thirdly, it seeks to safeguard claims of Chinese supremacy and land. The third specific push of China's foreign policy is the uncompromising effort to protect Chinese sovereignty. This policy agenda is likely to remain unchanged in the event of political or economic instability within China. However, the manner in which China carries out policies to protect its sovereignty may change in the event of an economic slowdown and political uncertainty. The crisis with Japan over Diaoyu/Senkaku Islands is alive. Territorial disputes with the Philippines and Vietnam in South China Sea are hurting Asian peace processes. It has offended India three times in 2013 and intruded into the latter's territory. The next section gives the details.

Fourthly, running parallel to these three trends is the theme of China's "peaceful rise." China has made great strides in the past three decades in integrating its market into the global economy. It is the largest single trading partner of 12-plus countries, including Japan, India, Peru and Angola. Its economic integration with foreign countries has greatly helped in its domestic development. This growth has given the new PM diplomatic leverage and lethal power. After the Wall Street crisis, China gave 4 trillion Yuan ($570 billion) as a relief package. It is a major force of global growth. China has also pledged a $43 billion contribution to the recapitalization of IMF. In the current worldwide financial crises. This has made it a mad bull, given that global polity pundits can easily assess that they cannot think about a diplomatic world sans China.

Foreign Policy of China towards India is Hostile

China went 19 km inside Ladakh which has been declared disputed by both nations. The Chinese built make-shift camps and were ready to face firing from India in May 2013. Manmohan Singh remained calm; so did the Russians. The US hoped that the crisis would diffuse. Before the visit of foreign minister Salman Khurshid, the Chinese went back to their previous position in Ladakh. The Indian Army chief had stated that its boys could teach a befitting lesson to the intruders. But diplomacy worked and Manmohan did succeed in brining the new Chinese PM to India too (May 2013). But the Chinese premier did not talk about the intrusion issue. The two countries decided to settle claims peacefully. It is clear that the claims on land will not be altered by a change in Chinese leadership. Japan is worried about North Korea which has aimed its N-missiles on its territory. Japan does not have N-ambitions but if the North Korean threat persists, it may have its anti-nuclear defence system soon. China supports North Korea and Pakistan to the hilt. Nuclear programmes of these two nations are the outcome of the dole given by China. Hence, any attack by the West on North Korea could trigger a minor conflict between China and the enemies of North Korea, whosoever they may be. China is likely to take even stronger measures to protect Chinese sovereignty in the disputed maritime areas. The recent anti-Japanese riots in Chinese cities serve as a reminder than many common Chinese people are more inclined to take a military approach to resolving these disputes than their leaders. The leadership sees no contradiction between the stated goal of "China's Peaceful Rise" and taking a hard line approach to resolving territorial disputes. The Chinese cannot be acting aggressively if they are protecting the sovereignty of their own country. China is not being treated with the proper fear and respect due to a major power in disputes with obviously less powerful nations. That is why it has triggered disputes with India, Vietnam, Japan and other nations to prove that its border disputes ought to be looked into pretty soon.

Thus, we can conclude that Chindia (a strategic combination of China and India) is not a reality, at least for the time being. The rivalry between China and India is one of the main problems for the BRICS organization. There are also differences between members due to their diverse political and economic systems. Trade between them is booming. But it is a small fraction of world commerce. IMF and World Bank call the shots in the world. Creation of a new economic forum is a big challenge in these troubled times.

China's Expansionist Policy through SCO and Pakistan

The Shanghai Cooperation Organization or SCO is a Eurasian political, economic and military organization. It was founded in 2001 in Shanghai by the leaders of China, Kazakhstan, Kyrghyzstan, Russia, Tajikistan and Uzbekistan. Four members of Shanghai Five are part of the SCO. Note that Shanghai Five was created in 1996. The fifth member of the SCO is Uzbekistan which joined SCO in 2001. Thus, Shanghai Five became SCO and is a regional organization run mainly by the communist dictators of Beijing. China gives preferences to its partners in the SCO. True, it is cooperating in BRICS but its main focus is on keeping the SCO intact and making it a more powerful economic player in Asia. Through BRICS, it wants to please Russia. In the SCO, its domination is absolute. Thus, it would use SCO as a major economic tool to capture markets of Asia. This is a reason to worry for the new leadership of New Delhi. Modi has yet to understand China's game plan even while shaking hands with China's top brass. Pakistan and China are very close.

Further, China has declared in February 2015 that Pakistan is its "all wheather" friend. Their military and economic alliances are known to all. This proximity with China gives Pakistan advantage in the sense that it keeps irritating the peaceful environment on the Indo-Pakistani border every now and then. Indiscriminate firing and mortar firing are done regularly and militants are sent to India under the cover of such firing. Pakistan has got military and information support from China in this context and India must not forget this evil fact. Through its allies and a handful of organization that it can dominate, China has been able to create a clout in the entire Gulf region, the Indian Ocean region and the Pacific Ocean rim region. It is also building ports for Pakistan and Sri Lanka. It does not have a single aircraft carrier but it has a fine range of nuclear arsenal and fighter aircraft which it had purchased from Russia not so long ago. The defence equipment of China and India are comparable. China has better missile systems. Except the Brahmos (made in collaboration with Russia), India does not have very lethal missiles that could match those of China. Pakistan has acquired Guangdong missiles from China and would procure more from its friend in the near future. Thus, China and Pakistan have enough destructive capabilities. Modi's policy of "Make in India" should be squarely applied to Defence Production at Home or DPH. Private sector players must be invited to make top—notch arsenal for the armed forces of the country. That move would be able to give a befitting reply to China and its hawkish allies.

Economic Slowdown and China's Initiatives

The current government policy of investing massive amounts foreign-currency reserves in US debt is deeply unpopular among the Chinese populace. Many Chinese are similarly displeased with the government's huge loans to poorer nations. Chinese labourers and peasants would much rather see their country's billions of dollars in foreign currency invested in domestic improvements in education, infrastructure and healthcare. If China's leaders are forced by changing political realities to be more sensitive to the popular sentiment, the country may be a less reliable source of desperately needed liquidity for both poor and rich nations.

As economic growth in China slows, one may expect the government to focus more upon upgrading its naval capabilities and other military assets. Economic development has been the prime source of CCP legitimacy for the past three decades. As the rate of economic growth slows down, the leadership may make a push for flashy military hardware to shore up domestic political support. These capabilities are unlikely to be deployed in a manner that directly threatens other major powers. Rather, the leadership can take a more active role in international missions that enhance Chinese prestige while limiting geopolitical risks, such as UN peacekeeping and international anti-piracy efforts.

China's Policy towards Pakistan

In mid-2013, Pakistan handed over the controversial Gwadar Sea Port to China. The latter would develop it in strategic terms, although both nations claim that it would be used to re-route international trade cargo. Pakistan has already secret ties with China in Karachi. Further, it also has a presence at one sea port of Sri Lanka. The Gwadar port is the third one. Thus, China has managed to engulf Indian peninsula by keeping its navy and army on these three ports. Evil is one who is seen with evil. Pakistan and China have the same mindset. China has set its eyes on Kashmir and Arunachal Pradesh and Ladakh. Pakistan has been looking at Kashmir like an evil eagle for the past 65-odd years. Together, they make a formidable combination. India's arms inventory is poor. We have yet to procure war-time helicopters, fine-quality battle tanks and ammunition for our latest weapon systems. We are importing most of our defence equipment and fighter aircraft. It is high time we started making these vital military hardware items at home and develop our own technologies for their manufacture and refinement. This would call for a major shift in our foreign policy, though.

Latest Determinants of Foreign Policy of China

They are as follows:

1. Relationships with the USA: China and the USA are partners in trade, technology and UNO. Beyond the gamuts of these three realms, they are rivals. China is also part of the UNSC and NSG. Many Chinese businessmen have purchased huge land areas, buildings and various industrial establishments in the USA. Likewise, the USA has also invested in China. Competition is fierce in every branch of business. Chinese economy, now moving at the rate of five or six percent per annum, is not likely to do well in the years to come. American economy is ahead of Chinese economy. There is a dual policy of both nations to help each other and also try to pull the carpet off each other's feat.
2. Relationships with Russia: China enjoys good relationships with Russia. It has repaired its relationships with India at the behest of Russia only. China, Russia and India are together in the war against terror.
3. Relationships with the Middle East: China has not tried to influence the vents there. Terror elements have not affected any part of China either.
4. Relationships with African Nations: Business is on the agenda of Chinese authorities and business firm even as they look forward to enhancing relationships with African nations. However, Nigeria South-west Africa and Kenya unstable due to the domination of Boko Haram and other organizations in those countries or regions. The latest scenarios of these countries would define the policy of the Chinese government towards Africa in the future.
5. Relationships with Allies: North Korea, Pakistan Kazakhastan, Kyrghyzstan, Russia, Tajikistan and Uzbekistan are traditional allies of China. Shanghai Five is also a group to reckon with in the global political circles. China has not irritated its allies at any point of time. Its amazing diplomacy with its allies makes it a superior diplomatic player of the new era.

6. Relationships with India, Japan, Myanmar and Other Neighbours: China has problems with almost all of its neighbours. The boundary disputes with all neighbours force it to become arrogant, even violent at times. Japan and India have been the victims of its wrath in the past. Boundary disputes are very old and cannot be resolved so quickly. Pakistan is also a supporter of the expansionist policies of China. It has been supporting China at the risk of irritating the United States, a key provider of arms, ammunition and economic aid to Pakistan over the past four decades. Thus, we can realize that the clout of the Chinese leadership over Chinese allies is very strong. This feature of Chinese foreign policy may hurt Indian ambitions and negotiations for the purpose of finalizing boundary issues.

Foreign Economic Policy of China

Chinese economy has grown seven-fold since 2000. In 2014, the real GDP of this communist-cum capitalist nation grew at the rate of 7.4 percent. The Chinese yuan is not an international hard currency. The recent fall in oil prices in January 2015 has helped China acquire huge stocks of oil. Everyone knows that if oil prices are low due to political reasons in January 2015, they are likely to rise to new levels in June 2015 due to economic reasons. In fact, oil prices started rising in the middle of February 2015. In India, petrol and diesel prices were raised on February 15, 2015. Everyone needs oil, even if it is costly. China is amassing dollars and euros to keep its economy strong and stable. Its exports are growing by leaps and bounds. It produces low-cost toys, electronic gadgets, FMCG items, clothes, cloth, jackets, T-shirts, TVs, refrigerators, microwave ovens, defence equipment like LMGs, ammunition, missile parts, nuclear power plant equipment etc. Its markets are growing around the globe. It charges low prices on its goods, which do not have very high quality. The goods its sells in global markets do not have good life. Thus, they are either worn out or declared outdated by consumers. This obsolescence due to poor quality triggers more orders from the international markets. That is how Chinese economy works. Its work force is fully employed. No one is unemployed in China. People may get poor salaries but nevertheless they get money to sustain and even grow. The standards of living of Chinese masses are rising. They have access to modern electronic devices and equipment. Tourism is a sunshine industry in China. Many medical colleges and engineering institutions are giving education to foreigners. True, the standards of these colleges and universities are not so good but Chinese academic circles are also becoming more knowledgeable and competent by the day. Education in China is cheap. Education in the West is costly. So, people try to get education from China, especially technical education. Language is a barrier to the growth of academic markets of China, though. Hence, sale of defence equipment, toys, electronic items, garments, jackets, education services and tourism are the forte areas that define and control China's foreign economic policy. It has been predicted that China's economic growth rate would fall to 5-6 percent in the next five years. After the fall in the growth of Europe (2.1 percent on a Quarter to Quarter basis in January 2015), China would also face the heat of slow industrial growth. Earlier, China had registered a growth rate of 10-12 percent but those golden days are gone. China had started the theme of "Make in China." Thus, it had established factories and shopping arcades across its length and breadth with private sector's participation. This Herculean effort required raw material for construction and other industrial inputs. Hence, industry grew in China by leaps and bounds till 2012. The Chinese masses also consumed cheap products and thus added to the growth of economy. Then, China, exported cheaply made goods abroad and in fact, became the biggest exporter of cheap and low-cost goods. This honeymoon continued for many years. However, the Chinese stopped building infrastructure and roads. At the same time, Europe and America reduced their imports from China in the wake of global recession which had hit all markets in February 2008. Thus, Chinese face recession. Their growth rate plummeted despite their hard work. As already stated, China would register a growth rate of 5-6 percent in 2015 and 2016. Its masses are facing the wrath of recession. They are unable to purchase even cheap goods made at home. Thus, China has to align its economic system with those of the world.

Another interesting feature of Chinese economy is corruption. Nearly 45 Chinese leaders were found to be corrupt. In collusion with private firms, they all had earned big sums of money during the past 15 years. The former railways minister of China was sentenced only recently on account of corruption. Note that due to corruption, Chinese economy had been growing. But when the Polit Bureau of the Communist Party of China punished the culprits with vengeance, the economy suffered to the tune of 0.1 or 0.2 percent. Even this percentage of reduction was a big blow to Chinese economy. The reduction in rate of growth has forced China to take austerity measures on various fronts. The powerful Chinese corporate lobby is forcing Chinese government to open up the economy. Investments are being done in China by USA, UK, India and EU. But recently, all these nations or unions have withdrawn funds from the Chinese economic mechanisms primarily due to recession. The US has come out of recession but its growth is still not certain. It is not increasing imports from China and that is why China may be forced to explore markets of Africa. Since Africa is in the vortex of communal turmoil, China cannot expect orders from there either. This is a jinx and the Chinese must come out of it soon. That is because major markets of China are located in Europe and the USA. We do not consider even this rate as a dismal performance, given that countries like Greece, Spain and Portugal are going through severe recession phases. At this point of time, Chinese economy can show the way to other developing economies of the world, even if it grows at a slow pace. China would have to explore new markets in Asia and Europe. Its traditional items like garments, toys and electronic gadgets must do well in all parts of the world. Its chief competitors are Korea, India, Japan, Taiwan and the USA.

Conclusion: China Is Not Likely to Lead the World

The leadership and masses of China want respect. They will seek to earn this respect through economic might, military capabilities and an uncompromising stance toward territorial disputes. So long as the international system can provide China with economic opportunity, multilateral missions in which to display military might and the respect due to a world superpower, China's rise can remain peaceful. However, the dragon has always been looked with suspicion and awe in the past. Its relations with Pakistan and North Korea are objectionable, given that these two nations are the most unstable areas of the globe. It is also supporting the machinations of these nations by giving them nuclear arsenal, weapons, funds, army support and advice.

CHAPTER 8

French Growth Engine has a Lucid Foreign Policy

Introduction

The new President of France has decided to be tough on reforms. France is doing well on the economic front. France, Britain and Germany are the three main fund donors of EU for giving dole to Greece, Spain and Monte Carlo. Since French economy is strong, it calls the shots in EU, just like Britain and Germany.

A Framework of Analysis for France

On January 7 2015, three armed gunmen attacked a magazine office in Paris and killed ten journalists, editors and cartoonists. Besides, two French police officers were also killed. Then, another group of terrorists attacked a mosque in a Leon, quite close to Paris. These terror elements were objecting to the cartoons published by the magazine about the Holy Prophet. This incident has shaken France, which is a very beautiful and calm nation by any norm. The fear of reprisals against the Muslim community is a cause of concern. France has been inviting people from Muslim countries to create a multi-cultural and multi-racial society. However, the incidents of the beginning of 2015 amply demonstrate the fact that freedom of Press is not something liked by terror organizations. France is free beyond freedom and the French masses have taken a vow that they would continue to have the utmost freedom of expression. Francois Hollande, the French president, has declared that France would continue to believe in democratic norms and the freedom of expression. Sarkozy, the former President of France, also gave full support to Hollande on January 8, 2015 even as the latter addressed a huge gathering of the Press personnel in Paris. Thus, France, the most recent target of terror attacks, would redefine its foreign policy. It may also review its immigration policy, which was hitherto liberal and supportive of other sects. The entire world has condemned these attacks and supported the French cause of freedom of expression. In our view, the Holy Prophet's cartoons should not have been published. It is a wrong idea to condemn, criticize and mock at any religious icon or preacher. The sentiments of people are linked with their prophets and religious leaders. Freedom of expression is fine but we should stop our finger where the nose of the other person starts. Thus, in the context of the attacks on Paris and Leon in 2015, we would like to restrict the freedom of Press (especially the freedom to make cartoons or mock at any religious leader) to decent limits. We must not offend any person, sect or religious icon in any way. Human wit and decorum both demand this from all of human beings. Since France is very much free, it faced the ire of terror elements. Freedom too must have its limits! Define them carefully, keeping the sentiments of each religion in full view!

On other fronts, France is a strong power within Europe. Its industrial production is high and efficient. It contributes the maximum to the EU fund, along with Germany and Britain. It is a small country with decent and educated people. It supports the merger of all EU nations and the adoption of the Euro as a single country. It is an ally of the West, just like Germany and Britain. Its troops rarely go out for peace keeping operations. Its life styles are luxurious. These features make the French silent partners in Europe's progress. They are not vocal or volatile. They are just there and working hard to give Europe a new prosperous future.

French Policy on Quebec

France has revived the neutral policy on Quebec independence. Maro is delighted by Francois Hollande's move back to position abandoned by predecessor Sarkozy. France has revived its traditionally neutral policy on Quebec independence that was temporarily interrupted under the resolutely pro-Canadian unity era of Sarkozy, the previous President.

After meeting with Pauline Marois at the presidential palace in Paris during her first visit to France in 2013 (as Quebec premier), Hollande gave this lucid neutral policy. He made it pretty clear that his country would support a return to the so-called Ni-Ni approach. As per this approach, the negotiating party neither interferes nor is indifferent to the independence debate. Sarkozy had clearly stated his Yes for Canadian unity and had added that the world didn't need more divisions. But Hollande has taken a U-turn on Sarkozy's policy and opened a small gate for Quebec's freedom. Note that the non-interference, non-indifference policy was introduced in France in the 1970s. It was a halfway station between outright opposition to Quebec independence and full-out endorsement of the sort famously made in Charles de Gaulle's notorious *Vive le Québec Libre* speech (demanding the freedom of Quebec State of Canada).

Such an approach could France stay neutral in a hypothetical future sovereignty referendum and then recognize Quebec independence following a Yes vote. The pro-independence Parti Québécois has always energetically courted French support in the belief that foreign recognition would be the crucial key to becoming a country. Recent surveys placed support for independence at some of its lowest levels in decades, with one poll suggesting a mere 28 percent of Quebec's respondents favoured separation.

French-EU Policy towards Iran

In 2013 European Union foreign ministers agreed to slap tough new financial and trade sanctions against Iran that would achieve a breakthrough in stalled talks on Tehran's contested nuclear programme. British Foreign Secretary William Hague stated that EU will step up the pressure to achieve success. The new package targets EU dealings with Iran's banks, shipping and gas imports. Washington welcomed the accord as further strengthening international efforts to pressure and isolate the Iranian government. Under the package, the EU would ban all transactions between European and Iranian banks unless authorized in advance by national authorities. Import of Iranian gas will be prohibited, a symbolic gesture since the amounts involved are small but the move sits alongside the much more significant July ban on imports of Iranian oil. Sales of graphite and metals of potential use to Iran's nuclear or ballistic missile programmes are also to be closed down. Some other measures target Iran's shipping industry. The package also bans the use of EU vessels for transporting or storing Iranian oil. An EU asset freeze and travel ban will be imposed on 34 additional entities, especially in the oil, gas and financial sectors. Iran can act responsibly and bring these sanctions to an end, the foreign ministers of EU added.

After long denying the impact of Western economic sanctions, Iranian leaders have changed their rhetoric and now regularly condemn the (illegal) Western-imposed economic war against Iran. They acknowledge that the economy is suffering in particular due to the cuts in oil exports and production. Note that oil is the main source of the country's revenue. Iran's supreme leader, Mr. Ayatollah Ali Khamenei, said before the EU decision that Iran's enemies were seeking to disrupt the calmness in the country through economic confrontation. Note that EU's decision on Iran is being supported by France.

Latest Determinants of Foreign Policy of France

They are as follows:

1. Relationships with EU Members: France supports the concept of unified Europe. Its major allies, Britain and Germany, want to unify Europe even while retaining their financial structures within the union. Britain would not do away with pound Sterling. Germany loves Deutsche mark. France has its own currency, the franc. The other members of EU are not able to exert enough influence over these three nations. rather, these three nations are demanding economic reforms processes to be expedited in the EU so that a way could be paved for final European integration. The financially weak entities consider it an autocratic stance of these three nations. This is the crux of the issue. If situation goes out of control, the dream of unified Europe can end in a damp squib. Greece, Portugal and Ireland do not want France, the UK and Germany to become masters of the destiny of the entire continent. Greece did not budge an inch from its stand on reforms and asked for a bridge loan to meet its financial needs post general elections. Other poor nations of Europe might also challenge the arm-twisting measures of this trio. So, the foreign policy of France would be dictated by its relationships with poor nations of Europe.

2. Relationships with Ultra-religious Forces: France was the victim of terror operations because of the caricatures its artists and editors had made and got published in the *Charlie Hebdo* magazine. In our view, the French must not have done all this. Now, all French people are in the line of fire of major terror groups of the world because of their common ideology and global linkages. France would be vulnerable to more attacks of the genre which we witnessed in France in the beginning of year 2015. How could France take a plunge into the deep ocean of terror which is full of chaos, given that the USA, super power has withdrawn from all war theatres of the globe? France cannot protect its citizens at all times and places. Tragedy can strike them anywhere. A situation of compromise never arises in most cases. There are no rules in these wars and minor skirmishes. Innocent civilians were killed in attacks on French public places. The armed forces and police were least affected. Terror elements are looking for soft targets in France; they are adept at finding them and shooting them at will. This stalemate is likely to continue in 2015.
3. Relationships with African Nations: France has offered full support for the cause of African peoples. Its trade with African nations is on the rise.
4. Relationships with China's Allies: France has opposed the nuclear ambitions of Iran and North Korea. Thus, its policy would be dictated by the comprehensive policy of NATO in this context.

Foreign Economic Policy of France

Although the franc is not a hard currency, it is a good currency worth relying on. The Euro is fully supported by France. Hence, France would eventually come into Euro Zone. Greece may opt out of the Euro Zone on the plea that its economy suffered since the time it had adopted Euro. For France, the opposite has happened. The Euro currency has helped France in ways more than one. Its industrial production has risen. Its experts are linked to the Euro. France is a major economic player of Europe but not an economic leader in the true sense of the world. Britain and Germany have an edge over France insofar as economic supremacy is concerned.

Another important development of February 2015 was the visit of German Chancellor Angela Merkel and French President Francois Holland to Kremlin. Both leaders met Russian President, Vladimir Putin and discussed the Ukraine crisis with him. The gist of the issue has lethal insinuations. The USA wants to supply arms to Ukraine on an official basis. Russia does not want to withdraw its support from the rebel militia that is operating in the eastern part of Ukraine. Russia hopes that the eastern part of Ukraine would come under its dominion within say two years. Thus, Russia is not doing anything except supplying enough weapons and money to rebels in eastern part of Ukraine. If the USA sends arms and military support to the government of Ukraine, it would lead to the escalation of tension between two superpowers. If the USA takes this drastic step, Russia would withdraw its investments from Europe. It would also stop supplying oil to Europe which is a lifeline for this cold continent. France and Germany do not want any trouble to brew in Europe. Russia is their backyard. If a problem occurs there, their economies would be affected. The growth rates achieved by France, Germany and Britain are enviable, given that more than half of this world is under the grip of either recession or mini wars. That is why Germany and France joined hands and pleaded to the Russians not to take drastic steps in Ukraine. Putin played it cool. He even cold-shouldered the requests of French and German CEOs. Economic stability and peaceful Europe were on the agenda of Holland and Merkel when they met Putin. No doubt, Putin visibly agreed with its European cousins. It also does not want to confront the USA or Ukraine in war zones. Thus, he is not likely to escalate tension with Ukraine for the time being. If the US sends arms to Ukraine, the sensitive balance of Europe would be disturbed and Russia might even declare a full-fledged war against Ukraine. It would find an alibi to release eastern Ukraine from the clutches of the Ukrainian government. This can lead to a war in Europe. That is what Germany and France would like to avoid at all costs. Thus, the situation is precarious for France and Germany both.

Conclusion: France Is a Good EU Leader

France has pro-West policy and it supports EU, NATO and free-market-based powers around the world. The attack on *Charlie Hebdo*'s office was a big blow for the freedom of France. It was supporting the USA in the latter's war against terror. It may not take active part in future encounters in Europe or the Middle East. The freedom of expression proved costly to the French. It has also taught us a very important lesson—do not criticize any person organization or outfit, whatever may be its genre or goal. Had the editors and cartoonists not made those caricatures or articles, they all could have been alive! We must learn to respect all great people, sages and prophets. We must not keep an element of bias towards any one. That is because one's deeds automatically express themselves as one's results. We need not point out that such and such person, country or outfit is bad or dangerous. The person, country or outfit in question would automatically get whatever he deserves according to its or his *karma*. French people are also concerned about the divisive forces within Ukraine which threaten to destabilize Europe. Their concerns are based on very solid grounds and they could be deeply hurt at least in economic terms if a war starts in Ukraine at the behest of Russia. That is why Holland and Merkel had gone to Russia to appease Mr. Putin on February 8, 2015. France is a peaceful and beautiful nation. Its growth model must be emulated by all developing countries. It is a strong democracy of Europe. It is a major contributor to the EU fund. Hence, it has become a powerful political-cum-economic entity of Europe. Its policies would affect the future of EU.

CHAPTER 9 Same Old Foreign Policy of Pakistan under Sharif

Introduction

The arrival of Nawaz Sharif on the chaotic political stage of Islamabad has made political experts dumb. He was not expected to win majority but did. Imran Khan's party (Tehriq-e-Insaf) and PPP have not been able to make an indelible mark on Pakistan's political canvas. Sharif was on exile and he had also faced threats from the militant groups in the past. But he staged a miraculous comeback. Musharraf was banned for life from taking part in the electoral process of any genre. He is being tried in court in connection with the murder of Benazir Bhutto. Thus, army, militant groups, government and helpless peoples are the four major pillars of Pakistan's internal polity. The foreign policies of this trouble-torn nation can be judged by anyone; they do not exist!

A Framework of Analysis for Pakistan

This trouble-torn country on our north-western borders has been facing the wrath of militancy ever since its inception. In the years of infancy of Pakistan, the Pakistani rulers and army cadres used to train terror elements to send them to fight against the forces of Russia in Afghanistan. Those trainees were called Taliban in Pakistan. Osama bin Laden was also part of these forces. Later, the Taliban grew to become a huge organizational set-up. Today, the Taliban of Pakistan and Afghanistan have different ideologies. The courts, armed forces and benign political machines of that country are unable to check the rise of the Taliban. Even NATO forces could not do much to control them.

On February 17, 2015, a bomb blast occurred outside the headquarters of Lahore Police. The man had strapped a bomb on his person. He died as well as killed five more persons and injured another 25. It was learnt later that Jamaat-ul-Ahrar, a splinter group of the TTP, had claimed the responsibility for this attack. Thus, the Taliban and its sub-groups have spread their networks in entire Pakistan.

Pakistan's last tryst with peace was Malala Yusufzai, who had won the Nobel Prize for peace in December 2014, along with Mr. Kailash Satyarthi of India. Beyond that peak, Pakistan cannot hope to achieve anything in terms of peace or at global political forums. Its army is fighting against India, the TTP and other splinter groups operating in the Af-Pak region. The claim of Pakistan for Kashmir is intact. The areas of FATA, Baltistan, Peshawar, North Waziristan and NWFP are infested by ultra-violent elements. This chapter would reveal how cruel the groups operating in that country could be. If Pakistan is declared a defunct State, things would not be resolved. Pakistani society cannot work under the UN Peace Keeping Force, UN agencies or any neutral groups of nations. That is because violence and chaos are the order of the day in that country. There is dialogue with terror elements. Only things that are exchanged with them are bullets, mortars and shells. No negotiation is also a chief negotiation (or a sign of no resolution of conflict)! Let us read how Pakistan fares as a major power.

Pakistan's Latest Terror Moves and Indian Stand

Pakistan has adopted a totally negative policy towards India. It sent a boat full of terrorists and ammunition from Karachi towards Porbandar. These terrorists wanted to do a 26/11 in Gujarat. They had set out from Karachi on the night of December 31, 2014. The Indian Coast Guard intercepted the boat of January 1, 2015 at a distance of 360 kilometres from the Porbandar coast. The terrorists blew up the boat. They also blew themselves up. The boat sank along with their bodies. Thus, a major disaster was avoided at the Gujarat coast due to the alertness of Indian Coast Guard. The Indian navy was not involved in this operation. Pakistan also fired incessantly at 104 BSF posts in February 2015. It is a ploy to send militants into the Indian territory under the shadow of mortar fire and gunfire. But the BSF acts wisely each time Pakistani rangers play their evil games. Our jawans are killed many times at the border. Many Pakistani rangers are also killed. This activity is clearly not under the control of Nawaz Sharif. Thus, in a democratic Pakistan, the army still rules the roost. The other major entity is militant outfits. Pakistan has become a defunct State. However, its innocent civilians love India. They respect Indian democratic values. They would like to emulate India in economic and academic terms. Currently, they are in a mess because of insurgency problem of FATA, Peshawar, North Waziristan and Baltistan. The Pakistani Supreme Court lifted that ban on execution in December 2014. After this, many militants were hanged in several Pakistani prisons. But the wave of militancy continues to sweep across this nation. There are no solutions of this problem. The foreign policy of Pakistani leaders is decided by Washington. The economic policy is also decided by Washington. The help from the West is not sufficient to create factories and shopping complexes in Pakistan. That is because a major part of this dole is spent to buy arms, ammunition and other supplies for the Pakistani armed forces. Then, Pakistan also spends a part of this dole to spread terror in India. Thus, India is at a receiving end, insofar as the activities of armed forces and terror groups based in Pakistan are concerned. The war never starts but border skirmishes go on relentlessly. The Indians do respond more alertly than before because of their bad experience in 26/11 attack on Mumbai.

Nawaz Must Remain Quiet

If he does not do so, he would be shown the way Benazir was sent on. The new government chief has stated that he would make peace with all parties, including India. However, Nawaz would continue to toe the American policies inside and outside Pakistan. Even if the US clears the war theatre in 2014, Sharif would continue to follow the diktats of his American masters. Pakistan is surviving on dole given by the US and West. Its economy is in shambles. Its society has revolted many times for political change and removal of the stains of militancy from its thickly religious fabric. But no government could succeed in Pakistan on any front, internal or external.

Malala: The Representative of Liberal Pakistani Society

Malala Yousufzai was awarded Pakistan's first national peace prize and nominated for the International Children's Peace Prize by an advocacy group (Kids Rights Foundation) for being an inspiration to her friends, by standing up against the repression of the Taliban insurgency. Malala was shot and wounded on her way home from school. She campaigned for girl's education in the valley of Swat in North West Pakistan came to public attention in 2009 by writing an online diary for the British Broadcasting Corporation. Malala Yusufzai has also been awarded the Nobel Peace Prize for 2014 in Norway; the ceremony was held in December 2014. Malala wants to study and work for the welfare of Muslim woman. She has good intentions. She is the positive face of Pakistan. If she succeeds (and is not bothered any more by terror elements), she can bring about dramatic changes in conditions of Pakistani women. She is young and highly motivated; she has also got the support of the West. Women like her can change the history of Pakistan.

In the diary written by her, Malala (under pen name **Gul Makai**) had painfully narrated the suffering of the people of Swat at the hands of the Taliban militants who had occupied her city, known to the Western holiday makers for its hospitality, lush green meadows, sparkling water falls, clear flowing waters and scenic valleys. Terrorists called out her name to identify and then opened sporadic fire on the school van carrying her and other students. The Taliban, under the leadership of Maulana Fazalullah unleashed a campaign of terror and violence, oppressing innocent civilians and destroying several girls' schools in 2009. The insurgents were eventually ousted by the army after displacing two million people. The Taliban have accepted responsibility for the attempt on Malala's life. They have accused her of spreading anti-Taliban and secular thoughts among the youth of the area. Pakistan's soft suave attitude would not be accepted by any militant operating from its soil. The new government cannot tame them, for no other government was ever able to do so since 1947. Malala can fight the case for women but cannot win. That is because fundamentalists would not let any liberal woman win any case in their favour.

Pakistan at a Crossroads

Domestic economic weaknesses, security competition with India and an antagonistic relationship with Afghanistan are the Pakistani issues. Pakistan has sought external alliances with strong powers and pursued an offensive security policy. Nevertheless, there has been a realization in Islamabad that a new approach is necessary. As a result, Pakistan's foreign and defense policies are undergoing important transformations, including a normalization of relations with neighbours and a renewed focus on domestic security threats.

With a low growth rate, high inflation, budget deficits and unsustainable debt, economic weakness is the single biggest challenge for Pakistan. A major energy shortage, which both results from limited economic development and causes further economic losses, is another pressing problem. Meanwhile, Pakistan's primary security threats now come from unconventional actors, such as insurgent and terrorist groups, who form a motley crew of tribal rebels, criminal groups and national and transnational Islamist militants. By extension, then, radicalization and extremism remain real risks within Pakistan. India also poses a security threat with the modernization and expansion of its nuclear capabilities, its Cold Start Doctrine (CSD) and its support for nationalist separatist forces within Pakistan.

Latest Determinants of Foreign Policy of Pakistan

They are as follows:

1. Proximity with China: Pakistan would remain a long-term, nee all-wheather as was stated recently, friend of China. It would get its covert strategic directives from China.
2. Proximity with the USA: Pakistan would get its overt strategic directives from Uncle Sam. It gets enough money from the USA to sustain its economy without producing or growing enough goods and services. That is because its

men are busy in either war zones of its borders along Afghanistan and FATA or the border with India.

3. Role in Gulf: Pakistan has Shia and Sunni populations. There are clashes in Karachi due to the presence of these two sects. Nothing could be done by the Pakistani government to remove this anomaly. We hope the two sects would resolve issues soon. Pakistan's social fabric is slightly traditional. That is why it is not apt to comment about their in-house matter like the Shia-Sunni conflict.
4. Economic Considerations: Pakistan's foreign policy is not affected by economic considerations. That is because it gets enough dollars from the USA to sustain its economic stability.

Foreign Economic Policy of Pakistan

Since Pakistan is either busy containing terror elements on its soil or involved in efforts to perpetuate terror on the Indian soil, it has not much to do with its economic stability. Its exports and imports are any person's guess. The country is not producing enough for its own peoples. The USA gives it funds so that it may fight terror elements. There is no money available for industrial growth. Plants and machinery are not being imported. Goods and vehicles are imported. Traditional crops are exported. India has also purchased onions from it in the distant past. Indo-Pakistani trade is at its lowest ebb. As the world comes out of recession in 2015, we can expect the Pakistani industrial units to improve their performances. Industrial growth and transnational trade go hand in hand; they complement each other. Pakistani economy must improve so that its peoples are able to sustain themselves. India and Pakistan can join hand on many economic and industrial fronts but a collaboration in the future seems a Utopian possibility. SAARC and NAM forums can help Pakistan come out of the phase of poverty, though. Pakistani leaders and masses must review their economic system and try to get into the global mainstream that is dedicated to industrial growth. Pakistan's population is not high. Hence, it can easily grow in economic terms to enhance the living standards of its peoples. Unlike India, Pakistan can grow quickly to become a major economic power. However, it has chosen to become a major strategic power. That way, its peoples would suffer. In the future, they still may have guns to fire at enemies but no wheat to eat!

Conclusion: Pakistan's Policy Is Not Clear on Terror

The Taliban, Al Qaeda and the Pakistani army are three major players in Pakistan. PML (N) had won the national elections but Nawaz Sharif is as helpless as were Benazir Bhutto, Asif Ali Zardari and Yusuf Raza Gilani. The foreign policy of Pakistan is a conflict between two policy poles—the fight against militancy and the fight against India. It is sad to note that Pakistan has not made much progress on the economic front simply because it spent 60-odd years fighting major and minor wars against India. Its army had created militants which had fought against Russia in the war that had started during 1980s. Today, the same men (or their disciples) have grown up to create militant outfits in Pakistan and Afghanistan. Now, the government has to fight against India at all global political forums like the UNOI. At home, it has two important duties—support good militants but eliminate bad ones. Its foreign policy is not its own. Global recession has also affected its exports. Thus, Pakistan cannot become a major power in the near future, given that the militant outfits have captured a huge part of its territory. It is busy handling its internal problems. True, it has strong army; that is what it has achieved after its separation from India. It would not pose any threat to India. Its militant outfits can do more harm to India than its armed forces. Its proximity with China has not turned tables on India. Russia, China and India have declared that they would fight all genres of terrorism jointly and through mutual cooperation. Thus, China would eventually become a friend of India, given that trade between these nations is growing by leaps and bounds. Pakistan can try to tread a normal path only after eliminating the insurgency problem from its soil. Current, this does not seem feasible. We shall apprise our valued leaders about the latest happenings in Pakistan in the very next edition of this volume.

Sheepish Yet Resurgent India Failed on Many Diplomatic Fronts in the Recent Past

CHAPTER 10

Introduction

India has formal diplomatic relations with most nations; it is world's second most populous country, the world's most-populous democracy and one of the fastest growing major economies. It has world's seventh largest military expenditure. It is ninth largest economy by nominal rates and third largest by purchasing power parity. India is a regional power, a nascent great power and a potential superpower. It is one of the founding members of several international organizations, most notably the United Nations, ADB, G20 and NAM. India has also played an important and influential role in other international organizations like East Asia Summit, World Trade Organization, International Monetary Fund (IMF), G8+5 and IBSA Dialogue Forum. India is part of SAARC, BRICS and BIMSTEC. It has taken part in several UN peacekeeping missions. It is seeking a permanent seat in the UN Security Council, along with the group of G4 nations.

A Framework of Analysis for India

The UPA government under Sonia Gandhi and Manmohan Singh failed on the foreign policy front on many fronts. They are as follows:

1. The inability of Indian troops to ward off Chinese troops and send them out of the disputed territory. Chinese came, built barracks and went back on their own.
2. India could not nab and punish underworld don who have indulged in bomb blasts, match fixing, murders and extortions over the past four decades.
3. India could not get back Kashmir territory from China.
4. Most neighbours are unhappy with India.

Recent foreign policy victories of India were as follows:

1. PM Indo-US Honeymoon Begins: Modi was able to bring President Obama to the Republic Day parade on January 26, 2015. India and the USA has signed many contracts.
2. The Trio: China, India and Russia have agreed to fight against terror as one single unit.
3. Neighbourhood Relationships: PM Modi and Sushma Swaraj have made best efforts to woo the neighbours of India and refine relationships with them. Thus, they have indulged in political diplomacy (or cricket diplomacy) with Sri Lanka, Pakistan, Bhutan, Nepal and China during the past eight months. The results are encouraging.
4. Neutral towards ISIS: Our nurses, drivers and other workers were safely taken out of Iraq and Syria, despite the fact that ISIS had inflicted heavy casualties in those two countries. If we do not hurt the feelings of ISIS cadres, we can remain safe in all parts of the world. Please note that when war would be over, our workers would go back to Iraq and Syria to start various construction and engineering projects. Thus, India is a neutral party in this conflict and wishes the welfare of all those concerned.

Role of Prime Minister

Nehru assumed a strong personal role for the post of PM but a weak institutional structure. Nehru served as PM and Minister of External Affairs; he made all major foreign policy decisions himself after consulting with his advisers. He was the founder of Panchsheel. China decimated this tenet in the 1962 war, although India still sticks to it. The Chinese incursions of 2013 do not prove that it is committed towards any inter-country negotiation or peace effort. Nehru's failure is our present. His successors exercise control over India's international dealings, although they generally appointed separate ministers of external affairs. Lal Bahadur Shastri (1964-66) expanded the PMO and enlarged its powers. By the 1970s, the Office of the Prime Minister had become the *de facto* coordinator and supra-ministry of the government. The enhanced role of the office strengthened the prime minister's control over foreign policy making at the expense of the Ministry of External Affairs.

Advisers in the office provided channels of information and policy recommendations in addition to those offered by the Ministry of External Affairs. A subordinate part of the office—the Research and Analysis Wing (RAW)—functioned in ways that expanded the information available to PM and his advisers. The RAW gathered intelligence, provided intelligence analysis to PMO and executed covert operations abroad.

PM's control on personal advisers in PMO was typically strong (and visible) under the tenures of Mrs. Indira Gandhi (1966–77 and 1980–84) and Rajiv Gandhi (1984–89). But PM's hold was weaker during the periods of coalition governments. Observers find it difficult to determine whether the locus of decision-making authority on any particular issue lies with the Ministry of External Affairs, the Council of Ministers, the Office of the Prime Minister, or the prime minister himself.

The Prime Minister is free to appoint advisers and special committees to examine various foreign policy options and areas of interest. Manmohan Singh appointed K. Subramaniam in 2005 to head a special government task force to study Global Strategic Developments over the next decade. The Task Force submitted its conclusions to the Prime Minister in 2006. The report has not yet been released in the public domain.

Ministry of External Affairs

In the mid-1990s, India attracted the world attention towards the Pakistan-backed terrorism in Kashmir. The Kargil War resulted in a major diplomatic victory for India. The United States and European Union recognized the fact that Pakistani military had illegally infiltrated into Indian territory and pressurized Pakistan to withdraw from Kargil. Several anti-India militant groups based in Pakistan were labeled as terrorist groups by the United States and European Union.

In 1998, India tested nuclear weapons for the second time (Pokharan-II) which resulted in several U.S., Japanese and European sanctions on India. India's former defense minister, George Fernandes, had said that India's nuclear program was necessary as it provided a deterrence to potential Chinese nuclear threat. Most sanctions imposed on India were removed by 2001.

After the 9/11 massacre in New York City in 2001, Indian intelligence agencies provided the USA with significant information on Al-Qaeda and related groups' activities in Pakistan and Afghanistan. India's extensive contribution to the War on Terror, coupled with a surge in its economy, has helped India's diplomatic relations with several countries. Over the past three years, India has held numerous joint military exercises with US and European nations that have resulted in a strengthened US-India and EU-India bilateral relationships.

India has been pushing for reforms in the UN and WTO with mixed results. India's candidature for a permanent seat at the UN Security Council is currently backed by several countries including France, Russia, the United Kingdom, Germany, Japan, Brazil, Australia and UAE. In 2004, the United States signed a nuclear co-operation agreement with India even though the latter is not a part of the Nuclear Non-Proliferation Treaty. The US argued that India's strong nuclear non-proliferation record made it an exception. However, this has not persuaded other Nuclear Suppliers Group members to sign similar deals with India. During a state visit to India in November 2010, Obama had announced the US support for India's bid for permanent membership to UN Security Council as well as India's entry into the Nuclear Suppliers Group, Wassenaar Arrangement, Australia Group and Missile Technology Control Regime.

Strategic Partners

India's growing economy, strategic location, friendly foreign policy and large and vibrant Diaspora has won it more allies than enemies. India has friendly relations with several countries in the developing world. Though India is not a part of any major military alliance, it has close strategic and military relationship with most of the major powers.

Countries considered India's closest include the Russian Federation, Israel, Afghanistan, France, Bhutan and Bangladesh. Russia is the largest supplier of military equipment to India, followed by Israel and France. According to some analysts, Israel is set to overtake Russia as India's largest military and strategic partner. The two countries also collaborate extensively in the sphere of counter-terrorism and space technology. India also enjoys strong military relations with several other countries, including the United Kingdom, the United States, Japan, Singapore, Brazil, South Africa and Italy. In addition, India operates an airbase in Tajikistan and has signed a landmark defense accord with Qatar (2008).

Make in India: New Plans of PM Modi for the Indian Navy

On February 17, 2015, the Modi government cleared the projects for the construction of seven stealth frigates, six nuclear submarines. The total project cost would be more than 1,00,000 crore; frigates would cost 50,000 crore rupees and submarines would cost 60,000 crore rupees. They would be made with foreign collaboration (in India). Thus, Modi has fulfilled his promise of "Make in India." Three nuclear submarines are already being built at Vizag; they can carry SSBNs. This is being done to boost the strength and reach of Indian Navy. The Cabinet Committee on Security took these decisions in tune with the critical necessity for India to bolster its overall deterrence capability in the Indian Ocean region. The primary zone of strategic interests of India stretches from the Persian Gulf to the Malacca Strait. The project of frigate construction was designated Project 17-A. Four frigates would be made at Mazagon Docks (Mumbai). Three frigates would be made at Garden reach Shipbuilders and Engineers (Kolkata). The project of submarine construction was named Project 75. It will take ten years to roll out the very first submarine of the diesel-electric power genre. All of them would be made in India. It may be noted that India has 140 warships at present. Besides, it has two aircraft carriers, 48 major combatants and 14 submarines. Thus, the government has done well by placing tenders for or ordering the purchase-cum-manufacture of 41 warships in all. This number includes one aircraft carrier, six destroyers and six submarines. The total cost to Indian exchequer would be more than INR 2,00,000 crore. The term "purchase-cum-manufacture" means that foreign technologies and gadgets would be imported according to the needs of the naval device being built but it would be made in India only.

INS Arihant began its 18-month sea trials in December 2014. INS Aridhman is now ready for launch into Indian waters. Another aircraft carrier is being built in India. These three subprojects are under the ATV Project. They would give a big fillip to India's naval abilities. INS Chakra is the nuclear powered Akula-II class SSN and has been taken on a lease of ten years from Russia. It may not be armed with long-range missiles due to international treaties. But it has Khub-S land-attack cruise missiles and advanced torpedoes.

Note that 13 diesel—electric submarines of India are very old and must be done away with. That is why Modi has taken steps to make more naval war vessels with foreign collaboration. Defence production at home is no longer a distant dream. The BJP government initiated the process and this would help the Indian engineering industry as well, albeit in the long run. Currently, all war vessels are being manufactured at government facilities, mainly at Vizag. Thus, we will redefine our naval capabilities within a decade or so from now.

Indo-China Conflict: Incursions into Indian Territory

India's trade relations in the Indian Ocean region have progressed chiefly along bilateral lines. But with China's economic overtures increasingly frequent and backed by commercial heft, India finds that it can no longer take its geo-economic position in the region for granted. To counter China, India seems to be trying to establish a multilateral mechanism for trade and investment that China may have to join.

Indo-China Cooperation and Support from NSG

The annual plenary meeting of the Nuclear Suppliers Group (NSG) later this month in Prague will focus attention once again on India's application for membership in the group. Since 2008, India has been campaigning to join the NSG, which governs all legal transfer of nuclear technology and material globally. While the India-U.S. civilian nuclear deal concluded that year raised India's hopes of inclusion, the NSG remains bitterly divided over the issue, with a U.S.-led bloc supporting India's candidature and a China-led bloc vehemently opposing its entry into the group.

The stand-off has frustrated India's deep-seated desire to become an equal of the major nuclear powers. But it also has implications for the future of the NSG and the nuclear non-proliferation regime more broadly.

During deliberations in Vienna in 2013, the NSG once again failed to reach a decision on India's membership. The 46-nation group works by consensus, making any opposition on effective veto. To India's frustration, disagreement within the group actually seems to be growing, which is especially puzzling given that four of the five major nuclear powers—Britain, the U.S., Russia and France—support India's bid to join the NSG. Many observers argue that India's status as a non-signatory to the Nuclear Non-Proliferation Treaty (NPT) is the main cause of this impasse but stiff resistance to India's membership appears to be rooted in geopolitics; China is the major obstacle because it links nuclear supplies with border disputes.

India's Policy towards USA

After the 11 September attacks in 2001, Indian intelligence agencies provided the US with significant information on Al-Qaeda and related groups' activities in Pakistan and Afghanistan. India's contribution to the War on Terror has helped India's diplomatic relations with several countries. Over the past few years, India has held numerous joint military exercises with U.S. and European nations. India's bilateral trade with Europe and U.S. has more than doubled in the last five years.

India has been pushing for reforms in the UN and WTO with mixed results. India's candidature for a permanent seat at the UN Security Council is currently backed by several countries including United Kingdom, France, Germany, Japan, Brazil, African Union nations, USA and China. In 2005, the United States signed a nuclear co-operation agreement with India even though the latter is not a part of the Nuclear Non-Proliferation Treaty. The US argued that India's strong nuclear non-proliferation record made it an exception and persuaded other Nuclear Suppliers Group members to sign similar deals with India.

On March 2, 2006 India and the USA signed the Indo-US Nuclear Pact on co-operation in civilian nuclear field. This was signed during the four days state visit of USA President George

Bush in India. On its part, India would separate its civilian and military nuclear programs and the civilian programs would be brought under the safeguards of IAEA. US would sell India the reactor technologies and the nuclear fuel for setting up and upgrading its civilian nuclear program. The US Congress needs to ratify this pact since U.S. federal law prohibits the trading of nuclear technologies and materials outside the framework of the Nuclear Suppliers Group (NSG).

One of the very interesting features of Indo-USA relations of recent times is the changes on the terms of engagement between the two countries on the issue of nuclear proliferation. While earlier, in the USA strategic thinking on nuclear proliferation, India figured mainly because of American concern about latter's nuclear and missile programmes. Now, the Americans are increasingly realizing the futility of insisting on a rollback of India's nuclear programme. They, rather, want to leverage India's growing power and influence in favour of their broader non-proliferation and counter proliferation objectives.

The promotion of democracy around the world is one of the most important foreign policy objective of USA. India is the largest democracy of the world. So, India can hardly be ignored by the USA. India is a founding member of the Community of Democracies, a prominent endeavour of USA on promotion of democracy. India rejected the suggestion of the USA about setting up a Centre for Asian Democracy.

While much of the world's attention was focused on the birth of Britain's Prince George (July 2013), US Vice President Joe Biden came to India in an attempt to get the bilateral relationship between the world's oldest and largest democracies back on track. New Delhi is understandably wary of the Obama administration. India's policymakers are concerned about a possible US rush for the exit in Afghanistan after 2014, especially if it involves a deal with the Taliban that would allow the militants to exercise real authority in the country and undercut Indian interests. India has real issues with China, including continued tensions over unresolved border issues. But it is not anxious to be drawn into playing a supporting role in Washington's strategic pivot to Asia. Nor does it want to assume new commitments on behalf of the US for underwriting US security preferences for the Indian Ocean basin.

US states that the Indian government has not done enough to open up the prospects of the vast Indian market to US business firms by removing trade barriers that continue to provide preferential protection for domestic industries. Indo-US nuclear deal is not being discussed. India needs nuclear fuel but no one is giving it to India.

We are trade partners of US and our peoples live there. But India does not have deep defence ties with US due to our proximity with Russia. Our policy towards US is more commercial and less strategic. Nuclear deal will take more time.

India's Policy towards Afghanistan

Bilateral relations between India and Afghanistan have been traditionally strong and friendly. While India was the only South Asian country to recognize the Soviet-backed Democratic Republic of Afghanistan in the 1980s, its relations were diminished during the Afghan civil wars and the rule of the Islamist Taliban in the 1990s. India helped in the overthrow of Taliban and became the largest regional provider of humanitarian and reconstruction aid.

The new democratically elected Afghan government strengthened its ties with India in wake of persisting tensions and problems with Pakistan, which was suspected of continuing to shelter and support the Taliban. India pursues a policy of close cooperation to bolster its standing as a regional power and contain its rival Pakistan, which it maintains in supporting Islamic militants in Kashmir and other parts of India. India is the largest regional investor in Afghanistan, having committed more than US$2.2 billion for reconstruction purposes.

India's Policy towards Bangladesh

Both states are part of the Indian subcontinent and have had a long common cultural, economic and political history. India played a crucial part in Bangladesh's independence from Pakistan. In recent years India provides co-operation and assistance during annual natural calamities. India is 8th largest exporter to Bangladesh. Most differences are regarding sharing of water resources between the two countries. Regarding the Ganges, Bangladesh accuses India of diverting her waters to Kolkata through Farakka Barrage. The terror camps are on in Bangladesh and Sheikh Hasina cannot control terror elements on her own soil. India is friendly towards the present government but BSF is equally alert.

India's Policy towards Myanmar

India is a major customer of Burmese oil and gas. In 2007, Indian exports to Burma totaled US$185 million while its imports from Burma were valued at around US$ 810 million, consisting mostly of oil and gas. India has granted US$100 million credit to fund highway infrastructure projects in Burma, while US$ 57 million has been offered to upgrade Burmese railways. A further US$ 27 million in grants has been pledged for road and rail projects. India provided military assistance to Burmese military junta. However, there has been increasing pressure on India to cut some of its military supplies to Burma. Relations between the two remain close which was evident in the aftermath of Cyclone (Nargis) when India was one of the few countries whose relief and rescue aid proposals were accepted by Burma's ruling junta. Elections have been held in Myanmar. Now, it is a half-democracy. India and Myanmar have good relations.

Foreign Policy towards China

India claims Aksai Chin and Trans-Karakoram Tract, as part of Jammu and Kashmir. China claims most of Arunachal Pradesh, a contested disputed territory of north-east India by not recognizing the McMahon Line. Two regions are claimed by both India and China. Aksai Chin is in the disputed territory of Kashmir, at the junction of India, Tibet and Azad Kashmir. India claims the 38,000-square-kilometre territory, currently administered by China. India also considers the cessation of Shaksam Valley to China by Pakistan as illegal and a part of its territory. Arunachal Pradesh is a state of India in the country's northeast, bordering on Bhutan, Burma and China. Though it is under Indian administration, China calls the 90,000-square-kilometre area as South Tibet. Also the boundary between the North Indian states of Himachal Pradesh and Uttaranchal with China's Tibet is not properly demarcated with some portions under India. These are the unpleasant landmarks in the chequered Indo-Chinese history. The incursions of 2013 by Chinese soldiers in Ladakh have made both sides chary, ready for conflict and offensive.

India is deploying 50,000 troops in Ladakh and Aksai Chin areas to ward off attacks by Chinese troops. India's defence minister, AK Antony visited China in June 2013 and received the bashing of one of their generals. The Chinese say that India has captured their territories illegally. Indians also say so. The policy debacle here is that India does not want to take major decisions in boundary disputes. There are many reasons behind this decision. Firstly, general elections (2014) are around the corner and international diplomacy has taken a backseat in all institutions, government or private. Secondly, PM Manmohan Singh and UPA chairperson Sonia Gandhi do not enjoy support in Parliament. Thirdly, the present government thinks that the new government in power should take up vital issues with Chinese. Thus, Dr. Singh has not sent a bold reply to Chinese intrusions; this fiasco could prove fatal for the UPA government in 2014 elections. General Bikram Singh, the former army chief of India, had stated that his men could give befitting replies to Chinese dragon's machinations. But PM told him to keep his cool. We consider this as a major foreign policy failure. We should have responded to the sabotage and incursion of Chinese troops in 2013. The non-performance of our armed forced sends wrong signals. As a result, the morale of the armed men sitting at the border goes down. If enemy fires one shot, we ought to fire three at him!

The commercial aspects of the foreign policy are equally pleasing. Bilateral trade surpassed US$60 billion in 2010; this made China the single largest trading partner of India. Despite suspicions lingering from the 1962 Sino-Indian War and continuing boundary disputes over Aksai Chin, Ladakh and Arunachal Pradesh, Sino-Indian relations have improved gradually since 1988.

India's Policy towards Nepal

Relations between India and Nepal are close yet fraught with difficulties stemming from geography, economics, the problems inherent in big power-small power relations, and common ethnic and linguistic identities that overlap the two countries' borders. Pakistan has created problems in Indo-Nepalese relations.

India's Policy towards Pakistan

In 1998, India carried out the Pokharan-II nuclear tests which was followed by Pakistan's Chagai-I tests. Following the Lahore Declaration in February 1999, relations briefly improved. A few months later, Pakistani paramilitary forces, terrorists and Pakistani Army infiltrated in large numbers into Kargil district of Indian Kashmir. This initiated the Kargil conflict after India moved in thousands of troops to successfully flush out infiltrators. The relations between the two reached all-time low which worsened even further following the involvement of Pakistan-based terrorists in the hijacking of the Indian Airlines IC814 plane in December 1999. Attempts to normalize relations, such as the Agra summit held in July 2001 failed. An attack on the Indian Parliament in December 2001 (blamed on Pakistan) which had condemned the attack. It caused a military standoff between the two countries which lasted for nearly a year raising fears of a nuclear conflict.

However, a peace process (2003) led to improved relations in the following years. The 26/11 attacks worsened the relationship again. The attack on the Indian Parliament proved lethal for the relations. The bomb blasts in Jaipur and elsewhere left many dead. All these incidents and the support of Indian Mujahideen to terror elements in Pakistan convinced Indian authorities that there was no need to talk to Pakistan on any issues. Today, talks are held for namesake. India's policy is clear—we cannot talk and even if we do, neither of us would be able to deliver.

Since the initiation of the peace process, several Confidence Building Measures (CBMs) between India and Pakistan have taken shape. The Samjhauta Express and Delhi–Lahore Bus service are two of these successful measures which have played a crucial role in expanding people-to-people contact between the two countries. The initiation of Srinagar–Muzaffarabad Bus service in 2005 and opening of a historic trade route across the Line of Control in 2008 further reflects increasing eagerness between the two sides to improve relations. Although bilateral trade between India and Pakistan was a modest US$ 1.7 billion in March 2007, it is expected to cross US$10 billion by 2010. After the Kashmir earthquake in 2005, India sent aid to affected areas in Pakistani Kashmir and Punjab.

The Mumbai attacks (2008) seriously undermined the relations between the two countries. Ten men had attacked various places in Mumbai. Nine of them died during the combat operation. The last one, Kasab, was hanged by India in 2012.

Afzal Guru, the mastermind of attacks on Indian Parliament, was hanged in March 2013. The policy of retribution between both nations can be attributed to one single reason—Kashmir. India's Pakistan policy is clear but weak. When they come, they kill us. When we nab them, we hang them. In 2013, two Indian (Hindu) soldiers were killed by Pakistan's Baluch Regiment. Their beheaded bodies were put back at the LoC. Pakistan is a tough customer; it needs a final befitting reply. But India is afraid of China and UN. It has not attacked any country in the past 10,000 years. How can it become a major power in the future?

India's Policy towards Sri Lanka

India-Sri Lanka relations have undergone a qualitative and quantitative transformation in the recent past. Political relations are close, trade and investments have increased dramatically, infrastructural linkages are constantly being augmented, defence collaboration has increased and there is a general, broad-based improvement across all sectors of bilateral cooperation. India was the first country to respond to Sri Lanka's request for assistance after the tsunami in December 2004. In July 2006, India evacuated 430 Sri Lankan nationals from Lebanon, first to Cyprus by Indian Navy ships and then to Delhi and Colombo by special Air India flights.

There exists a broad consensus within the Sri Lankan polity on the primacy of India in Sri Lanka's external relations matrix. Both the major political parties in Sri Lanka, the Sri Lanka Freedom Party and the United Nationalist Party have contributed to the rapid development of bilateral relations in the last ten years.

Sri Lanka has supported India's candidature to the permanent membership of the UN Security Council.

India's Policy towards Americas

India's relations with developing nations in Latin America, especially Brazil and Mexico have continued to grow. India and Brazil continue to work together on the reform of Security Council through the G4 nations which have also increased strategic and economic cooperation through the IBSA Dialogue Forum. The process of finalizing Preferential Trade Agreement (PTA) with MERCOSUR (Brazil, Argentina, Uruguay, and Paraguay) is on the itinerary and negotiations are being held with Chile. Brazilian President Luiz Inacio Lula da Silva was the guest of honour at the Republic Day celebrations in New Delhi in 2004.

India's Policy towards Canada

Indo-Canadian relationships are the longstanding bilateral relations between India and Canada, which are built upon a mutual commitment to democracy, pluralism and people-to-people links, according to the government of Canada. The Pokharan-II tests did irritate Canada. Now, India is very friendly towards Canada. Many Indians live and work there. In 2014, the anniversary of the fateful incident of Kamagatamaru ship was celebrated all over India. This incident took place in Vancouver in 1914. The ship went to Vancouver with 357-plus passengers, most of them being Sikhs. The ship was sent back after torturing the passengers and attacking the ship with artillery guns. The ship had to come back to Baj Baj port of Calcutta (now Kolkata). These brave passengers were arrested, beaten, jailed and even fired at upon their arrival in Calcutta. The Sikhs took these incidents seriously and most of them joined the Ghadar Party to avenge their losses during the course of this fateful tragedy. Eventually, the Ghadar Party also lost its battles against the Punjab police. Most of its cadres were either killed in encounters or arrested by the police of the Punjab province (of undivided India). Kartar Singh Sarabha and Ras Bihari Bose were the two major stalwarts of the Ghadar Movement. They were hanged to death by the British. Many other patriots were also hanged at the end of the Ghadar Movement.

The Canadian government was forced to file an apology for oppressing the passengers of the Kamagatamaru. Finally, Mr. Stefan Harper, the PM of Canada, did ask for an apology on August 3, 2008 in Surrey (British Columbia). The year 2014 was a very important year in Canadian history as well as history of Indian rebellion. Today, India and Canada enjoy great relationships with each other. Canada has also given technical and economic support to the peaceful nuclear programmes of India in the past. It would continue to do so in the future, for India does not have any nuclear ambition. The memories of the fateful incident of Kamagatamaru would never fade from the annals of Sikh history. They had fought bravely against the government of Canada at that time because it was biased against the Asians and Sikhs on racial and colour grounds. Because of the sacrifices made by our forefathers, we are able to send our people to Canada for the sake of working and living there.

India's Policy towards the EU

India was one of the first countries to develop relations with the Union, signing bilateral agreements in 1973, when the United Kingdom joined. The most recent cooperation agreement was signed in 1994 and an action plan was signed in 2005. As of April 2007 the Commission is pursuing a free trade agreement with India.

The Union is India's largest trading partner, accounting for 20% of Indian trade. However, India accounts for only 1.8 percent of the EU's trade and attracts only 0.3 percent of European Foreign Direct Investment, although still provides India's largest source. During 2005 EU-India trade grew by 20.3 percent.

In 2006, Mittal Steel decided to take-over the Luxembourg-based steel company, Arcelor. The move of Lakshmi Mittal was opposed with hostility by France and Luxembourg but was passed by the Commission later. The Tata group took over Corus, another steel giant, in a bid to remain at the top of the steel production chain around the world.

EU and India agreed on 29 September, 2008 at the EU-India summit in Marseille, France's largest commercial port, to expand their cooperation in the fields of nuclear energy and environmental protection and deepen their strategic partnership. The former

French President, Nicolas Sarkozy, stated, "The EU welcomes India, as a large country, to engage in developing nuclear energy, adding that this clean energy will be helpful for the world to deal with the global climate change." Later, Francois Holland took over as the new French president. He also supported India as a growing economy and society and extended all kinds of support to it.

In 2015, when the office of *Charlie Hebdo* magazine was attacked, the Indian media and peoples stood along with the French masses to give them support. Thus, France and India have same views on terror and preservation of human values and freedom.

European Commission President José Manuel Barroso expounded the joint action plan on adjustments of EU's strategic partnership with India, saying the two sides will strengthen cooperation on world peace and safety, sustainable development, cooperation in science and technology and cultural exchanges.

Earlier, in 2013-14, while reviewing efforts of two sides in developing the bilateral strategic partnership, the joint action plan reckoned that in politics, dialogue and cooperation have enhanced through regular summits and exchanges of visits and that in economy, mutual investments have increased dramatically in recent years, dialogue in macro-economic policies and financial services has established and cooperation in energy, science and technology and environment has been launched. Under the joint action plan, EU and India would enhance consultation and dialogue on human rights within the UN framework, strengthen cooperation in world peacekeeping mission, fight against terror and non-proliferation of arms, promote cooperation and exchange in developing civil nuclear energy and strike a free trade deal as soon as possible. France, which relies heavily on nuclear power and is a major exporter of nuclear technology, is expected to sign a deal that would allow it to provide nuclear fuel to India.

India's Policy towards UK

Switzerland has an embassy in New Delhi and a consulate in Bangalore and Mumbai. India has an embassy in Bern and consulates in Geneva and Zurich. India is one of Switzerland's most important partners in Asia. Bilateral and political contacts are constantly developing, and trade and scientific cooperation between the two countries are flourishing. Switzerland was the first country in the world to sign a treaty with India in 1947.

India's Policy towards UK

Since 1947, India's relations with the United Kingdom have been bilateral and through the Commonwealth of Nations. India and the UK have many enduring links. This is in part due to the significant number of people of Indian origin living in the UK. Economically the relationship between Britain and India is strong. India is the second largest investor in Britain after the US. Britain is also one of the largest investors in India. In 2008, Britain gave India the 825-million-pound aid package to help India develop its health and education systems. Our policy towards Britain is a copy of our policy towards EU which is friendly and trade-oriented.

India's Policy towards France

France, Russia and Israel were the only countries that did not condemn India's decision to go nuclear in 1998. In 2003, France became the largest supplier of nuclear fuel and technology to India and remains a large military and economic trade partner. India's permanent member aspirations in the UN Security Council have found very strong support from former French president and former Prime Minister, Mr. Nicholas Sarkozy. The recent decision by the Indian government to purchase French Scorpène class submarines worth US$ 3 billion and 43 Airbus aircraft for Air India worth US$ 2.5 billion has further cemented the strategic, military and economic co-operation between India and France.

Nicolas Sarkozy visited India in January 2008 and was the Chief Guest of the Republic Day parade in New Delhi. France was the first country to sign a nuclear energy co-operation agreement with India. It was done during PM's visit, following the waiver by the Nuclear Suppliers Group. During the Bastille Day celebrations on July 14, 2009, a detachment of 400 Indian troops marched along with the French troops. Dr. Manmohan Singh was the guest of honour. We have deep strategic and commercial relations with France.

Joint Policy of India, China and Russia towards Terrorism

India, China and Russia have taken a vow to fight an all-out war against terrorism. On February 2, 2015, Chinese, Indian and Russian foreign ministers sat together in the 13th trilateral meeting in Beijing (China) and vowed to fight terrorism. During the course of this meeting, it was also decided that India was the right candidate to join the Asia Pacific Economic Cooperation (APEC). Mrs. Sushma Swaraj (the Foreign Minister of India), Mr. Wang Ti (the Foreign Minister of China) and Mr. Sergey Lavrov (the Foreign Minister of Russia) met in Beijing in February 2015 to confirm that they were one single entity, insofar as the fight against terror was an issue. This trilateral relationship is a new development in international political circles. Till date, only bilateral or multilateral relations were considered as conducive to global political transactions. But China, India and Russia have taken their trilateral binding to new level. That could be a blow to Sino-Pakistani relations. The governor of a Pakistani province had tendered his resignation simply because President Obama had not visited Pakistan after visiting India in January 2015. This sad state of affairs can be changed only by Pakistan if it changes is stance towards terror.

India's Policy towards Germany

India is a friend of Germany. It has adopted mutually-benefitting policy towards this EU nation. The policies of India are applicable to Germany as well. Germany is a big trade partner of India.

India's Policy towards the Arab World

India and the Arab states of the Persian Gulf enjoy strong cultural and economic ties. This is reflected in the fact that more than 50% of the oil consumed by India comes from the Persian Gulf countries and Indian nationals form the largest expatriate community in the Arabian peninsula. The annual remittance by Indian expatriates in the region amounted to US$20 billion in 2007. India is one of the largest trading partners of the CCASG with non-oil trade between India and Dubai alone to the tune of US$19 billion in 2007. The Persian Gulf countries have also played an important role in addressing India's energy security concerns, with Saudi Arabia and Kuwait regularly increasing their oil supply to India to meet the country's rising energy demand. In 2005, Kuwait increased its oil exports to India by 10% increasing the net oil trade between the two to US$4.5 billion. In the year 2008, Qatar decided to invest US$5 billion in India's energy sector.

India has maritime security arrangement in place with Oman and Qatar. In 2008, a landmark defense pact was signed. Thus India has committed its military assets to protect Qatar from external threats. There has been progress in a proposed deep-sea gas pipeline from Qatar, via the Oman route, to India.

Egypt–India relationships

Modern Egypt-India relations go back to the contacts between Saad Zaghloul and Mohandas Gandhi on the common goals of their respective movements of independence. In 1955, Egypt under Gamal Abdul Nasser and India under Jawaharlal Nehru became the founders of the Non-Aligned Movement. During the 1956 War, Nehru stood supporting Egypt to the point of threatening to withdraw his country from the Commonwealth of Nations. In 1967, following the Arab-Israeli war, India supported Egypt and the Arabs. In 1977, New Delhi described the visit of President Anwar al-Sadat to Jerusalem as a "brave" move and considered the peace treaty between Egypt and Israel a primary step on the path of a just settlement of the Middle East problem. Major Egyptian exports to India include raw cotton, raw and manufactured fertilizers, oil and oil products, organic and non-organic chemicals, leather and iron products. Major imports into Egypt from India are cotton yarn, sesame, coffee, herbs, tobacco, lentils, pharmaceutical products and transport equipment. The Egyptian Ministry of Petroleum is also currently negotiating the establishment of a natural gas-operated fertilizer plant with another Indian company. In 2004, the Gas Authority of India Limited, bought 15 percent of Egypt Natural Gas distribution and marketing company. In 2008 Egyptian investment in India was worth some 750 million dollars, according to the Egyptian ambassador. After Arab Spring of 2011, with ousting of Hosni

Mubarak, Egypt has asked for help of India in conducting nationwide elections.

Foreign Policy towards Iran

After the Iranian Revolution of 1979, Iran withdrew from CENTO and dissociated itself from US-friendly countries, including Pakistan, which automatically entailed improved relationship with the Republic of India.

Currently, the two countries have friendly relations in many areas. There are significant trade ties, particularly in crude oil imports into India and diesel exports to Iran. Iran frequently objected to Pakistan's attempts to draft anti-India resolutions at international organizations such as the OIC. India welcomed Iran's inclusion as an observer state in the SAARC regional organization. Lucknow continues to be a major centre of Shiite culture and Persian study in the subcontinent.

In the 1990s, India and Iran both supported the Northern Alliance in Afghanistan against the Taliban regime. They continue to collaborate in supporting the broad-based anti-Taliban government led by Hamid Karzai and backed by the United States.

However, one complex issue in Indo-Iran relations is the issue of Iran's nuclear program. In this intricate issue, India tries to make a delicate balance. According to Rejaul Laskar, an Indian expert on International Relations, "India's position on Iran's nuclear programme has been consistent, principled and balanced, and makes an endeavour to reconcile Iran's quest for energy security with the international community's concerns on proliferation. So, while India acknowledges and supports Iran's ambitions to achieve energy security and in particular, its quest for peaceful use of nuclear energy, it is also India's principled position that Iran must meet all its obligations under the international law, particularly its obligations under the nuclear Non Proliferation Treaty (NPT) and other such treaties to which it is a signatory."

Following an attack on an Israeli diplomat in India in February 2012, the Delhi Police contended that the Iranian Revolutionary Guard Corps had some involvement in the attack. This was subsequently confirmed in July 2012, after a report by the Delhi Police found evidence that members of Iranian Revolutionary

Guard Corps had been involved in the February 13 bomb attack in the capital.

India's Policy towards Iraq and Syria

Iraq was one of the few countries in the Middle East with which India established diplomatic relations at the embassy level immediately after its independence in 1947. Both nations signed the "Treaty of Perpetual Peace and Friendship" in 1952 and an agreement of cooperation on cultural affairs in 1954. India was amongst the first to recognize the Baath Party-led government, and Iraq remained neutral during the Indo-Pakistani War of 1965. However, Iraq sided alongside other Persian Gulf states in supporting Pakistan against India during the Indo-Pakistani War of 1971, which saw the creation of Bangladesh. The eight-year long Iran–Iraq War caused a steep decline in trade and commerce between the two nations.

During the 1991 Persian Gulf War, India remained neutral but permitted refueling for U.S. airplanes. It opposed U.N. sanctions on Iraq, but the period of war and Iraq's isolation further diminished India's commercial and diplomatic ties. From 1999 onwards, Iraq and India began to work towards a stronger relationship. Iraq had supported India's right to conduct nuclear tests following its tests of five nuclear weapons on May 11 and 13 1998. In 2000, the then-Vice President of Iraq Taha Yassin Ramadan visited India. On 6 August, 2002, President Saddam Hussein had conveyed Iraq's unwavering support to India over the Kashmir dispute with Pakistan. India and Iraq established joint ministerial committees and trade delegations to promote extensive bilateral cooperation. Although initially disrupted during the 2003 invasion of Iraq, diplomatic and commercial ties between India and the new democratic government of Iraq have since been normalized.

After the rise of ISIS to power in Iraq and Syria, India had to take a defensive stance. We had to remove our workers and nursing staff from that country in a bid to save their lives. Mr. Bhagwant Singh Mann, the MP of India belonging to the Aam Aadmi Party, took personal care to get the Indians evacuated through such air routes as were safe. Currently, none of our peoples is staying there. The embassies in Iraq and Syria are working only for namesake. War is taking its toll in Iraq and Syria. India has played its card well by not interfering in the affairs of Iraq and Syria. When situation becomes normal in that region, our workers would go back once again and start working for the construction of the parts ravaged by war. Many Indians were treated badly by the cadres of the ISIS. That is a bad news, given that we have good relationships with all countries of the Gulf region. When the conditions become conducive for the entry of the Indians to those two countries, the government would take a decision to send its peoples there. As of now, the situation is volatile there and we cannot do much to change it.

India's Policy towards Israel

The creation of Israel at the end of World War II was a complex issue. India, along with Iran and Yugoslavia had recommended a single state with Arab and Jewish majority provinces with an aim to prevent partition of historic Palestine and prevent any conflict that might follow based on its own experience during partition. However, the final UN resolution decided to partition historic Palestine into Arab and Jewish states based on religious and ethnic majority which India opposed in the final vote as it did not agree with concept of partition on the basis of religion.

However, due to the security threat from a US aided Pakistan and its nuclear program in the 80s, Israel and India started a clandestine relationship that involved cooperation between their respective intelligence agencies. Israel shared India's concerns about the growing danger posed by Pakistan and nuclear proliferation to Iran and other Arab states. After the end of the Cold War, formal relations with Israel started improving significantly.

Since the establishment of full diplomatic relations with Israel in 1992, India has improved its relation with the Jewish State. India is regarded as Israel's strongest ally in Asia, and Israel is India's second largest arms supplier.

India has entertained Israeli Prime Minister in a visit in 2003 and Israel has entertained Indian dignitaries such as Finance Minister Jaswant Singh in diplomatic visits. India and Israel collaborate in scientific and technological endeavours. Israel's Minister for Science and Technology has expressed interest in collaborating with the Indian Space Research Organization (ISRO) towards utilizing satellites for better management of land and other resources. Israel has also expressed interest in participating in the ISRO's Chandrayan Mission involving an unmanned mission to the moon. On January 21, 2008, India successfully launched an Israeli spy satellite into orbit from Sriharikota space station in southern India.

Israel and India share intelligence on terrorist groups. They have developed close defense and security ties since establishing diplomatic relations in 1992. Israel is India's second-biggest arms supplier, after Russia. India has bought more than $5 billion worth of Israeli equipment since 2002. In addition, Israel is training Indian military units and discussing an arrangement to give Indian commandos instruction in counter-terrorist tactics and urban warfare. In December 2008, Israel and India signed a memorandum to set up an Indo-Israel Legal Colloquium to facilitate discussions and exchange programs between judges and jurists of the two countries.

India's Policy towards Saudi Arabia

India and Saudi Arabia are actively cooperating in the field of science and technology. CSIR and the Saudi Arabian Standards Organization (SASO) have an ongoing programme of technical cooperation (POC) since June 1993. Under this programme, Indian experts in different scientific areas, particularly in the field of measurement and calibration, are deputed to Saudi Arabia on regular basis. Similarly, several Saudi experts and have undergone advanced training in India. National Physical Laboratory has provided expertise and technology for two important SASO projects related to calibration and the tele-clock system. CSIR and the King Abdulaziz City for Science and Technology (KACST) signed an MoU for bilateral cooperation in 1997 and have an ongoing programme of cooperation, particularly in the field of space science, remote sensing and installation of Internet. Recently a three-member delegation from CSIR, NPL and CFTRI visited SASO during January 2004 and both sides agreed to renew the POC.

India's Policy towards Russia

India's ties with the Russian Federation are time-tested and based on continuity, trust and mutual understanding. There is national consensus in both the countries on the need to preserve and strengthen India-Russia relations and further consolidate the strategic partnership between the two countries. A Declaration on Strategic Partnership was signed between present Russian President Vladimir Putin and former Indian Prime Minister Atal Bihari Vajpayee in October 2000. Joint Indo-Russian BrahMos nuclear cruise missile has a top speed of Mach 2.8, making it the world's fastest supersonic cruise missile.

Russia and India have decided not to renew the 1971 Indo-Soviet Peace and Friendship Treaty and have sought to follow what both describe as a more pragmatic, less ideological relationship. Ties have grown stronger with President Vladimir Putin's 2004 visit. The pace of high-level visits has since increased, as has discussion of major defence purchases. Russia, is working for the development of the Koodankulam Nuclear Power Plant that will be capable of producing 1000 MW of electricity. Gazprom is working for the development of oil and natural gas in the Bay of Bengal. India and Russia have collaborated extensively on space technology. Other areas of collaboration include software, Ayurvedic medicines etc. India and Russia have decided to enhance trade to US$10 billion. Cooperation between clothing and hosiery manufacturers of two countries continues to strengthen. India and Russia signed an agreement on joint efforts to increase investment and trade volumes in the textile industry in both countries. The signing of the document included representatives of the Russian Union of Entrepreneurs of Textile and Light Industry Council and apparel exports of India (AEPC). A cooperation agreement provides, inter alia, exchange of technology and know-how in textile production. For this purpose, a special Commission on Affairs textile (Textile Communication Committee). Counter-terrorism techniques are also in place between Russia and India. President Vladimir Putin was guest of honour at Republic Day celebration on 26 January, 2007. The year 2008 was declared by both countries as the Russia-India Friendship Year. Bollywood films are quite popular in Russia. The Indian public sector oil company ONGC bought Imperial Energy in 2008. In December 2008, during new President

Medvedev's visit to New Delhi, India and Russia signed a nuclear energy co-operation agreement. In March, 2010, Russian Prime Minister Vladimir Putin signed an additional 19 pacts with India which included civilian nuclear energy, space and military co-operation and the final sale of Admiral Gorshkov (Aircraft Carrier) along with MiG-29K fighter jets. M1G aircraft were destroyed and many of our men had died in the crashes. We have taken up the issue with Russia. If these fighters do not suit us, India must stop their purchase from Russia. The aircraft of Dassault could be more suitable. In sum, India is a key ally of Russia.

India's Policy towards Kazakhastan, Uzbekistan, Slovania, Ukraine, Mongolia and Other States of Central Asia

India enjoys good relations with them. It has friendly policy towards all of them. It seeks more deeper commercial ties with them. Defence ties are not being sought. Diplomatic relations between India and Ukraine were established in January 1992. Indian Embassy in Kiev was opened in May 1992 and Ukraine opened its mission in New Delhi in February 1993. The Consulate General of India in Odessa functioned from 1962 till its closure in March 1999. India has an embassy in Belgrade. Serbia has an embassy in New Delhi and an honorary consulate in Chennai. India has an embassy in Ljubljana. Slovenia has an embassy in New Delhi.

India's Foreign Policy towards Africa

As of year 2011, India's total trade with Africa is over US$46 billion and total investment is over US$11 billion with US$5.7 billion line of credit for executing various projects in Africa.

India enjoys good relationships with most sub-Saharan African nations for most of its history. In the Prime Minister's visit to Mauritius in 1997, the two countries secured a deal to a new Credit Agreement of INR 10.5 crore (US$ 3.0 million) to finance import by Mauritius of capital goods, consultancy services and consumer durable from India. The government of India secured a rice and medicine agreement with the people of Seychelles. India continued to build upon its historically close relations with Ethiopia, Kenya, Uganda and Tanzania. Visits from political ministers from Ethiopia provided opportunities for strengthening bilateral cooperation between the two countries in the fields of education and technical training, water resources management and development of small industries. This has allowed India to gain benefits from nations that are generally forgotten by other Western Nations. The South African President, Thabo Mbeki has called for a strategic relationship between India and South Africa to avoid imposition by Western Nations. India continued to build upon its close and friendly relations with Angola, Botswana, Lesotho, Malawi, Mozambique, Namibia, Swaziland, Zambia and Zimbabwe. The Minister of Foreign Affairs arranged for the sending of Special Envoys to each of these countries during 1996–97 as a reaffirmation of India's assurance to strengthening cooperation with these countries in a spirit of South-South partnership. These relations have created a position of strength with African nations that other nations may not possess.

Foreign Policy towards Mauritius

The relations between India and Mauritius have existed since 1730 AD. But diplomatic relations were established in 1948, before Mauritius became an independent State. The relationship is very cordial due to cultural affinities and long historical ties that exist between the two nations. More than 68 percent of the Mauritian population are of the Indian origin, most commonly known as Indo-Mauritian. Economic and commercial cooperation has been increasing over the years. India has become Mauritius' largest source of imports since 2007 and Mauritius imported US$816 million worth of goods in the April 2010-March 2011 financial year. Mauritius has remained the largest source of FDI for India for more than a decade with FDI equity inflows totaling US$55.2 billion in the period April 2000 to April 2011. India and Mauritius cooperate in combating piracy which has emerged as a major threat in the Indian Ocean region and support India's stand against terrorism.

India's Foreign Policy towards Nigeria

India has close relations with this oil rich West African country. Twenty percent of India's crude oil needs are met by Nigeria.

India gets 40,000 barrels (per day) of oil from Nigeria. Trade, between these two countries stands at $875 million in 2005–2006. Indian companies have also invested in manufacturing, pharmaceuticals, iron ore, steel, information technology and communications, amongst other things. Both India and Nigeria are members of the Commonwealth of Nations, G-77 and NAM. The Nigerian President, Olusegun Obasanjo, was the guest of honour at the Republic Day parade in 1999. Prime Minister Manmohan Singh visited Nigeria in 2007 and addressed the Nigerian Parliament. Nigeria is under the grip of terror now-a-days. Indian leaders hope that things would turn out to be better for Nigerian peoples. A few untoward incidents occurred in India in which Nigerian students were allegedly involved. They were accused of carrying drugs to India. In our view, this should not be done by any African student or citizen, given that India is committed towards the overall growth of African nations.

Foreign Policy towards South Africa

India and South Africa, have always had strong relations even though India revoked diplomatic relations in protest to the apartheid regime in the mid 20th century. The history of British rule connects both lands. There is a large group of South Africans of Indian descent. Mahatma Gandhi, spent many years in South Africa, during this time, he fought for the rights of the ethnic Indians. Nelson Mandela was inspired by Gandhi. After India's independence, India strongly condemned apartheid, and refused diplomatic relations while apartheid was conducted as state policy in South Africa.

The two countries, now have close economic, political, and sports relationships. Trade between the two countries grew from $3 million in 1992–1993 to $4 billion in 2005–2006, and aim to reach trade of $12 billion by 2010. One third of India's imports from South Africa comprise gold bullion. Diamonds that are mined from South Africa are polished in India. Nelson Mandela was awarded the Gandhi Peace Prize. The two countries are also members of the IBSA Dialogue Forum, with Brazil. India hopes to get large amounts of uranium, from resource rich South Africa, for India's growing civilian nuclear energy sector.

International Territorial Disputes

India's territorial disputes with neighbouring Pakistan and People's Republic of China have played a crucial role in its foreign policy. India is also involved in minor territorial disputes with neighbouring Bangladesh, Nepal and Maldives. India currently maintains two manned stations in Antarctica but has made some unofficial territorial claims, which are yet to be clarified.

Major International Disputes India Must Resolve

India is involved in the following international disputes (these are affecting our global position and foreign policy doctrine):

1. Bangladesh:

The 6.5-kilometre-long border between India and Bangladesh remains to be demarcated. The discussion is on with Bangladesh to exchange 162 minuscule enclaves between two nations.

2. Nepal:

Kalapani village of India is claimed by Nepal and Nawalparasi district of Nepal is claimed by India. The dispute between India and Nepal involves about 29 square miles of area in Kalapani, where China, India and Nepal meet. Indian forces occupied the area in 1962 after China and India had fought their bitter war. Three villages are located in the disputed zone of Kuti, Gunji and Knabe. India and Nepal disagree about how to interpret the Sugauli treaty (1816 AD) between the British East India Company and Nepal which delimited the boundary along the Maha Kali River (Sarda in India). The dispute intensified in 1997 as the Nepalese Parliament considered a treaty on hydroelectric development of the river. India and Nepal differ as to which stream constitutes the source of the river. Nepal considers the Limpiyadhura as the source. India claims it is the Lipu Lekh. Nepal has tabled a map of 1856 from the British India Office to support its position. The countries have held several meetings about the dispute and discussed to resolve the issue. The Indo-Nepalese dispute was aggravated in 1962 due the war between China and India. The disputed area lies near the Sino-Indian frontier.

3. British Indian Ocean Territories:

There is a dispute over the British Indian Ocean Territories and Coco Islands with former colonial powers. India regards these islands as part of its Lakshadweep Indo-sphere strategy as part of its oceanic vicinity of its sovereignty and a threat to its integrity of its emerging geopolitical might and does not recognize the Crown's rule over these Indian islands.

4. Maldives:

Maldives claims that Minicoy Island is Maldivian, although there is no official Maldivian claim to this atoll. In addition, Maldives and India have made arrangements to allow Maldivians to travel directly to Minicoy without any visa. The Framework Agreement on Cooperation for Development, which was signed by former Maldivian President Mohamed Nasheed and the former Indian Prime Minister, Dr. Manmohan Singh, during his recent visit to the Maldives, includes an article on establishing a transport network between the Maldives and Minicoy. The earlier policy required Maldivians to get a visa from New Delhi before boarding a ferry en route to Minicoy from Kochi (India). The Government of the Maldives has stressed that the ferry service must be established between Kulhudhuffushi in Haa Dhaal atoll and that Minicoy will also allow cargo to be transported between the Maldives and Minicoy. President Nasheed also expressed hope to start a regular passenger cargo ferry service between the Maldives and Minicoy in the near future.

5. Pakistan:

The unresolved Kashmir dispute and the status of Kashmir with Pakistan, India claims the disputed territories in Pakistan known as Azad Kashmir and Gilgit Baltistan while Pakistan disputes India's administration of Jammu and Kashmir. There is also a dispute over Sir Creek and the maritime boundary regarding the Rann of Kuchchh area of India. Water-sharing problems with Pakistan over the Indus River (Wular Barrage) are also a key area of concern. Further, the Indus Water Treaty is to be renewed; it must support both nations. Finally, the international border with Pakistan has not been defined in Siachen Glacier. That task was left uncompleted during the 1950s.

6. People's Republic of China:

India claims Aksai Chin and Trans-Karakoram Tract as part of Jammu and Kashmir. China claims most of Arunachal Pradesh, a disputed territory of north-eastern India, by not recognizing the McMahon Line. Two regions are claimed by both India and China as their own. Aksai Chin is in the disputed territory of Kashmir, at the junction of India, Tibet and Azad Kashmir. India claims the 38,000-square-kilometre territory, currently administered by China, as its own area. India also considers the cessation of Saksham Valley to China by Pakistan as illegal and considers its part of its own territory. Arunachal Pradesh is a state of India in the country's northeast, bordering Bhutan, Burma and China; it was called NEFA earlier. Though it is under Indian administration, China calls this 90,000-square-kilometre area as South Tibet. The boundary between North Indian states of Himachal Pradesh and Uttarakhand with China's Tibet has not been properly demarcated; some portions of this region are under the administration of India.

Latest Determinants of the Foreign Policy of India

They are as follows:

1. Make in India and Defence Production Independence: PM Modi's slogan "Make in India" has received good responses from all circles. Note that the DRDO has 53 research centres all over the country. There are 39 ordnance factories dotted across India. There are four full-fledged dockyards in India that can make latest naval vessels. They make clothes, tents, minor ammunition and light weapons for armed forces. India is making 40 percent of its defence material requirements. It is importing the rest from outside. We do not have world class submarines, heavy fighter choppers and fine guns like AB Bofors. If India has to start making 70 percent of its defence material needs, it must invest heavily in the defence sector. Mr., Uday Bhaskar, a defence analyst, has stated that the target of 70 percent in-house production is difficult but not impossible to achieve. It would take nearly 15 years to achieve this target, defence experts aver. Thus, India

must invite the private sector for making defence equipment and ammunition. Thus, the government has risen to the occasion by extending the limit of equity participation by the private sector from 24 percent to 49 percent. Thus, the private sector would play a key role in India's defence quarters. This would affect our foreign policy because we would import less equipment and arsenal. Then, we would import the advanced technologies alone. Manufacturing would be done in India. The Indian entrepreneurs would work under the control and technical guidance of the armed forces and nine PSUs that are already making defence equipment and weapons. We have imported equipment and ammunition from the USA, France, Russia and Israel. The Westland helicopter deal was vital for us but we lost it because of corruption in our own house. We cannot depend on Tejas, the LCA developed by DRDO because of its poor performance. We do not have good submarines either. China has 65 submarines and we have only 30-plus. Indigenous technology is not dependable, hence there is a need to import technologies from abroad. India should make 50 percent of its defence arsenal at home and import the rest from abroad. Then, after ten years, it should change its policy of import of tangible equipment. Then, it should import only technologies and make nearly 80 percent of equipment and army supplies at home. The private sector from abroad should also be allowed to participate in the defence production activities of India.

2. Pakistan is a Nuisance: Sadly, nothing can be done to stop Pakistan from disturbing our north-western border. Our policy of defence against Pakistani shelling must continue. The Kashmir imbroglio does not have any solution, as of now.
3. China is Not a Friend: We cannot trust China either. Pakistan and China work together to destabilize India. China works covertly. Pakistan works overtly. This is a strategy of grinding the enemy between two stones, one hot and the other cool. India must see through this trick. Border disputes are vital for the stability of south Asia. Pakistan

and China must change their old stances. Currently, this does not seem to be happening. Our China policy must take care of its past record.

4. Middle East Is Burning and India Is Losing Business: Instead of taking sides with any sect, India must request the players to create peace and settle their mutual differences. They are not likely to listen to Indian demands. But India has to send its engineers, nurses, managers, businessmen, teachers and students to Gulf countries. Our revenues are suffering due to war in the Gulf. We are also not able to go to Libya, Lebanon, Jordan and Egypt because of volatile situations there. We must mend walls with every nation of Asia and Africa to ensure that we are able to send our workers there (when battles come end in those war theatres). Primarily, we are working hard to become a growing economy, not a strategic super power. Our defence abilities or ambitions are not signals of our growing lust for power but they are our minimal deterrents for thwarting the attempts of enemies to enslave us. Hence, we must not lose sight of happenings in the Gulf. We mean business and must not forget that when the region becomes peaceful, our people would go there to work, yet again.

Foreign Economic Policy of India

Indian economy has grown three-fold since 2000. The economy is growing at 4.5 percent per annum. The BJP government claims that by the end of 2015, the economy would grow at the rate of 6.5 percent or more. These are theoretical assumptions, though. Stock markets are doing well. The RBI has changed the base year, for the purpose of judging the GDP growth rate and other vital economic indicators, as 2011-12. Thus, as per calculations done by Shri Arun Jaitley, India's Finance Minister, the GDP growth rate is 6.5 percent or so at present.

In October-December quarter of 2014, India registered a growth rate of 7.5 percent in GDP; it was the highest in the world. In 2014-15, the growth rate in GDP is likely to be 7.5 percent (if we take 2011-12 as the base year for calculation. This value was 6.9 percent in 2013-14. This would help the RBI get clear pictures of economy in the current chaotic scenario. This may also boost our global image as an exporter whose economy is fine-tuned to the needs of the new era.

FIIs have started bringing money back to India. Industrial growth rate is dismal but not negative. The unemployment rate is high. Petrol and diesel prices have been slashed due to the global oil recession. Last time, they were slashed in the first week of February 2015. However, the government did not give full benefit of oil price slide to ultimate consumers. The government has not transferred the entire benefit of this fall to ultimate customers. That is because the government is building buffers of a huge kind so that when prices rise in international markets, it would not increase prices of petrol and diesel. That way, common people would not suffer and buffer funds would take care of the losses being incurred by oil marketing companies. This is the domestic scene in 2015. Let us review the foreign economic policy of our country now. Modi has given the slogan "Make in India." It is not a bad idea and we have mentioned this concept elsewhere in this volume as well. However, we talked to experts in economy and global relations. They averred that China's policy of "Make in China" had ended in a whimper. China is suffering due to low production, rising prices, unemployment and the lack of new infrastructure projects. It was making cheap goods at home but today, there are no buyers left to lift its stocks. Then, experts asked the author, how can Modi succeed by making goods in India? Would we be able to consume all stocks that we produce under this policy? The experts also told the author that the concept of "Make in India" should be applied more to service production, not to product production. Currently, Indian economy is based on product creation, not on service creation. American economy is service-based. Our economy is partly service based (which is low percentage in the economy) and majority of its bedrock is tangible goods production (which is a high percentage in the economy). We would have to bring drastic changes in our infrastructure to make our economy predominantly service based. India's exports are not rising at the speed at which its imports are rising. The RBI has not changed its rapo rate or interest rate. It wants the economy to remain afloat on its own. Our imports have become liberal in the last five-odd years. Oil prices have gone down, so our economy has received a big boost in the last few months of 2014. The export outlook of 2015 is very positive. We can export our products and services at low rates if oil prices remain low in 2015. However, problems in Middle East and Africa can hurt our exports. These regions demand weapons, not rice. We do not export arms and ammunition. Hence, we are supposed to explore new markets for our traditional agricultural products. We must also export technology and technical services. Currently, we are not exporting much of technology or engineering goods. The reason could be our poor-grade technologies and products, which do not fetch nice prices abroad. Hence, India must invest in R&D and become highly innovative like other advanced nations of the world. Rural areas are potential export houses of our country. Industrial machines can be made in small towns and export processing zones. Further, we are partners in the BRICS, G-20, ASEAN and SAARC. We must use these regional forums to enhance our exports. Finally the concept of "Make in India" should also include the tenet of production and supply of services at home. We must also export services like education, railway engineering, management consultancy, satellite propulsion into space, exploration of oil in various parts of the world etc. We are giving many of such services but our impetus should be on technical services. Our technical manpower is the largest in terms of number.

After inflation, it is the time of deflation to enter India. Low oil prices and quite reasonable wholesale price indices have helped Indian consumers to the hilt. They are out in the markets to buy things and services because they have much more disposable incomes than before. This rising spending on FMCGs and durable goods would give a fillip to our economy. Modi's arrival has augured well for Indian economy. This trend is likely to continue. We have been informed that there is a big surge in the sales and revenues of publishing industry of India; this news was picked up by us in February 2015. Similarly, economic outlooks of other sectors are also healthy.

In February 2015, the Government of India completed its enquiry about the foreign bank accounts of 350 Indians. A total of 1195 Indians have accounts in the Swiss branch of the HSBC, the government revealed in the last week of December 2014. They own more than 25000 crore INR in those accounts. The names of Annu Tandon, Anil Ambani, Mukesh Ambani, Harsimrat Kaur and many others were revealed by the media. The enquiry is still going on. The HSBC office in Switzerland was raided in February 2015. The bank was accused of colluding with its Indian clients who avoided paying taxes and other charges to the Indian government. Obviously, if this money was not earned through proper export procedures (which was really the case in some accounts), it must have been given to these people through illicit means. This is black money (in most of the accounts being scrutinized). This bank and accused Indians are guilty due to *prima facie* evidences. Mr. Shanti Bhushan of the Aam Aadmi Party stated in February 2015 that mere declarations about these accounts would not suffice. He added that court cases must be filed against these persons because they had betrayed India and Indian economy, even as they knew well that they were not supposed to amass huge fortunes in illegal ways. Thus, it is hoped that a huge chunk of this money would come to India. This event disproves that myth that the Indians are poor. Thus, we confirm that slightly more than ten percent of Indian people are superrich. Had they earned their millions through legal means, we, as Indians, would have become proud. But they would lose huge parts of their wealth. That way, the Indian NRIs and businessmen may not like to invest in India. Let us hope that the government does not act harshly to clean up this mess. The return of this capital to India would make it very powerful in economic terms. Our image as a dirty businessman would also be established abroad. These pros and cons are always part of trade. Now, the World Bank would ask, "You have stashed millions in the Swiss accounts. Why are you demanding loan or dole from us?" But we have an answer—this money belongs to only ten-odd percent of the masses. The rest of Indians are quite poor and still facing the brunt of unemployment, resource shortage, market uncertainty and inflation. In our view, PM Modi must take a liberal view about this wealth. We agree that these businessmen have made huge mistakes and that such acts of money laundry are deemed crimes against the Indian nation. But the system can be cleaned up and these accounts can still be maintained in Swiss banks. All these businessmen have to do is clean up their conscience and do fair dealings in the future. That would help boost our image abroad as a neat and clean business nation. Currently, we are plausibly the most corrupt nation on the earth. We should change this *status quo* if we want to make India a respectful nation. All Indians are responsible for taking up this noble task. It is very difficult, though not impossible, to be honest.

Conclusion

India is a weak tiger with sharp claws. It has absolutely failed to deal with the State-sponsored terror of Pakistan. Its soldiers and civilians are dying or getting hurt almost every day. On January 1, 2015, a Pakistani boat came towards India with tones of explosives. It was intercepted but the Pakistanis destroyed it on high seas, off the coast of Porbander. Our army personnel and villagers die almost every day at the Indo-Pakistani border due to shelling and firing by Pakistani rangers. Pakistan is burning due to Shiite-Sunni clashes. Bomb blasts occur in its mosques almost every day. Terror groups operate freely in that country. The government of Pakistan keeps differentiating between good and bad terror elements but is not able to save even its children from such people. Thus, Pakistani rulers or terror elements continue to attack India every now and then to divert the attention of the world from the internal chaos of that country. In the wake of recent happenings, we suggest that India take up the Kashmir issue at the United Nations in an official way. India must stake its claim on Kashmir on the plea that we have been living there since times immemorial. Pakistan was created in 1947. It cannot stake its claim on a territory that is religiously and emotionally linked to India. India, an old nation by all norms, is stable and peaceful. It has accommodated even those militants in its territory who are against its policies. We can quote the examples of Maoists, Naxalites, Kashmiri militants, the SIMI and other organizations in this context. The government talks to these groups and tries to find out how solutions can be chalked out. The government does not act in an autocratic manner. It does not send the army to destroy these groups. True, clashes take place in all parts of the country and terror elements are also killed by police and paramilitary jawans in encounters. But our jawans are also ambushed in various encounters by these terror groups. Then, how can the armed forces, who have been the duty to protect this land mass, remain idle when they are being shot at and ambushed daily? Talks must be conducted and they are being conducted every now and then. The problem is that insurgents do not want to take up democratic courses to resolve problems. Add to it the support of arms and money by China and Pakistan. Thus, our home terror problem is no longer a domestic issue. It has become an international issue. Our foreign policy with respect to Pakistan and China is not stern. We go to these countries, indulge in some sweet nothings and come back. China and Pakistan are supporting many terror groups of India. They also have hold over a major Kashmiri territory. India has not been able to get that territory from them. It sends troops and police to defend people and armed forces. Had this country been ruled by Idi Amin, all terror groups would have been destroyed within a month! Our Constitution is based on peace and human dignity. We are not a terror State but Pakistan really is.

Another plea in favour of our claim over Kashmir is that Indian armed forces and civilians have given so much sacrifices for the sake of Kashmir that its only compensation should be the unconditional return of all Kashmiri territories under Chinese and Pakistani control to India. China also has 5,180 square kilometers of the Kashmiri territory under its control. Pakistan also has some part of Kashmir under its control. We should not lose even a square inch of Kashmir to any country because our religious beliefs, sacrifices made over the last 65 years and centuries-old tolerance naturally make Kashmir the crown in India's glory. India must take up this issue in the UNO and lobby for its release from clutches of Pakistan and China.

Every nation is involved with every other nation in commercial, political and social terms. Even Russia would not help us if an Indo-China war breaks out. Even China did not help Pakistan in 1999 when India and Pakistan went to war in Kargil. The realities of recession and regional stability are very harsh. We cannot expect loans and investments from China in one inhale and ask for battle tanks from Russia (against China) in the following exhale.

Our proximity with the USA has irked both Pakistan and Russia in just one go. Thus, our old friend, Russia, is not happy because of the super successful tour of President Obama to India in January 2015. Mrs. Sushma Swaraj, our Foreign Minister went to China in February 2015 and took part in bilateral and trilateral negotiations (with Russia). We are superficially mending our walls with China. Real issues remain as such. Our economy must grow at the rate of 8 percent per annum or more. If this is to be done, all border disputes must be settled. Further, all terror groups must be reined in to create a peaceful climate in all parts of the country. Then, industry and business doyen should use their manpower, technologies and money to allow various parts of the country. These plans are only on paper for the governments of states and union. We have a long way to go. We have only started our journey and many challenges face us, some of them pretty harsh to the core.

India has military power, economic strength and technological prowess. But it has not been able to exert its influence even in its south-Asian region in the past decade, leave alone the global arena. Indian leaders have proved weak, although they are diplomatic and wise to the core. We do not underestimate the diplomatic strength of any government or political party. However, we must contend that India must resolve all of its pending disputes with its neighbours. Then alone, can it become a major power of the world.

Finally, as already stated, PM Modi should be fair towards our businessmen who had stashed millions in a Swiss bank of the HSBC. These people should be told to deposit some parts of this wealth in India so that our economy may get the benefit of this big amount. According to the Press and TV, a total wealth of more than 25,000 crore INR has been deposited in the Swiss branch of the HSBC (in the names of 1195 Indians only). The businessmen must be allowed to maintain their Swiss bank accounts without hassles. We also expect them to be more transparent and honest in the future. They can pay the fines and other dues to the Indian government and come out clean from this shabby racket.

Foreign Policy of the EU Is Superb, Economically and Technologically

CHAPTER 11

Introduction

European integration goes on and the European Union is increasingly being seen as a great power in its own right. It has representation at the WTO and at G8 and G-20 summits. This is most notable in areas where it has exclusive competence or economic prowess. It also reflects a non-traditional conception of Europe's role as a global civilian power, exercising collective influence in the functional spheres of trade and diplomacy, as an alternative to military dominance.

A Framework of Analysis for the EU

The European Union is a supranational union and not a sovereign state. It has limited scope in the areas of foreign affairs and defense policy. These remain with the member States of the European Union. EU has three great powers—France, Germany and the United Kingdom. Together, they are called EU Three.

EU Policy towards Palestine

Relations between the European Union and the Palestine Liberation Organization (PLO) were established in 1975 as part of the Euro-Arab Dialogue. The EU is a member of the Quartet and is the single largest donor of foreign aid to Palestinians.

The EU maintains an office in Ramallah, accredited to the PNA. The PLO's general delegation in Brussels, accredited to the EU was first established as an information and liaison bureau in September 1976. Other representations are maintained in almost every European capital, many of which have been accorded complete diplomatic status. In western Europe, Spain was the first country granting diplomatic status to a PLO representative, followed by Portugal, Austria, France, Italy and Greece. EU has insisted that it will not recognize any changes to the 1967 borders other than those agreed between the parties. Israel's settlement program has therefore led to some tensions and EU considers these settlements illegal.

In July 2009, EU foreign policy chief called for the United Nations to recognize the Palestinian state by a set deadline even if a settlement had not been reached. The official said that the mediator has to set the timetable. If the parties are not able to stick to it, then a solution backed by the global community should be put on table. After a fixed deadline, a UN Security Council resolution can accept the Palestinian state as a full member of the UN and set a calendar for implementation, the chief had concluded.

In 2011, the Palestinian government called on the EU to recognize the State of Palestine in a United Nations resolution scheduled for September 20. EU member States were divided over the issue. Some, including Spain, France and the United Kingdom, stated that they might recognize Palestine if talks did not make any progress. Others, including Germany and Italy, refused to oblige. Ms. Catherine Ashton said that the EU position would depend upon the words of this proposal.

EU Policy towards South Africa

South Africa has strong cultural and historical links with European Union, particularly through immigration from the Netherlands, the United Kingdom, Germany, France and Greece. The EU is South Africa's biggest investor.

Since the end of South Africa's apartheid-based policies, EU-South Africa relations have flourished. They began a Strategic Partnership in 2007. In 1999, the two sides had signed a Trade, Development and Cooperation Agreement (TDCA) which entered into force in 2004, with some provisions being applied from 2000. The TDCA covered a wide range of issues from political cooperation, development and the formation of a free trade area.

South Africa is the EU's largest trading partner in Southern Africa and has a FTA with the EU. South Africa's main exports to the EU are fuels and mining products (27 percent), machinery and transport equipment (18 percent) and other semi-manufactured goods (16 percent). However they are growing and becoming more diverse. European exports to South Africa are primarily machinery and transport equipment (50 percent), chemicals (15 percent) and other semi-machinery (10 percent).

EU Policy towards the Caribbean Region

The independent countries of the Caribbean region (Namely the Caribbean Community (CARICOM) and Dominican Republic are known by the European Union as CARIFORUM (under the Lomé Convention and Cotonou Agreement). CARIFORUM makes up one of three parts of the African, Caribbean and Pacific Group of States. CARIFORUM remains the only region of the ACP to have concluded with the EU an Economic Partnership Agreement. Under the EPA, the EU maintains an active joint ACP–EU Joint Parliamentary Assembly.

EU Policy towards Latin America

The EU has been developing ties with other regional bodies such as the Andean Community and MERCOSUR, with plans for association agreements between the EU and the two other blocs under way to help trade, research, democracy and human rights. Chile and Mexico have an Association Agreement with the EU. A 2.6-billion euro financial package for Latin America was also put forward with 840-million euro for Central America. A major forum for European relations with Latin America is the Latin America, the Caribbean and the European Union Summit, a biannual meeting of heads of state and government held since 1999.

EU Policy towards the USA

The European Union and the United States have held diplomatic relations since 1953. The relationship between the EU and the US is a major relation. They are the biggest economic and military powers in the world. But the EU does not have a common defence policy. They dominate global trade. They play key roles in international political relations. But they have regularly disagreed with each other on a wide range of specific issues. In the past, they had different political, economic and social agendas. Understanding the relationship today amounts to reviewing developments that predate the creation of the European Economic Community.

Both the United States and European Union had an arms embargo against China (PRC) in 2005. It was installed in 1989 after the events of Tiananmen Square. The US and some EU members continue to support the ban but others, headed by France, have been attempting to persuade the EU to lift the ban. They contend that more effective measures can be imposed. The trade relations between China and certain EU states are the major factor that would lift this embargo. The US strongly opposes this and after the PRC passed an anti-secession law against Taiwan (PRC), the likelihood of the ban being lifted reduced.

EU Policy towards Australia

Australia and the European Union (EU) have strong historical and cultural ties. The two have solid relations and increasingly see eye-to-eye on international issues. The EU-Australian relations are founded on a Partnership Framework, first agreed in 2008. It covers not just economic relations, but broader political issues and cooperation.

The EU is Australia's second largest trading partner, after China and Australia is the EU's seventeenth. Australia's exports are dominated by mineral and agricultural goods. It has stopped mining and exporting gold. Nearly 37 percent of trade is in commercial services, especially in transportation and travel. EU corporations have a strong presence in Australia (2360) with an estimated turnover of €200 billion (more than 14 percent of total sales in Australia). These companies directly created 5,00,000 jobs in Australia. The EU is Australia's second largest destination of overseas investment and the EU is by far Australia's largest source of foreign investment € 2.8 billion in 2009 (€11.6 billion in 2008). Trade was growing but ebbed in 2009 due to the global financial crisis.

EU Policy towards China

The EU is China's largest trading partner and China is the EU's second largest trading partner. Most of this trade is in industrial and manufactured goods. Between 2009 and 2010 alone EU exports to China increased by 38 percent and China's exports to the EU increased by 31 percent. However there are sources of tension, such as human rights and the EU's arms embargo on China. Both the United States and the European Union as of 2005 have an arms embargo against the PRC, put in place in 1989 after the events of Tiananmen Square. The US and some EU members continue to support the ban but others, spearheaded by France, have been attempting to persuade the EU to lift the ban, arguing that more effective measures can be imposed, but also to improve trade relations between the PRC and certain EU states. The US strongly opposes this, and after the PRC passed an anti-secession law against Taiwan the likelihood of the ban being lifted diminished somewhat.

There have been some disputes, such as the dispute over textile imports into the EU (see below). China and the EU are increasingly seeking cooperation, for example China joined the Galileo project investing € 230 million and has been buying Airbus planes in return for a construction plant to be built in China; in 2006 China placed an order for 150 planes during a visit by the French President. Also, despite the arms embargo, a leaked US diplomatic cable suggested that in 2003 the EU sold China € 400 million of defence exports and later, other military grade submarine and radar technology.

Interest in closer relations started to rise as economic contacts increased and interest in a multi-polar system grew. Although initially imposing an arms embargo on China after Tiananmen (see arms embargo section below), European leaders eased off China's isolation. China's growing economy became the focus for many European visitors and Chinese businessmen began to make frequent trips to Europe. Many Chinese have settled in Europe and are doing roaring businesses there. Europe's interest in China led to the EU becoming unusually active with China during the 1990s with high-level exchanges. The EU-Chinese trade increased faster than the Chinese economy itself, becoming three times in ten years (from US$ 14.3 billion in 1985 to US$ 45.6 billion in 1994).

Political and security co-operation was hampered with China seeing little chance of headway there. Europe was leading the desire for NATO expansion and intervention in Kosovo, which China opposed as it saw them as extending US influence. However by 2001 China moderated its anti-US stance in the hopes that Europe would cancel its arms embargo but pressure from the US led to the embargo remaining in place. Due to this, China saw the EU as being too weak, divided and dependent on the US to be a significant power. Furthermore, it shared too many of the US' concerns about China's authoritarian system and threats of force over Taiwan. Even in the economic sphere, China was angered at protectionist measures against its exports to Europe and the EU's opposition to giving China the status of market economy in order to join the WTO.

Economic cooperation continued, with the EU's New Asia Strategy, the first Asia–Europe Meeting in 1996, EU-China summit (1998) and frequent policy documents desiring closer partnerships with China. Although the 1997 Asian Financial Crisis dampened investors enthusiasm, China weathered the crisis well and continued to be a major focus of EU trade. Trade in 1993 saw a 63 percent increase from the previous year. China became Europe's fourth largest trading partner at this time. Even following the financial crisis in 1997, the EU-Chinese trade increased by 15 percent in 1998.

The EU Policy towards India

India was one of the first countries to develop relations with the Union, signing bilateral agreements in 1973, when the United Kingdom joined. The most recent cooperation agreement was signed in 1994 and an action plan was signed in 2005. As of April 2007 the Commission is pursuing a free trade agreement with India.

The Union is India's largest trading partner, accounting for 20 percent of Indian trade. However, India accounts for only 1.8 percent of the EU's trade and attracts only 0.3 percent of European Foreign Direct Investment. But it still is India's largest external financial resource. During 2005 the EU-India trade grew at the rate of 20.3 percent.

A controversy had started in 2006 when the Indian Mittal Steel Company sought to take over the Luxembourg-based steel company, Arcelor. The approach met with opposition from France and Luxembourg. But it was passed by the Commission which stated that it was judging it on competition grounds only.

Mittal finally took over Arcelor. Now, Mittal-Arcelor is the largest steel conglomerate in the world.

The European Union (EU) and India agreed on September 29 2008 (at the EU-India summit in Marseille) France's largest commercial port, to expand their cooperation in the fields of nuclear energy and environmental protection and deepen their strategic partnership. French President Nicolas Sarkozy, the EU's rotating president, said at a joint press conference at the summit that "EU welcomes India, as a large country, to engage in developing nuclear energy, adding that this clean energy will be helpful for the world to deal with the global climate change." Sarkozy also said the EU and Indian Prime Minister Manmohan pledged to accelerate talks on a free trade deal and expected to finish the deal by 2009. The Indian prime minister was also cautiously optimistic about cooperation on nuclear energy. "Tomorrow we have a bilateral summit with France. This matter will come up and I hope some good results will emerge out of that meeting", Singh said when asked about the issue. Singh said that he was "Very satisfied" with the results of the summit. He added that EU and India have "Common values" and the two economies are complementary to each other. In 2013, EU came up with new programmes for India. We are trying to buy fighter aircraft from Dassault (France). We had got Sea Harriers from Britain in the past.

The European Commission President, José Manuel Barroso, delineated the joint action plan on adjustments of EU's strategic partnership with India. He stated that the two sides will strengthen cooperation on world peace and safety, sustainable development, cooperation in science and technology and cultural exchanges.

EU Policy towards Japan

The EU and Japan share values of democracy, human rights and market economics. Both are global actors and cooperate in international forums. They also cooperate in each other's regions: Japan contributes to the reconstruction of the western Balkans and the EU supports international efforts to maintain peace in Korea and the rest of Asia.

The EU-Japan relationship is anchored on two documents: the Joint Declaration of 1991 and the Action Plan for EU-Japan Cooperation of 2001. There are also many forums between the two, including an annual summit of leaders and an inter-parliamentary body. Both sides have now agreed to work towards a deep and comprehensive free trade agreement. Four agreements have been signed by the two sides. They are as follows:

1. The EU-Japan Mutual Recognition Agreement (entered force on January 1, 2002).
2. An Agreement on Co-operation on Anti-competitive Activities (adopted June 16, 2003).
3. A Science and Technology Agreement between the EU and Japan (signed on November 30, 2009).
4. The Agreement on Co-operation and Mutual Administrative Assistance (enforced on February 1, 2008).

Japan is the EU's sixth largest export market (3.2 percent in 2010 with a value of 44 billion). EU exports are primarily in machinery and transport equipment (31.3 percent), chemical products (14.1 percent) and agricultural products (11.0 percent). Despite a global growth in EU exports, since 2006 EU exports to Japan have been declining slightly. In 2009, due to the global financial crisis, exports saw a 14.7 percent drop; however in 2010 they recovered again by 21.3 percent. Japan is also the 6th largest source of imports to the EU (4.3 percent in 2010 with a value of €65 billion). Japanese exports to Europe are primarily machinery and transport equipment (66.7 percent). The EU is Japan's third largest trading partner (11.1 percent of imports, 13.3 percent exports). Trade in commercial services were to the tune of €17.2 billion from the EU to Japan and to the tune of €12.7 billion from Japan to the EU.

The trade relationship has been characterized by strong trade surpluses for Japan; it has reduced in 2000s. Doing business and investing in Japan can be difficult for European countries and there have been some trade disputes between the two parties. The slowdown in the Japanese economy encouraged it to open up more to EU business and investments. While working on reducing trade barriers, the main focus is on opening up investment flows.

The EU Policy towards South Korea

The Republic of Korea (South Korea) and the European Union (EU) are important trade partners: Korea is the EU's ninth largest trading partner and the EU is Korea's second largest export market. The two have signed a free trade agreement which will be provisionally applied by the end of 2011.

The first EU-South Korea agreement was the Agreement on Co-operation and Mutual Administrative Assistance in Customs Matters (signed on May 13, 1997). This agreement allows sharing of competition policy between two parties. The second agreement, the Framework Agreement on Trade and Co-operation (enacted on 1 April, 2001). The framework attempts to increase co-operation on several industries, including transport, energy, science and technology, industry, environment and culture.

In 2010, the EU and Korea signed a new framework agreement and a FTA which is the EU's first FTA with an Asian country and removes virtually all tariffs and many non-tariff barriers. On the basis of this, the EU and Korea decided in October 2010 to upgrade their relationship to a Strategic Partnership. These agreements will be provisionally in force by the end of 2011.

EU-Korea summits have taken place in 2002 (Copenhagen), 2004 (Hanoi) and 2006 (Helsinki) on the sidelines of ASEM meetings. In 2009, the first stand alone bilateral meeting was held in Seoul. The European Parliament delegation for relations with Korea visits the country twice a year for discussions with their Korean counterparts. Meetings at foreign minister level take place at least once a year on the sidelines of the ASEAN regional forum meetings. But these meetings between the Korean foreign minister and the EU have occurred more frequently at G20 meetings and at other forums. Ad-hoc meetings between officials occur monthly.

The EU Policy towards ASEAN

There are annual meetings between the EU and the ASEAN Plus Three. But relations have been strained with Association of Southeast Asian Nations (ASEAN) since Burma (Myanmar) joined the group which is facing EU pressure over human rights abuses by its military regime. The European Union threatened to boycott an EU-ASEAN meeting when Myanmar was due to take over the presidency of ASEAN. Myanmar gave up the presidency. In April 2007, the Commission implemented a free trade agreement with ASEAN.

Latest Determinants of the Foreign Policy of the EU

They are as follows:

1. Greece Has Threatened to Exit the Euro: Greece was close to an exit from the Euro currency system in mid-February 2015. The finance ministers of the EU told Greece that financial support would not be given to Greece unless it requested for an extension of its existing bailout programme. This discussion was done in Brussels. The new Greek PM, Mr. Alexis Tsipras and the new Finance Minister, Mr. Yanis Varoufakis, refused to bow to the demands of EU. The current aid agreement would expire after February 2015. If Greece does not obey the EU, it would not get more money to survive. Then, it would run out of cash by the end of March 2015. That way, Tsipras would be deemed to have broken his election promise, which were the statements due to which his arrival as PM had been made possible. Alternatively, Tsipras can introduce a new Greek currency. Greece accused Joeroen Dijsselbloem of backtracking on an agreement he had made with Mr. Tsipras a week ago (in February 2015). Dijsselbloem hoped that Greece would extend the existing programme (and thus remain a member of the Euro system). The Greek government said that it was an absurd idea. If Greece leaves the Euro system of currency, it can spell disaster for entire Europe. Even with a new currency of its own, Greece cannot survive in financial terms. Thus, the EU would like to persuade PM Tsipras to come home. It would not be easy for the EU to retain Greece, though.
2. The EU Does Not Want the USA to Intervene in Ukraine: If the USA intervenes in the Ukraine-Russia conflict directly or indirectly, Russia would be irritated beyond compare. Germany and France do not want this to happen. Other EU nations are also against the idea of the US send-

ing arms, tanks and armed men to Ukraine to give decisive military support to Kiev.

3. Common Immigration Policy: The EU wants to devise a common immigration policy for all outsiders. Despite many internal voices of protests, the EU may become fully united on deciding one single policy for immigration.
4. War against Terror: The EU is united with the USA and NATO forces in war against terror. Much to the chagrin of European citizens, the recent attacks on offices and civilians have caused much more pain to the democratic fabrics of all EU nations. The acts of terror are being carried out despite the fact the INTERPOLE and various police departments of EU nations are quite efficient in handling sudden conspiracies. A new policy may have to be delineated to counter threats of terror.
5. **Relationships with Islamic Fortresses:** Saudi Arabia and Iran are the two opposite religious poles or Islamic fortresses of the world today. Europe has been affected due to the battles between these two countries. This is a war of ideologies and the EU cannot do much about it. The sympathy of Saudi Arabia for anti-Shia militancy was identified in leaked official American documents. The then US Secretary of State, Ms. Hillary Clinton, wrote in December 2009 in a cable released by Wikileaks. Thus, she wrote: "Saudi Arabia remains a critical financial support base for Al-Qaeda, the Taliban, the LeT in Pakistan and other terrorist groups. She went on to add that in so far as Saudi Arabia did act against Al-Qaeda, it was as a domestic threat and not because of its activities abroad. This policy may now be changing with the dismissal of Prince Bandar (of Saudi Arabia, who was retired from Saudi government only recently) as head of intelligence. But the change is very recent, still ambivalent and may be too late. The EU is victim of wars against terror as well as a middle party if the Shias and Sunnis clash on the European soil. Both ways, this peaceful continent is going to suffer. The EU may have to change its policies to counter these threats from outside.

Latest Foreign Economic Policy of the EU

The European Union has shown a negative growth rate of 2.1 percent in January 2015 (on a quarter to quarter basis). Therefore, despite herculean efforts of France, Britain and Germany on the economic front, other nations of the EU have let it down. Industrial growth is minimal in east Europe. West Europe has also faced the heat of recession. The oil market has plummeted to dollar 50 per barrel. Russian recession has also affected EU markets in an adverse manner. If Russia sells oil to EU, it gets Euros. It purchases a lot of things from the EU and Asia with this money. This cycle has been broken, primarily due to the oil glut. Further, political events of recent times have forced the EU to do away with its traditional policies. For example, Greece has voted in December 2014 and the results are yet to pour in. If Greece wants to opt out of EU and euro currency, this would not be a setback to EU. However, this exit would lead to speculations that Spain and Portugal, who suffered since the time they joined the Euro Zone, may also think along these lines. Only a few countries have gained after joining the Euro Zone. The recession in Greece, Portugal and Spain is attributed to the fact that they all had adopted the Euro as the common currency of Europe. Germany benefited from the Euro, not Greece, hence the dilly-dally attitude of the Greek peoples towards the Euro. Time would tell what the EU would do on the Euro front. Currently, at rupees 101 per Euro (January 2015), this currency is a hard international currency by any norm. It can compete against the US dollar and British pound Sterling. The cracks within the European Union indicate that EU economy is not a one set, as people from outside Europe visualize. They countries of the EU do not want to part with their respective currencies and economic mechanisms. A common EU policy for immigration and investment is being considered but for several years, it has not taken a final shape due to the cracks within the EU.

The EU cannot survive without the consent of Britain, France and Germany. Out of these three powerful nations, Germany is the only odd man out, the other two being traditional NATO allies. Hence, Britain and Germany may face each other even as they stake their claims for leading the unified Europe. The US would naturally support Britain. Germany may have to do some lobbying in Eastern Europe because it can get support from Balkan states, Turkey and traditional allies of Russia. Once the pauper states of Europe stand back on their feet, the process of merger of nations would star in the European continent. It is easier said than done though. That is because Britain would not like to lose its currency. The Euro did not suit many nations that adopted it. Thus, the Euro must be strengthened to make it a currency with credibility in global markets. Merger of nations would take place much later. Many nations still oppose the merger of all EU nations into one single nation. If that happens—again, we can only make an honest guess—the EU would become the most powerful entity next only to the United States.

Millions of dollars and Euros have been stashed by global business firms and persons in Swiss banks. The EU is a major beneficiary of this wealth. Many Indians have also kept their money in Swiss banks. The EU's financial prowess is a lesson for economically feeble nations like India. We should also have banks that could attract foreign capital. Currently, we have to do a lot of lobbying abroad to attract investments of FIIs and FDIs. This *status quo* must change because we cannot do much with foreign capital. It is sad to note that the investments of the EU and USA in China are much more than they are in India. Why does the EU not look at us from the investment viewpoint? Why are we not a hot destination for foreign business firms? The current spate of recession could have been overcome, had the EU invested its millions of dollars or euros in our business ventures and industrial empires. World's best cars are being made in Europe. But their numbers are far fewer than those of India. We are a promising global market but still our growth rate is mere five-odd percent per annum.

Conclusion: EU Could Be the New Pole

Our valued Cosmos readers must have taken the cue that Europe is a bone of contention between America and Russia. We have discussed the policies of all major powers. We have seen EU as only a commercial power, not a strategic power. If EU does not become a strategic power, supported by its members independently, it cannot come out of the shadows of Russia, the USA or any other military bloc. Japan is an economic power but not a strategic one. Pakistan is stronger than Japan today; and the Japanese understand this concept. Money is a power but military is a bigger power. Today, the crisis before EU is hunger of some of its members. A time would come when it would overcome this recession phase. In the future, the EU must start building its own defense systems, without taking Russia and US into account. This can happen only if EU bosses listen. After all, India has its own policies. No one dictates its foreign policies. China is also in the same league. If EU is integrating in economic terms, why cannot it have its own armed forces? If Britain, Sweden and France can deliver most modern war gadgets to the world, why cannot they state that they shall become part of a new strategic alliance? It could be the European Alliance or EUAL!

Foreign Policy of Japan

CHAPTER 12

Introduction

Japan is a major economic power, not a military power. It aspires to become a military power now. Shinzo Abe, the current Japanese premier, has decided to remove dirt off the Japanese traditional robe and make Japan a major power in the real sense of the world. Let us study how this Asian tiger, hitherto hibernating due to strong American influences, has decided to come out of the shadows of the West and create a new path for ensuring its global presence.

A Framework of Analysis for Japan

By 1990, Japan's foreign policy choices often challenged the leadership's tendency to avoid radical shifts and to rely on incremental adjustments. Although still generally supportive of close ties, including the alliance relationship with the United States, Japanese leaders were well aware of strong American frustrations with Japanese economic practices and Japan's growing economic power relative to US in world affairs. Senior United States leaders were calling upon Japanese officials to work with them in crafting "a new conceptual framework" for Japan-United States relations that would take account of altered strategic and economic realities and changes in Japanese and United States views about the bilateral relationship. The results of this effort were far from clear. Some optimistically predicted "a new global partnership" in which the United States and Japan would work together as truly equal partners in dealing with global problems. Pessimists predicted that negative feelings generated by the realignment in United States and Japanese economic power and persistent trade frictions would prompt Japan to strike out more on its own, without the "guidance" of the United States. Given the growing economic dominance of Japan in Asia, Tokyo was seen as most likely to strike out independently there first, translating its economic power into political and perhaps, eventually, military influence.

Still, the image of Japan as a "military dwarf" was in a sense ironic, as Japan had one of the biggest defense budgets in the world throughout the 1980s and 1990s and defense expenditure is one of the most frequently used indicators of military power. It also had very advanced naval and air self-defense capabilities.

The collapse of the Soviet Union and the growing preoccupation of its former republics and the East European nations with internal political and economic problems increased the importance of economic competition, rather than military power, to Japan. These formerly communist countries were anxiously seeking aid, trade, and technical benefits from the developed countries, such as Japan. The power of Japan's ally, the United States, was also seen by many as warning. The United States were forced to look increasingly to Japan and others to shoulder the financial burdens entailed in the transformation of former communist economies in Eastern Europe and other urgent international requirements that fall upon the shoulders of world leaders.

Japanese industries and enterprises were among the most capable in the world. High savings and investment rates and high-quality education solidified the international leadership of these enterprises during the mid- to late 1990s. Its economic power gave Japan a steadily growing role in the World Bank, the International Monetary Fund, and other international financial institutions. Investment and trade flows give Japan by far the dominant economic role in Asia, and Japanese aid and investment were widely sought after in other parts of the world. It appears to be only a matter of time before such economic power would be translated into greater political power. The crucial issue for the United States and many other world governments focuses on how Japan will employ this growing economic power.

Inside Japan, both elite and popular opinion expressed growing support for a more prominent international role, proportionate to the nation's economic power, foreign assistance, trade, and investment. But the traditional post–World War II reluctance to take a greater military role in the world remained. A firm consensus continued to support the 1960 Treaty of Mutual Cooperation and Security and other bilateral agreements with the United States as the keystones of Japan's security policy. However, Japanese officials were increasingly active in using their economic and financial resources in seeking a greater voice in international financial and political organizations and in shaping the policies of the developed countries toward international trouble spots, especially in Asia.

Role of Domestic Politics

General satisfaction in Japan with the peace and prosperity that had been brought to the country made it hard for opposition parties to garner much support for a radical move to the left in Japan's foreign policy. The collapse of communism in Eastern Europe and the widely publicized brutalities of communist regimes in Asia in the late 1980s further dampened popular Japanese interest in shifting foreign policy to the left.

Anti-terrorism as Part of the Japanese Foreign Policy

Japan, since the end of the WW-II has operated via a policy of pacifism and passivism. This began to change in the late eighties and early nineties, in tandem with a shift in national identity, as understood via a change in its conception of its international role as a great economic power. Among the major catalysts were a shift in Japan's national security objectives, and widespread criticism of its "cheque book diplomacy" policy during the first Gulf War. This shift, ultimately, moved Japan from the realm of pacifism into a more activist assertive power. It was characterized by increased participation in international and regional organizations (monetarily) and by increased participation in global Peace-Keeping operations and in conflict resolution more broadly, under the umbrella of the UN. Japan's anti-terrorism policy can be seen as a part of this broader foreign policy platform, as it stems from these large objectives. Its anti-terrorism policy is an integral part of its larger foreign policy objectives. They are: (a) the maintenance of the US/Japanese security alliance; (b) continual global peace and security; and finally, (c) moderate defence buildup. The last objective shows some concern for the US as it signals the beginning of a more independent Japan in the future. It hasn't resulted in any significant increase in Japanese independence from the US in terms of foreign policy formation.

Latest Move of Japan to Fight Terror

Japan has contributed US$ 15.5 million to fight terrorism in the Middle east and Africa. Earlier, the Japanese Finance Minister, Mr. Fumio Kishida, had pledged in Brussels that Japan would give US$ 7.5 million. But due to the harrowing deaths of Japan's two reporters, Mr. Kishida has doubled the amount he had pledged to give in Brussels. This announcement was made on February 17 2015. Thus, Japan is trying to acquire more power in the international circles to fight against forces of terror.

Abe's Term as PM

Shinzo Abe is the new PM of Japan. In the new government's agenda, the Diet would certainly like Japan to assume a more independent strategic role in the Asian Pacific Rim. Japan is likely to come out of the American shadow but this process would take time. Let us delve deeply into the concept of Japanese slavery now. When two atom bombs were dropped over Hiroshima and Nagasaki in 1945, the death and destruction were so harrowing that the Japanese military came to a halt. The Japanese masses cried their hearts out for those who had died or become lame due to the bombs and their after effects. Thus, Japan surrendered to Allied Powers. It became the *de facto* prisoner of the USA. Japan was a prize for Uncle Sam in the Second World War. Later, American occupiers drafted a constitution for Japan. That Constitution still rules Japan. In this Constitution, it was written that Japan would never indulge in military expansion or any acts of atrocity over fellow human beings. The Japanese, shocked by the vagaries of the War and also awestruck by the hell let loose on their brothers and sisters due to the two nuclear explosions, decided to stick to it. They have still been following this Constitution (in 2015) because their hearts had really transformed for the benefit of mankind. They wanted to remain peaceful citizens of the world. Note that Japanese Constitution was never amended.

In the meantime, the domineering policies of the USA for Japan proved during the seventies of the last century that Japan would have to remain under the thumb of Uncle Sam. Eventually, Japan became an electronics power to reckon with during the late seventies of the century gone by. Its technology made all peoples of the world bow their heads with respect towards the real Japanese intelligentsia. Thus, within the framework of that sheepish Constitution, Japan achieved the impossible in less than 50 years.

Today, Japanese PM, Shinzo Abe, talks of breaking loose from the American dominance. He declared on February 5, 2015 that Japan was ready to bring serious changes in its Constitution. In particular, Abe informed the Japanese Parliament that the Article 9 of Japanese Constitution, which bars Japan from using armed forces to resolve international disputes. If Article 9 is revised, Japan would have two benefits. Firstly, it would be able to send its troops against militant outfits around the world. Its two journalists were butchered mercilessly by militants in February 2015. It could not pay the ransom fee. This would not happen in Japan from the date on which its Constitution is altered. Secondly, it would also be able to put up a brave front against China, its traditional foe in boundary issues.

Thus, Japan has also decided to wear the mask of a major power in real sense of the world, experts opine. It was an economic power, not a major power because its military was in barracks, not in the war theatres of the world. Now, that *status quo* would change, much to the relief and ecstasy of the Japanese masses. If Article 9 alone is changed, Japanese forces would be able to move around the world to combat terror forces. Elections for the upper house of Diet would be held in the summer of 2016. Hajime Funada is a senior lawmaker of Shinzo Abe's party. He has been taken into confidence by Abe to implement this change in Constitution. If the Diet passes the amendment bill and if Article 9 is changed in favour of Japanese forces, this island nation would not look back. They have technology, money and machinery. They can surpass any power of the earth. That way, the total political scenario of the world would change. A likely change in the otherwise peaceful Constitution of Japan proves that people around the world would not put their hands on their cheeks if terror outfits strike them. Jordan, an Arab country, has taken the vow to eliminate terror outfits (we have mentioned that text in the chapter dedicated to the foreign policy of the USA, under the heading *The USA and Jordan*). Now, Japan is also on its way to freedom from terror of all kinds. Hence, we can observe that there is a growing resentment of countries against evil terror elements of the world.

Latest Determinants of the Foreign Policy of Japan

They are as follows:

1. A Decision to Come out of America's Shadow: If the Diet decides to break free from the American influence, Japan would become a very free and strong nation by all norms. The PM of Japan, Mr. Shinzo Abe, is trying his best to let that happen. If Japan has its own military policy, it would be able to make its own defence equipment. It would also be able to send its troops to fight against terror elements anywhere in the world. Combating terrorism has also come on the agenda of Japan only recently.
2. Japan Needs More Global Support for a New Land: The Pacific Ocean Rim is prone to tsunamis and earthquakes. Japan may ask for a huge land area in any safer part of the world. A safe country is a dream for every Japanese national. Nature has cause great damage to Japan's ecology and geography. On February 17, 2015, a minor Tsunami had hit northern Japan due to an undersea earthquake that had struck off the Pacific coast. The area of influence was the same as the one that had been hit by a killer tsunami in 2011. Note that more than half of Japanese economy was affected by the Tsunami of 2011. Japan's foreign policy would be dictated by its geographical agonies.
3. Economic Growth Rate Is Slow: A slow growth rate of Japanese economy would not change its foreign policy. That is because this is a yen- and dollar-rich nation and has superior technologies to ward off any challenge it faces.
4. Japan and Asia: The recent happenings in Asia would affect Japanese exports, especially the export of cars, technology and equipment. Japan wants to export to Asia

only if the latter is stable in political terms. Japan supports India on the latter's border dispute with China.

5. Japan and China are Not Friendly: Japan and China have centuries-old border issues to settle. China acts like a big brother in these disputes. Hence, Japan would like to devise a new policy to counter the evil-minded policies of China in border settlement mechanisms.
6. The UNSC Dream: If Japan becomes a major power by becoming a strategic partner of Russia and makes military equipment on its own, it can claim a seat in the UNSC. But it has a long way to go before it leaves its American shell and starts leading an independent existence. Note that all UNSC members have nuclear capabilities. Japan can acquire nuclear capabilities if it chooses to do the same.
7. Japan Cannot Fight against Terror Outfits on Its Own: That is because its war machinery was never built, post the Second World War. Thus, it may have to depend upon other major powers, especially Russia or India, to develop in strategic terms. It can make arms and ammunition. It can develop latest technologies in Electronic Warfare (EW), Guerilla Warfare (GW), Chemical Warfare (CW) and Satellite Warfare (SW). True, it would not like to step into the realm of Nuclear Warfare (NW) for the time being. Nevertheless, it has nuclear capabilities as well finest nuclear power plants on its soil. It can always lunge into this realm at any point of time due to its advanced technologies. But it has less military manpower to count on. Sixty-odd years of passive peace record have not made its soldiers strong enough to face the vagaries of GW or terror attacks. Thus, it would need the support of many nations to fight and win wars against terrorism.

Foreign Economic Policy of Japan

After coming out of the pangs of recession, the economy of Japan has finally running on the path of progress. In fact, Japan was not to be blamed for its poor performance since February 2008. That was because every country was going through a recession phase and Japan was no exception to this general trend. As the NYSE, Nikki and Hang Seng indices recovered in the end of January 2014 and as the Mumbai Sensex crossed the 27000-plus mark in February 2015, Japan also rose after a long economic slumber. Thus, in 2015, Japan is expected to bring out new electronic devices and gadgets that would be used by the entire world. The GDP growth rate will rise in that country, thanks to new ambitions for the year 2015. Oil prices fell and this augured well for Japanese car makers. Now, people are spending more on automobiles the world over. The Japanese have been giving liberal loans to India and other Asian nations. They have a very positive orientation towards India, it being the land of Holy Buddha. Japan has achieved a lot on technological fronts and its economy is also taking good shape in the year 2015. However, its islands are located in the Pacific Ocean Rim area. That is why it has to face the wrath of earthquakes and Tsunamis every year. In the last Tsunami, almost one half of its island was totally annihilated. But Japan is an economic superpower. Hence, it rebuilt the destroyed and submerged area once again. Nevertheless, its economy had received severe jolts due to the previous Tsunami.

Conclusion: Japan Is Rising

We expect Japan to become a major economic superpower and an independent country that would take its own decisions. It can become a military power if its changes its Article 9 of its Constitution. Given that Abe has been lobbying for this change in the media and at national forums, Japanese Constitution would get serious alterations most of which would empower it to become a major power of the world. It has not been able to play its military games in the war theatres of Europe and Asia. Two of its reporters were killed. It could not resolve its boundary disputes with China. Now, these conditions are likely to change in 2016 because the upper house of Diet goes to polls in that year. After the end of polls, Abe would certainly steer its country to a new era full of independence, self decision-making and prosperity.

Foreign Policy of Britain (UK)

CHAPTER 13

Introduction

The UK is one of the major powers of the world. Its monarchy had ruled over more than one half of the world during the past 700 years. If you believe, please be careful—the UK is still ruling nearly one half of the countries of this world, albeit indirectly. Its currency, the UK pound Sterling, is worth more than 100 Indian rupees. Its jaguar range of fighter aircraft is impeccably the most lethal of air forces in the world. It fought both World Wars and won. Its economy is based on sale of technology and defence equipment. The British rule the roost in education, research, defence production, economic growth and above all, political influence and manipulation. Although a small nation by all means, Great Britain is one of the few players of the world that can change the history of the world at any point of time.

A Framework of Analysis for the UK

King John had signed **Magna Carta** in 1600 AD. Since then, Britain has become a true symbol of democratic ideals and true human values. Its forces have fought battles in all parts of the world. Human freedom is the primary cause for concern for the British Diaspora as well as its leaders. This country has seen racial hatred, communal violence, the Great Fire of London, the infamous London plague, two World wars and a host of scientists (like Newton), poets (like Wordsworth), playwrights (like Shakespeare) and thinkers (like Bacon). The sun of British Empire remained in the horizon for nearly 200 years in the past. Today, it is the major ally of the USA, hence a mini super power, if we choose to call it so. Its military capabilities are amazing. It won the famous Falklands War in decisive terms under a woman PM, Mrs. Margaret Thatcher; then, the fiery brand of Maggie polity came to be known as Thatcherism.

Britain has been contributing to the EU in a big way. Its supremacy is coupled with those of France and Germany, the two other economic players of EU. Out of these three EU nations, Britain is the only nation that can change the course of EU. Britain does not want to do away with its currency because of its strength. The EU wants a single currency, the euro. The countries, which adopted the euro, failed on all economic fronts. Thus, the initial reluctance of the British towards the unification of European nations was justified. The British policy makers had thought well in advance that their currency was the best. Only US dollar, Japanese yen, Saudi rial and Kuwaiti dinar can compete against the pound Sterling. The GDP of this nation has more of a technology base than the physical output base that we see in India. Only technology files are transferred and they acquire big bucks. In India, we transfer wheat, rice, jute, machines, clothes, cotton bales and what not! But our exports do not match those of Britain. This fully developed nation has learnt the art and craft of international trade. It is never out of orders!

British polity is driven by two major groups—the Whigs and Tories. One of them is conservative and the other one is liberal. When Conservatives take the seat of power, the poor people of the world suffer. When Liberals take over, the poor of the world get great benefits. Britain supports the USA in all arenas. The war against terror is on its priority list. They have arms, ammunition and technologies. In fact, Britain has been giving major support to the reprisals of the West towards the armed terror encounters that are going on throughout the world. Take Kenya, Nigeria, Egypt, Syria, Iraq and other war theatres of the world into consideration. You would hear that the US or NATO is acting in all of them. That is not true. The US cannot act in any of these theatres without British support. The intelligence of British armed forces and the support of the INTERPOL (which the Britons carefully manage) are two contributing factors that help US and NATO forces succeed in all war zones of the world. British policy on terror is lucid—if you cannot change them, make them your enemies and when the time comes, decimate them. That is why terror elements have developed systems of intelligence gathering that may tell them in advance what the British are up to. The British know that the war against terror is a slow and painful exercise. The terror elements of today are driven by religion today. Tomorrow, they could be driven by another force, say money. Then, the policy of Britain would be quite different from what it is today. London bombings proved that they are also vulnerable to attacks by terror groups. Many UK citizens left Britain and went to get training in the name of Jihad (the holy war). The same thing happened in case of France when the staff of magazine *Charlie Hebdo* was attacked by militants in January 2015. The love of the British or French for people proved harmful for both of them. That was because they were the countries who had issued visas to people in the name of liberalism. These very people fled these two countries to get training. They came back after getting training. They attacked those very people in those very nations where they had prospered. This is a major lacuna of the British foreign policy. If someone kills a person anywhere in the world, he or she goes to London and seeks asylum there. He gets it immediately in the name of human freedom and liberalism. The same man could be a terror element or a small-time thief. When music magnate Gulshan Kumar was killed, Nadeem, the man accused of getting him killed, went to London; he is still there! Similarly, Mr. Lalit Modi, the former IPL Commissioner, went to London and dared to contest elections of the BCCI from there, even after his debacle in the IPL scam. The British do not give any consideration to the harsh fact that they are misused because they are too liberal to be safe. They give asylum and purchase a bag of agonies. The case of London Tube Bombings is a case that proves the point because terror elements knew well when and where to plant the bombs in the tube. They had done Reiki of London Tube. They knew London like the palm of their hand. Similarly, the terror elements had also conducted Reiki in the office or near the office of the magazine *Charlie Hebdo* before striking. These people belonged to France; they were not outsiders. They also knew the office of magazine *Charlie Hebdo*, Paris and even France, just like we know how to add two to two. Britain, just like France, does not differentiate between good and not-so-good people who would become any-but-good later, after skillful training.

The UK and Yemen

We have already pointed out in this volume that the USA and UK had to shut down their embassies in February 2015 in the wake of the rise of Huji Shiite group. Cadres of this group have captured the capital of Yemen. They are fighting against government forces. Britain supports the democratically elected government of Yemen which was given power in November 2015. Thus, the UK has to give support to the ousted government. It may have to send troops to Yemen which are likely to be part of NATO forces. Thus, the UK is likely to take active part in Gulf conflicts in the wake of recent developments in that region.

The UK and USA

The UK is the most trusted ally of the USA. The majority of British population comprises Anglo Saxons. These were the people whose ancestors had gone to the plantations of the USA to work there nearly 400 years ago. Since British blood flows through the veins of Anglo Saxons of America, we can take it for granted that the two nations are a singular entity whose parts are divided only by the Atlantic. Both nations have a common foreign policy on terror. The UK is part of NATO, probably the most vital pivot of this organization. The USA cannot move an inch in Europe without the logistic, political and technical support of the UK. In fact, the two World wars were fought to maintain the supremacy of the UK in Europe. That is why the UK has not agreed for the final unification of all nations of EU to form one single EU. Very few nations and individuals know about this fact. The EU is not a single entity because of the desire of the British to unite the European nations under their full control. Till the time this does not happen, the USA would continue to support the UK on all platforms. Mr. Gordon Brown has been consistently supporting the US policy on terror in the past. This would continue in the future as well.

The UK and India

We enjoy very good relationships with the UK. We have been traditional friends and foes, given that Indian history is full of many an incident of martyrdom due to the atrocities of the British inflicted on us during their rule of over 90 years in India. However, let bygones be bygones. India and the UK are supportive of each other at all political platforms of the globe.

The UK and Arab World

The UK is not heavily dependent upon nations like Saudi Arabia and Kuwait at the oil front. The UK is importing oil from Russia. Note that Russia is the largest producer of oil in the world, followed by Saudi Arabia, the USA and China, in that order. The UK does not depend upon the Arab world, although it has deep business relationships with all countries of the same. The reports of CNN and BBC give indications that the UK has not favourably seen the perpetrators of terror from the Saudi Arabian soil. That was because a majority of 9/11 attackers were from Saudi Arabia. The policy of the UK towards terror is clear. It does not want the terror elements of any nation or sect to operate from any soil. It supports human liberalism and is an icon of Western liberal policies at all UN forums. However, too much liberalism also has its own negative points. That is what traditional societies despise.

Saudi Arabia, the UK and USA are traditional friends and they do not include any other country in this trio. The policies of Saudi Arabia are supportive of a particular sect of Islam. That is why problems are cropping up in all parts of the Islamic world. We feel that the UK and USA must persuade Saudi authorities to take a neutral stance in the present spate of conflicts. For Saudi Arabia, all Muslims must have the same status. The traditional society and royal class of Saudi Arabia may be difficult to convince, though.

Latest Determinants of the Foreign Policy of the UK

They are as follows:

1. The UK Has Not Forgiven Russia Due Its desire for Eastern Ukraine: Towing its centuries-old policy of supporting every act of the USA, the UK has stated that it does not want Russia to support rebels in eastern parts of Ukraine. If the USA sends troops to Ukraine, the UK would also support them by sending its own armed force cadres. Then, the UK and USA may also send tanks and ammunition to Kiev in a bid to save Ukraine from Russia's grab.

2. Domineering British Policies Post Merger: Till the time the EU does not become a reality, the UK would support NATO forces and the Americans. After the merger, it would become a power to reckon with in Europe. Then, it would not need the support of Uncle Sam. But the European Diaspora is so diverse that a common European entity is still a distant dream. It this dream becomes a reality, the UK would like to see itself at the top of the mound.
3. Relationships with Germany: The UK would get stiff resistance from Germany post amalgamation of European States into one single union. Thus, Germany would be its archrival; currently, it is its friend and industrial partner. Thus, the UK may change its foreign policy even in the near future, fearing that it may not be able to distance itself from Deutschland post European merger.
4. War against Terror: The UK would extend all kinds of support to NATO forces and the USA in the long lasting war against terror. The British were the victims of the wrath of terror in distant past, immediate past and the present time.
5. Economic Problems of Eastern and Western Europe: The UK is worried about its financially weak European sisters. How can it help them? The answers are not so easy to find. Greece has refused to obey EU norms and may leave the Euro fold soon. If other nations follow suit, how would Britain stop the disintegration of Europe. That is a big question before the British leadership. In a unified Europe, Britain would get a big role to play. Thus, its territory would be enlarged and its decisions would be accepted by almost ninety percent of European populace, the rest being under the Russian influence. But when would that transpire? The poor nations of Europe are not allowing this continent to become one formidable entity in political and economic terms. Even the UK was not in favour of this plausible unification during the beginning of this century. Now that it sees itself as a leader (or one important player among three most powerful nations of the EU), it can dream big. Its policies would be directed towards bringing prosperity in poor nations and making

all nations sign on the dotted lines for the ultimate European unification.

Foreign Economic Policy of the UK

The UK is sitting pretty on its pounds! Its economic growth rate is nearly 6 to 7 percent per annum. European recession has not hurt its march towards amazing progress. Along with France and Germany, the UK is one of most powerful players in global political and economic arenas. No doubt, British economy had also witnessed recession after the stock market massacre of February 2008 in American markets. However, the British played their industry and economy cards well and came out of the pangs of recession. The UK is the chief contributor to the EU fund out of which Greece, Spain, Portugal and Ireland are given dole on an annual basis. Naturally, Britain will call the shots along with these two nations in all political and economic affairs of the EU.

Conclusion

The United Kingdom is truly a major power of the world. If it is viewed as the most prosperous and alert watchman of Europe, it is also viewed as the most trustworthy ally of the United States. Together, these two nations form a formidable team. The USA primarily looks after all interests of Britain through NATO operations. Political stability and industrial advancement of Britain are the two major factors that have catapulted to the position of major power. Germany is a rival for Britain. The British are Anglo Saxons. White Americans are also Anglo Saxons. That is why Britain has aligned its policies with those of the USA. However, the Germans are a different race altogether; they are Aryans. This is a racial divide that cannot be filled up. Thus, German supremacy in any field may be viewed by the British with suspicion. Britain and Germany had fiercely fought against each other in two World Wars. That era is over but wounds remain in hearts of both nations. In sum, the UK can become the major force in United Europe, when the union of all of its States becomes a reality. Britain is supporting NATO and the US in war against terror. That is why it is vulnerable to attacks of terrorist outfits at home and abroad.

